# Montana's Explorers

1805 THE PIONEER NATURALISTS 1864



NUMBER NINE

BY LARRY S. THOMPSON

PUBLISHED BY

Montana Magazine, Inc.

HELENA, MONTANA 59604

RICK GRAETZ, PUBLISHER
MARK THOMPSON, PUBLICATIONS EDITOR
CAROLYN CUNNINGHAM, EDITOR

This series intends to fill the need for in-depth information about Montana subjects. The geographic concept explores the historical color, the huge landscape and the resilient people of a single Montana subject area. Design by Len Visual Design, Helena, Montana. All camera prep work and layout production completed in Helena, Montana. Typesetting by Thurber Printing, Helena, Montana. Printed in Japan by DNP America, San Francisco.

MONTANA HISTORICAL SOCIETY, MUSEUM PURCHASE

# When the Land Belonged to God by Charles M. Russell

Montana Magazine Inc.
Box 5630
Helena, Montana 59604

ISBN 0-938314-09-2

# PREFACE

What present-day Montana explorer has not wished for a chance to know Montana when it was truly wild—when the land was ruled by the Indian and the bison, when immense herds of prairie elk grazed the Yellowstone Valley bottoms, when Audubon's bighorn clambered over eastern badlands, when the plains grizzly roamed free? Who has not wished for a chance to visit the northern Plains and Rockies in a time machine, to see the land and its wildlife as they were before the onslaught of civilization?

Fortunately a window exists through which we can view the wilderness that was Montana. This window is the writings, paintings, and photographs of the early explorers, those fortunates who knew Montana in its wild and truly primitive state.

This book features a special group of early Montana explorers, a group that left us with perhaps the most interesting and valuable legacy of all. These were the explorers who made careful observations of Montana wildlife, landscapes, geography, geology, and plant life, and who recorded these observations as written accounts and perhaps also as paintings, sketches, or collections of specimens. They were the first geographers, geologists, paleontologists, botanists, anthropologists, and zoologists — in short, the explorer-naturalists of Montana. Among their ranks were some of America's greatest wildlife and landscape artists as well as our first and foremost conservationists. Among them were European princes, American presidents, famous writers, and some of America's most influential scientists. The story of their discoveries is one of the most exciting chapters in Montana history.

In this first volume, we will explore Montana through the first-hand accounts of the earliest explorers, those who braved the hardships of wilderness travel to see the land before 1864, the year Montana became a territory of the United States of America. (Next year will see publication of a companion volume, covering explorations during the post-Civil War era.) We will share with them a glimpse of the living natural history laboratory that Montana presented (and still presents, although greatly changed). We will exult with them over the discovery in Montana of unknown species and landscapes, and we will suffer with them over the catastrophic losses of painstakingly-prepared scientific specimens in hair-raising wilderness accidents. Volume 2 will witness the coming of the railroads, the extermination of the bison, and the growing role of the federal government in scientific exploration.

*Lewis' Woodpecker.* (ALAN NELSON)

# CONTENTS

# Montana's Explorers



## The Author

Larry Thompson, a native of Kalispell now living in Helena, is a biologist who has authored more than 40 technical and popular articles appearing in Montana Magazine, Audubon Magazine and numerous scientific journals.

# DEDICATION

This book is dedicated to my parents, Roger and Lee, who have explored Montana together for over half a century.

# INTRODUCTION

In a work such as this, only the highlights of the exploration and scientific discovery of 19th-century Montana can be addressed. Volumes have been written about some of the explorers included in this account; virtually nothing has been written previously about others. The material in this book is just a hint of the fascinating reading of the first-hand accounts of the explorer-naturalists. To guide the reader to some of the more valuable primary and secondary sources, footnotes are used and a numbered list of selected references is provided at the end of each chapter. The first number in each footnote (followed by a colon [:]) refers to the work's number in the bibliography; the other numbers refer to volume (if any) and page number. For example, a footnote that reads "3:VII,231" refers to the third work listed in the bibliography, and its Volume VII, page 231. Some of the works cited have been out of print for a century or more, but most can be located through any of the larger libraries or examined at the Montana Historical Society Library in Helena.

From the roster of hundreds of 19th-century explorers, I have tried to select the most interesting and the most influential of those who also could be called naturalists. By my criteria, a naturalist in the early decades of the 19th century is virtually anyone who observed and wrote perceptively about wildlife and plant life. Some of these, like David Thompson, Father DeSmet and John Palliser, would scarcely be called naturalists by today's standards, but they did make a contribution to the literature on Montana flora, fauna, and geography. My criteria grew progressively more strict as exploration and discovery proliferated through the century, so that by the latter decades of the 19th century only those explorers who were also active and influential scientists are included. Regrettably, dozens of interesting biographies and hundreds of stories had to be excluded. The reader wishing a complete list of all early explorer-naturalists should consult Ewan and Ewan's book, *Biographical Dictionary of Rocky Mountain Naturalists.*

For the sake of readability, scientific names are used sparingly in the text. A complete list of common and scientific names used in this book will appear in Volume 2.

I sincerely hope you find as much enjoyment as I did in this vicarious visit to early nineteenth century Montana!

*The pinyon jay once was named the Maximilian's jay after explorer-adventurer Prince Maximilian.* (ALAN NELSON)

# ACKNOWLEDGEMENTS

The accuracy and readability of this volume has been greatly enhanced by the careful reviews so graciously offered by a number of very busy and very professional people. Dave Walter of the Montana Historical Society carefully read through the entire manuscript. Dave and others of the Montana Historical Society Library staff (especially Bob Clark and Dave Girshick) have my gratitude for their cheerful responses to my endless requests for documents of incredible obscurity and staggering size. Ray Breuninger, Mike Cronin, Paul Russell Cutright, Jerry DeSanto, Mick Hager, Jack Horner, David C. Hunt, Keir B. Sterling, and Ken Walcheck each provided careful reviews of one or more chapters. Many, many other people helped by answering questions, providing illustrations and photographs, helping to find documents, and providing moral support throughout the project. Sue Jackson of the Montana Historical Society kindly helped me to get started on this project. This book would have suffered without the assistance of these most capable and helpful people. Special thanks go to my wife Sue, who carefully proofed many long chapters and cheerfully tolerated my nights and weekends at the typewriter. To all these I owe a debt of gratitude as big as the Montana sky. I accept all responsibility, however, for any inaccuracies that may remain.

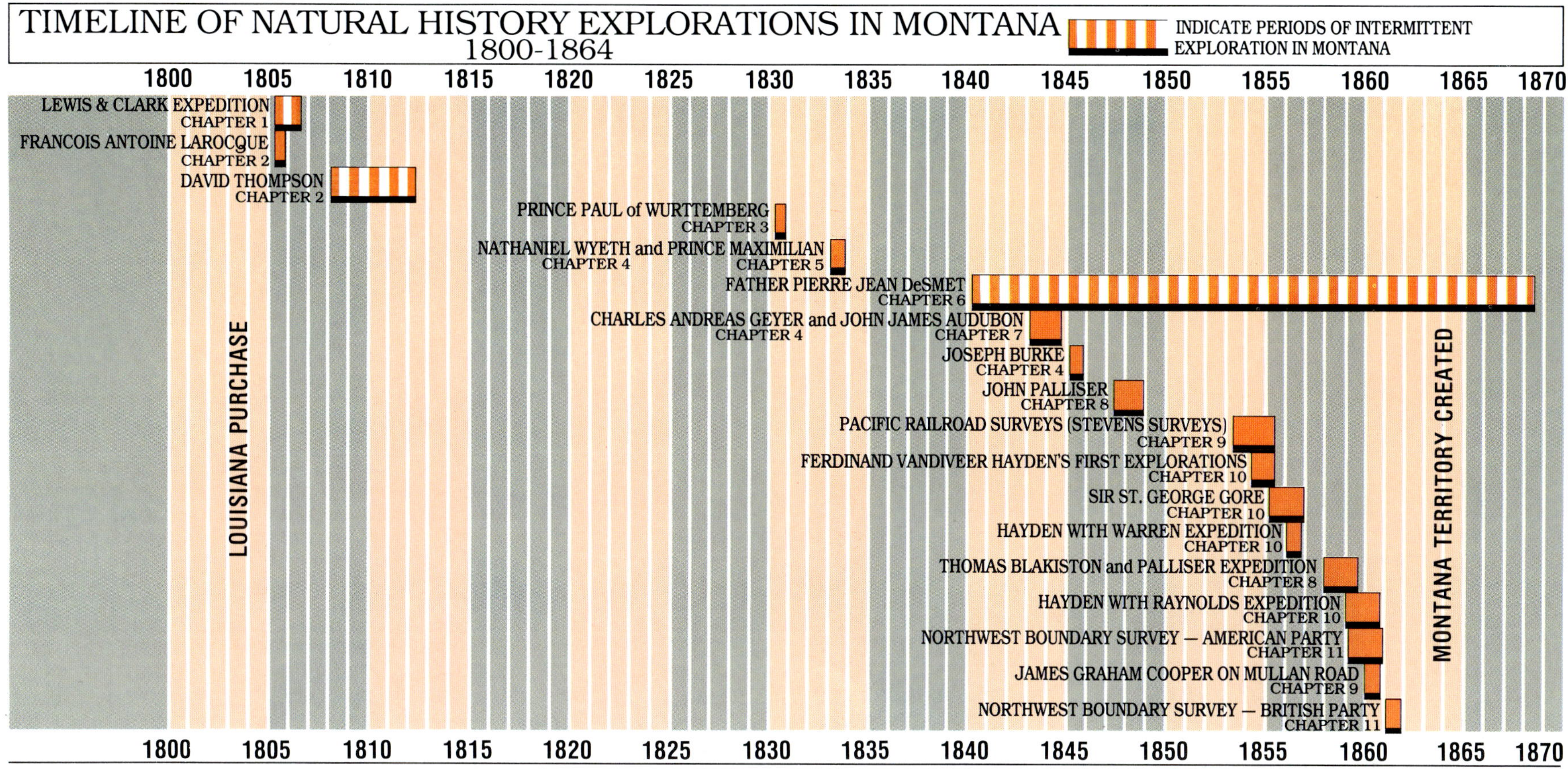


# REFERENCES

These sources contain information on many early naturalists and were used as sources for chapters throughout this volume.


1. Barber, L. *The Heyday of Natural History: 1820-1870.* Garden City, N.Y.: Doubleday, 1980.
2. Bartlett, R. A., and W. H. Goetzmann. *Exploring the American West, 1803-1879.* U.S.D.I. National Park Service Handbook 116. Washington: U.S. Government Printing Office, 1982.
3. Blankinship, J. W. "A Century of Botanical Exploration in Montana, 1805-1905." *Montana Agricultural College Scientific Studies* 1(1905):3-31.
4. Brown, M. H. *The Plainsmen of the Yellowstone.* New York: G. P. Putnam's Sons, 1961.
5. Elman, R. *First in the Field: America's Pioneering Naturalists.* Ontario: Van Nostrand Reinhold, 1977.
6. Ewan, J. *Rocky Mountain Naturalists.* Denver: Univ. of Denver Press, 1950.
7. Ewan, J., and N. D. Ewan. *Biographical Dictionary of Rocky Mountain Naturalists: A Guide to the Writings and Collections of Botanists, Zoologists, Artists, and Photographers, 1682-1932.* Hingham, Mass.: Kluwer, 1981.
8. Gilbert, E. W. *Exploration of Western America, 1800-1850: An Historical Geography.* Cambridge, England: Cambridge Univ. Press, 1933.
9. Goetzmann, W. H. *Army Exploration in the American West, 1803-1863.* New Haven, Conn.: Yale University, 1959.
10. Goetzmann, W. H. *Exploration and Empire: The Explorer and the Scientist in the Winning of the West.* New York: Alfred A. Knopf, 1967.
11. Hume, E. E. *Ornithologists of the United States Army Medical Corps.* Baltimore: Johns Hopkins Press, 1942.
12. Jenkins, A. K. *The Naturalists: Pioneers of Natural History.* Toronto: Nelson, 1979.
13. Kastner, J. *A Species of Eternity.* New York: Alfred A. Knopf, 1977.
14. Koch, E. "Big Game in Montana from Early Historical Records." *Journal of Wildlife Management* 5(1941):357-70.
15. McKelvey, S. D. *Botanical Exploration of the Trans-Mississippi West, 1790-1850.* Jamaica Plain, Mass.: Arnold Arboretum of Harvard University, 1955.
16. McFarling, L. *Exploring the Northern Plains, 1804-1876.* Caldwell, Idaho: Caxton, 1955.
17. Merrill, G. P. *The First One Hundred Years of American Geology.* Forestburgh, N.Y.: Lubrecht and Cramer, 1969.
18. Trenton, P., and P. H. Hassrick. *The Rocky Mountains: A Vision for Artists in the Nineteenth Century.* Norman: Univ. of Oklahoma Press, 1983.
19. Wagner, H. R., and C. Camp. *The Plains and the Rockies: A Bibliography of Original Narratives of Travel and Adventure, 1800-1865.* San Francisco: Charles C. Camp, 1953.


ALL ALDEN PAINTINGS COURTESY NATIONAL ARCHIVES, RECORD GROUP 76, ENTRY 221.

CHAPTER 1

# The Lewis and Clark Expedition

*Meriwether Lewis (left) and William Clark (right) shared command of the "Corps of Discovery." Lewis doubled as the expedition's chief naturalist and journalist, Clark as cartographer.* (COURTESY, MONTANA HISTORICAL SOCIETY)

Before the year 1805, Montana was *terra incognita* of the first order. Its major river valleys may have been worked by a few obscure trappers and traders, but these men were a reticent lot and shared their discoveries with few. The first real exploration of Montana was made by two of the greatest explorers our continent has ever known: Meriwether Lewis and William Clark.

The Lewis and Clark Expedition was the pet project of Thomas Jefferson, the man who wrote the Declaration of Independence, who served as third president of the fledgling United States, and who in 1803 purchased virtually the entire Great Plains region from France.

Jefferson was a respected naturalist in his own right. He was a competent botanist, a meticulous recorder of the comings and goings of migratory birds, a noted meteorologist, an investigator of Indian mounds, and a collector of native American vocabularies. As a paleontologist he studied the controversial mastodon fossils that contributed to Darwin's theory, and he discovered and described a new species of extinct giant ground sloth, later named *Megalonyx jeffersoni*. During his term as president, the East Room of the White House became a museum of sorts for his extensive fossil collection. Jefferson was one of the founders and for 17 years president of the most respected scientific organization in the New World, the American Philosophical Society of Philadelphia. In his own words, "Nature intended me for the tranquil pursuits of science, by rendering them my supreme delight." (5:1)

For almost 20 years Jefferson endeavored to engineer an expedition to explore the vast *terra incognita* in the interior of the continent. His early attempts failed to materialize, but international politics at the end of the 1700s lent increasing urgency to Jefferson's ambitious plan. The French, the British, and the Spanish were eyeing this ground more eagerly, and the first nation to explore and describe these unknown landscapes would have the most valid claim of territory. In 1801 Jefferson approached an old family friend, named Meriwether Lewis (then a paymaster in the "Army of the West)," and appointed him his private secretary, with a mind to train him for what would be Jefferson's fifth attempt to get the expedition going.

What kind of person was Meriwether Lewis that the President of the United States would select him to carry out vicariously his personal dream? In Jefferson's eyes, Lewis was "of courage undaunted; possessing a firmness and perseverance of purpose which nothing but impossibilities could divert from its direction; careful as a father of those committed to his charge, yet steady in the maintenance of order and discipline; ...guarded by exact observation of the vegetables and animals of his own country, against losing time in the description of objects already possessed; honest, disinterested, liberal, of sound understanding, and a fidelity to truth so scrupulous that whatever he should report would be as certain as if seen by ourselves." (9:I,xxvi)

Lewis had been born in 1774 near Charlottesville, Virginia, and grew up roaming the fields and woods, hunting, observing, learning, whetting the powers of observation that were to make his future journals sparkle with detailed and astute natural history observations. His mother was an herbalist and taught him at an early age the skills of a field botanist.

In 1794 Lewis joined General "Mad Anthony" Wayne's army, which was skirmishing with the British and Indians at the edge of the frontier. While fighting in the wilderness, he became a close friend of his commanding officer, Lieutenant William Clark, younger brother of Revolutionary War hero George Rogers Clark. This friendship was to shape the destiny of the American West.

So it was that, when Jefferson appointed Lewis as leader of his long-planned "Corps of Discovery," Lewis unhesitatingly asked his friend Clark to join him and to share the command. Clark, born in 1770 in Caroline County, Virginia, had been fighting Indians since the age of 19 but had retired from military service to his home in Kentucky, then practically a howling wilderness. Needless to say, when the invitation from Lewis arrived, he accepted at once.

Much has been written about the personalities of these two men and the traits that allowed them to share command of a danger-frought, grueling wilderness adventure for nearly three years without the slightest trace of friction or animosity. According to historian Paul Russell Cutright, "Lewis was a dreamer, intent, fine-drawn, reserved, unwavering, generally humorless. Clark was warm, companionable, a good judge of men, an easy conversationalist ... and highly successful in meeting the demands of actual living." (5:19) The two men differed greatly in training also. Lewis was fairly well-read and had just completed a two-month cram course at Philadephia, studying everything from astronomy to paleontology under some of the best-known scientists of his time. Lewis, of course, had also been tutored by Jefferson while serving as his secretary, learning from him such practical field techniques as how to prepare skins and skulls. More important, Jefferson taught him the skills of observation and careful description, the preeminent requirements of a successful field naturalist. The robust, red-headed Clark had not received much formal schooling — he was particularly deficient in spelling, as revealed by his journals — but possessed a vast amount of practical engineering skill, a knack for dealing with the Indians, and a consummate knowledge of the details of wilderness survival. Most of the expedition's maps were drawn by Clark.

*The mouth of the Yellowstone River near the point where the Lewis and Clark Expedition first entered Montana.* (PAINTING BY KARL BODMER. COURTESY, INTERNORTH ART FOUNDATION, JOSLYN ART MUSEUM, OMAHA, NEBRASKA)

On May 14, 1804, the expedition started up the Missouri from its winter campsite near St. Louis, scarcely noticed by the rest of the world. Thirty-three persons were part of the full expedition, and all returned safely but one (a man who died of appendicitis early in the voyage). To more than a ton of supplies, Lewis added a sizable scientific library, including at least two of Linnaeus's volumes on flora and fauna, plus a plant press which was given him by Dr. Benjamin Smith Barton (who had trained him in botany during his Philadelphia stay).

The band of explorers made its way slowly and laboriously up the Missouri, and by late October it arrived at the villages of a friendly group of Indians, the Mandans, near present-day Bismarck, North Dakota. There the men spent the winter of 1804-1805, studying the Indians and the countryside and making preparations for the next spring's assault on the Rocky Mountains. On April 7, 1805, the expedition struck out for the wilderness.

Lewis and Clark probably first entered what is now Montana on April 27, 1805. During the ensuing weeks in Montana they would encounter and describe many species of plants and animals that had never before been seen by European man. These species, first described by Lewis and Clark, are listed in Paul Russell Cutright's book, "Lewis and Clark: Pioneering Naturalists." (5) Our chapter highlights some of the scientific findings of the expedition, with emphasis on new discoveries, and gives some examples of the leaders' — particularly Lewis's — outstanding ability to draw ecological inferences based on careful observation.

No sooner had the Lewis and Clark expedition passed the mouth of the Yellowstone River than the first discovery intruded itself upon the party. This was the plains grizzly, which Lewis and Clark described at various times as the brown, yellow, or white bear because its color was generally lighter than that of the black bear with which they were familiar. Other

*Top left: Along the Missouri today.* (LEN ECKEL)
*Top right: Lewis and Clark grew to have a deep respect for that "furious and formidable anamal," the plains grizzly.* (BENGEYFIELD PHOTO)
*Bottom: Lewis described these remarkable stone walls along the Missouri River as "of tolerable workmanship, so perfect ... that I should have thought that Nature had attempted here to rival the human art of masonry ...."* (LARRY THOMPSON)

explorers, particularly Alexander Mackenzie, had noted the existence of the huge and ferocious bear prior to this date, and in fact Lewis and Clark themselves had seen grizzlies as far downstream as present-day Yankton, South Dakota. The bear that Lewis shot near what is now Culbertson, Montana, was the first grizzly to be scientifically examined and described in detail.

In comparing the grizzly to the black bear, Lewis wrote, "it is a much more furious and formidable anamal, and will frequently pursue the hunter when wounded. it is asstonishing to see the wounds they will bear before they can be put to death. the Indians may well fear this anamal ... but in the hands of skillfull riflemen they are by no means as formidable or dangerous as they have been represented." (9:I,351) Before the expedition would travel another hundred miles Lewis would share a new respect for this awesome bear with every member of the party.

A little farther upstream, where Wolf Point, Montana, now stands, a monstrous grizzly estimated to weigh 600 pounds was shot by Clark. It proved a little harder to pacify. "It was a most tremendious looking anamal, and extreemly hard to kill notwithstanding he had five balls through his lungs and five others in various parts he swam more than half the distance across the river to a sandbar, & it was at least twenty minutes before he died; he did not attempt to attack, but fled and made the most tremendous roaring from the moment he was shot." (9:I,372) Six days later, near the present site of Fort Peck Dam, a third grizzly was shot. It immediately turned on the rifleman and chased him half a mile, then continued a mile up the riverbottom with a bullet through its lungs and dug itself a two-foot deep hole. It finally taught Lewis what may be termed a proper respect. He wrote, "These bear being so hard to die reather intimedates us all, I must confess that I do not like the gentlemen and had reather fight two Indians than one bear; there is no other chance to conquer them by a single shot but by shooting them through the brains, and this becomes difficult in consequence of two large muscles which cover the sides of the forehead and the sharp projection of the center of the frontal bone, which is also of a pretty good thickness." (9:II,25)

During these blustery spring days on the lower Missouri, Lewis made some of his most astute observations. His narrative leaves little doubt that he was a first-rate observer and as perceptive a naturalist as ever worked the river. Often, while the rest of the party struggled upstream with the boats, Lewis would strike off on foot by himself and follow a buffalo trail along the river. Lewis noted that the bison followed the most direct routes, routes that would have made an engineer proud, cutting off river bends and following the most gentle slopes to minimize energy expended in travelling from place to place. The Indians had appropriated many of these trails, which had been worn up to ten feet wide. Today, many highways in eastern Montana follow these same trails.

On his strolls, Lewis must have stopped to examine every new plant and animal he encountered. He made note of each of the various conifers found along the Missouri near where his path first intercepted their present-day range. He described the ponderosa pine, Douglas fir, horizontal juniper, Rocky Mountain juniper, and even the limber pine, which has escaped the notice of many a highly trained naturalist. He noticed the difference between the leaves of silver sagebrush, a bottomland species, and big sagebrush, which prefers the slopes, and even commented on their different habitat characteristics.

While walking the floodplain of the Missouri, Lewis observed "traces of the ancient beds of the river," (9:I,362) which bespeak a shifting, changing topography, re-engineered each spring by the raging flood waters. This was a very remarkable observation for the time, since most of the world's noted geologists then believed that the shape of the landscape they observed was exactly as it was when it was first conjured into being by the Creator as described in Genesis. Lewis's understanding of the changing nature of the landscape was no doubt a result of Jefferson's training, for Jefferson was one of the earliest proponents of uniformitarianism — that is, the notion that the earth's surface features were created over millenia by the slow, steady work of wind and water, and that the landscape is continually changing.

Lewis observed that the snow geese were still congregating in large flocks in early May, and did not appear to be paired. From this he deduced correctly that these birds did not remain to breed but were merely stopping over during a long journey to breeding grounds far to the north.

Lewis clearly described the difference in habitat use between the mule deer and white-tailed deer, species that share a common range over much of Montana. "We have rarely found the mule deer in any except rough country; they prefer the open grounds and are seldom found in the woodlands near the river; when they are met with in the woodlands or river bottoms and are pursued, the[y] invariably run to the hills or open country as the Elk do. the contrary happens with the common [white-tailed] deer." (9:II,20) This is the first description of the behavioral and habitat differences between the two species, differences that have been described a hundred times since but never more succinctly. Lewis even used his knowledge of habitat preferences to predict which species he would most likely shoot for supper as the path of the expedition progressed through different types of habitat.

Lewis's observations of the predatory behavior of gray wolves — constant companions on the expedition — were no less incisive. "We have frequently seen the wolves in pursuit of the Antelope in the plains; they appear to decoy a single one from a flock, and then pursue it, alturnately relieving each other untill they take it." (9:I,351)

One of Lewis's most remarkable observations was that of water conservation in rodents which inhabit arid regions. Just above the mouth of the Musselshell River, Lewis encountered a large prairie-dog town. These animals, he wrote, "never visit the brooks or river for water; I am astonished how this anamal exists as it dose without water, particularly in a country like this where there is scarcely any rain during ¾ of the year and more rarely any due [dew]; yet we have sometimes found their villages at the distance of five or six miles from any water, and they are never found out of the limits of the ground which their burrows occupy ..." (9:II,63-4)

Scientists were not to discover for many decades that prairie dogs and other rodents of the arid plains can live largely on "metabolic water," water that is created from the oxidation of the carbohydrates that make up the bulk of their food. The kidneys and bladder of these rodents are highly adapted to re-absorb water from the urine, which as a consequence is highly concentrated. A biologist once kept a couple of prairie dogs alive for seven years without as much as a drop of drinking water. In 1804 Lewis and Clark shipped a prairie dog east to Jefferson. Amazingly, it survived the four-month, 4,000-mile journey to Washington. Its survival was more than likely due to its ability to subsist on metabolic water. Any animal requiring a regular dose of drinking water would probably have died if it had to depend on the shifting crews of river-boat men for its supply!

Most accounts of the natural history aspects of the expedition dwell almost exclusively on Lewis's accurate and perceptive descriptions, and fail to give proper credit to Clark. It is true that whenever the two explorers traveled together Clark's notes tended to be little more than badly misspelled paraphrases of Lewis's journal. On May 9, 1805, Lewis shot some unusual birds along the river that turned out to be willets, a species then unknown to science. Lewis penned a 300-word description of the bird that is a model of scientific exactitude and verbal imagery. Every part of the bird was described in exquisite detail: "the beak is black, 2½ inches in length, slightly tapering, streight, of a cilindric form and blontly or roundly pointed...." (9:II,17) Clark's entire account of the same birds reads: "Capt. Lewis killed 4 pleaver different from any I have ever before seen, larger & have white breast & the underfeathers of the wings are white &c." (9:II,19)

Clark, however, must be given credit for the first

*Above: Lewis observed that black-tailed prairie dogs never leave their colonies for drinking water; scientists were not to discover for more than a century that the rodents survive on metabolic water.* (LARRY THOMPSON)
*Below: The first description of the golden currant, a common Montana shrub, was written by Clark.* (CHARLES KAY)

*The Lewis and Clark Expedition spent many days at the junction of the Marias River (top) and the Missouri River (below), determining which was the Missouri. A wrong choice would have spelled disaster for the expedition.* (PACIFIC RAILROAD SURVEY LITHOGRAPH. LEN ECKEL PHOTO)

description of the golden currant, a plant which is common in Montana and which Lewis is often assumed to have first described. Near the mouth of the Yellowstone, Sacagawea brought Clark "a bush something like the currunt, which she said bore a delicious froot and that great quantitis grew on the Rocky Mountains. This shrub was in bloom has a yellow flower with a deep cup, the froot when ripe is yellow and hangs in bunches like cheries, Some of those berries yet remained on the bushes." (9:I,356) Clark later would prove to be a diligent observer when separated from Lewis.

The previous fall, Lewis and Clark had received reports of some strange "anamale with large circular horns" (9:I,176) inhabitating the wild and rugged mountains to the west. During the winter at Fort Mandan, the Indians had brought them a pair of horns, which provided tantalizing evidence of the reality of this mysterious beast. Finally, near the mouth of the Yellowstone River, a member of the expedition spotted some of them on the hoof during a solo walk. But Lewis the naturalist did not have the opportunity to view one closely until May 25, 1805, when one was shot from the steep cliffs along the river. Lewis then proceeded to pen the first, and to this day one of the most detailed, descriptions of Audubon's bighorn sheep, a now-extinct subspecies of the mountain sheep. In describing the horns, Lewis wrote that "they are compressed, bent backwards and lunated; the surface swelling into wavy rings which incircleing the horn continue to succeed each other from the base to the extremity and becoming less elivated and more distant as they recede from the head ... the horns of the female are small, but are also compressed and bent backwards and incircled with a succession of wavy rings." (9:II,73)

Even today, when wolves are practically extinct in Montana, mountain sheep select their habitat with wolves in mind. Whether in the western mountains or the eastern river breaks, mountain sheep go for the steepest, most inaccessible terrain in the area, and they seldom stray very far from this escape terrain where they are relatively safe from predators. As Lewis described their habitat, "the places they generally celect to lodg is the cranies or crevices of the rocks in the faces of inaccessable precepices, where the wolf nor bear can reach them and where indeed man himself would in many instancies find a similar deficiency; yet these anamals bound from rock to rock and stand apparently in the most careless manner on the sides of precipices of many hundred feet." (9:II,73-4)

Mountain sheep are primarily grazers, and most populations today subsist on a diet of bunchgrasses seasoned with a few mouthfuls of the tender tips of shrubs. But the Audubon's bighorn apparently had different tastes. Lewis wrote that they did eat grass but fed "principally on the arromatic herbs which grow on the clifts and inaccessable hights which they usually frequent." (9:II,73) These "arromatic herbs" probably included the salt desert shrubs, invaders from the Great Basin which are often the only vegetation growing on the steep cliffs and coulee walls of eastern Montana — Nuttall's saltbush, shadscale saltbush, winterfat, and several varieties of sagebrush. Mountain sheep have been re-introduced to their close relative's former habitat in eastern Montana, but these introductions have not met with as much success as had been hoped, possibly because their dietary preferences reflect some real evolutionary differences between the two subspecies.

Lewis and Clark reached the mouth of the Marias River on June 8, 1805. The party was stalled here for many days, unsure of which river fork was the real Missouri. The Marias was high, swift, and muddy, and every member of the party — except the two leaders — was convinced that it was really the Missouri.

This was one of the most important decisions of the journey. To make the wrong choice may well have meant the end of the expedition. Nevertheless, Lewis found the time to do a little bird watching. Walking the cottonwood bottom lands along the Missouri River, he compiled the first bird list ever made in Montana: "the river bottoms affording all the timber which is to be seen in the country they are filled with innumerable little birds that resort thither either for shelter or to build their nests. when sun began to shine today these birds appeared to be very gay and sung most inchantingly; I observed among them the brown thrush, Robbin, turtle dove linnit goaldfinch, the large and small blackbird, wren and several other birds of less note." (9:II,130) Lewis's account describes two important features of the eastern Montana avifauna. First, birds during the breeding season sing most actively right around sunrise; a birder who sleeps past 8:00 or so might as well stay home for all the birds he'll hear. Second, as Lewis so perceptively described, the riparian cottonwood forests harbor the greatest diversity of bird life of any habitat on the prairies. The birds he described are still common in these cottonwood bottoms today: the brown thrasher, American robin, mourning dove, American goldfinch, Brewer's blackbird, common grackle, and house wren.

The party finally continued up the southern fork — the correct one — but it wasn't until Lewis actually saw the Great Falls of the Missouri on June 13 that anyone felt certain that the right decision had been made. In traveling from the Marias River to the Great Falls, Lewis began noting some subtle changes in the wildlife of the river corridor. Belted kingfishers and river otters were much more common above the mouth of the muddy Marias River, where "the water has become sufficiently clear for them to take fish." (9:II,225) Also, Lewis noted that some species of fish began to disappear from the day's catch, while several new species appeared. The party was crossing the transition zone between the warm-water fishery of the lower river — where the river is the color of milk chocolate, sluggish, wide, and warm — and the cold-water fishery of the upper river — clearer, colder water, and a somewhat faster current, fed by mountain streams pouring in from the Continental Divide to the west.

Of course, different species of fish would be adapted to the different environments offered by the upper and lower river. Lewis noted that the channel catfish began to peter out above the mouth of the Marias River and that some new species made their appearance. At the Great Falls, Lewis discovered some large trout of a new species, which were "from sixteen to twenty three inches in length, precisely resemble our mountain or speckled trout in form and the position of their fins, but the specks on these are of a deep black instead of the red or goald colour of those common to the U'. States. these are furnished long sharp teeth on the pallet and tongue and have generally a small dash of red on each side behind the front ventral fins; the flesh is of a pale yellowish red, or when in good order, of a rose red." (9:II,150-1) These fish were the westslope cutthroat trout, once named *Salmo lewisi* after Lewis but now called *Salmo clarkii*, subspecies *lewisi*, in honor of both explorers.

The Great Falls of the Missouri, Lewis discovered, was the scene of a unique ecological occurrence. Bison were abundant in the plains above the falls, and herds were constantly descending to the river's edge for water. The river banks were steep and did not provide much room for the hundreds of jostling, shoving bovids. As a consequence, Lewis observed, "the hinder part of the herd press those in front out of their debth and the water instantly takes them over the cataracts where they are instantly crushed to death without the possibility of escaping. in this manner I have seen ten or a douzen disappear in a few minutes. their mangled carcases ly along the shores below the falls in considerable quantities and afford fine amusement for the bear wolves and birds of prey." (9:II,167)

*Lewis noted that bison attempting to swim the Missouri River above the Great Falls often would be swept to their deaths over the brink.* (TOM ULRICH)

The grizzlies were unusually abundant near the falls where they found a dependable and abundant food source. They were also unusually territorial here, and Lewis was chased into the river by one while he was scouting out a portage route. Bald eagles, also carrion eaters, were abundant as well. A huge nest, built atop a snag on a secure island just below one of the upper cataracts, was a local landmark for many years.

The expedition was forced to make an arduous, 18-mile portage around the impassable falls, a detour that delayed the expedition 11 days. The corps was at Great Falls from June 21 to July 15, 25 days in all. Lewis took advantage of this slower pace to explore the falls area in some detail. The first descriptions of the western meadowlark, thirteen-lined ground squirrel, bobcat, bushy-tailed woodrat, prairie rattlesnake, and swift fox

*The Swift Fox, now virtually extinct in Montana, was common in the vicinity of the Great Falls at the time of the Lewis and Clark Expedition.* (JOHN JAMES AUDUBON PAINTING)

were written by Lewis while the rest of the party made the long, slow portage. Lewis's description of the swift fox provides one of the few sources of information on the ecology of this species in Montana, as it was quickly driven to near-extinction along with the bison, plains grizzly, and gray wolf. According to Lewis, swift fox "associate in large communities and burrow in the praries...they are extreemly watchfull and take reffuge in their burrows which are very deep...their tallons appear longer than any species of fox I ever saw and seem therefore prepared more amply by nature for the purpose of burrowing." (9:II,213,216) The sight of burrowing foxes living in prairie dog-like colonies must have been a memorable event. Lewis was able to recognize the difference between his new discovery, the swift fox, and the kit fox, a related subspecies which occupies the deserts far to the south.

Those who believe that the problem of overgrazing is a new one will be surprised to read Lewis's account of the expedition's portage route around the Great Falls. That route intersected a major buffalo migration pathway, and the grassland had been so severely grazed and trampled that little vegetation was left except plains pricklypear. This cactus was so abundant that the men's feet quickly became agonizingly full of the spines. Actually, bison damage to the grassland was widespread, and almost everywhere the party left the river bottoms and crossed the uplands similar damage was seen. It was seen as a severe problem here simply because the 18 miles around the falls had to be covered on foot rather than by river.

While moving some gear around camp, Lewis discovered a bushy-tailed woodrat, one of the few creatures able to work around the pricklypear's defensive thorns and able to get at the juicy flesh inside. According to Lewis, "they feed very much on the fruit and seed of the prickly pear; or at least I have seen large quantities of the hulls of that fruit lying about their holes and in their nests." (9:II,205) Lewis probably wished that more creatures fed on the loathsome plants by the time the party reached the end of the portage.

It was not long after the expedition resumed its journey up the Missouri that Lewis discovered an unknown bird, a species that now bears his name. The party had just passed through the Gates of the Mountains near Helena when Lewis saw a "black woodpecker...about the size of the lark woodpecker as black as a crow...it is a distinct species of woodpecker; it has a long tail and flies a good deal like the jay bird." (9:II,252) Lewis must again be applauded for identifying this bird as a woodpecker, because its behavior is most un-woodpecker like. As Lewis noted, it flies with a jay-like arc rather than the undulating flight characteristic of most woodpeckers; it perches robin-like on branches rather than woodpecker-like on the tree trunk; it does most of its feeding on the ground and seldom plies its beak on a tree; in fact, it does not even excavate its own nest. Lewis collected one of these curious birds near the site of present-day Missoula during his return trip the following year; its skin is the only known bird specimen from the expedition that exists today. It is now housed at Harvard University's Museum of Comparative Zoology.

Two other birds new to science that Lewis discovered during his ascent of the Missouri were the blue grouse and the pinyon jay. Blue grouse were seen along the river bottom near present-day Whitehall; Lewis described them as "black or dark brown phesants." (9:II,295) Blue grouse undergo a curious reverse altitudinal migration; unlike most other resident bird species, they descend the mountains into the valleys in the spring and climb back up into the snow-covered mountains in fall. Lewis was lucky enough to catch them near the lowest point of their range. Nearby he saw a "blue bird about the size of the common robbin. it's action and form is somewhat that of the jay bird and never rests long in any one position but constantly flying or hoping from sprey to sprey... their note is loud and frequently repeated both flying and when at rest and is char-́ah, chár-ah, char-áh, as nearly as letters can express it." (9:II,295-6) This bird was next seen 28 years later, when Prince Maximilian saw it near Fort Union. Since the scientific aspects of Lewis and Clark's journey were not published until decades after the expedition, the bird came to be known as "Maximilian's jay" (later renamed the pinyon jay), and Maximilian received the credit for naming and discovering it.

Traveling upstream from the Gates of the Mountains, the party passed through the canyon where Canyon Ferry Dam is now located and into the lush and fertile floodplain that now lies beneath Canyon Ferry Reservoir. As reported by Lewis, "the river immediately on entering this valley assumes a different aspect and character, it spreads to a mile and upwards in width, crouded with Islands, some of them large." (9:II,255-6) If present today, this river section of braided channels, huge islands, and diverse wildlife would be a national treasure. Lewis believed that beaver were responsible for creating these intricately braided river channels. He noticed that beaver would dam channels up to 20 yards wide, forcing the current into other channels and causing the slackwater behind the dam to quickly fill with mud, sand, and driftwood. Lewis's intimate experience with all aspects of river hydrology — knowledge learned through life-and-death testing every hour on the river — led him to make this perceptive observation.

A little farther up the river, a new pest was added to the twin plagues of mosquitoes and pricklypear, which already had caused the expedition so much grief. This was needle-and-thread grass, a dominant species of the dry grasslands of the prairies. The expedition had undoubtedly encountered this grass over almost the entire route, but only in late July when the seed heads ripen and dry out was it brought painfully to their attention. The seeds of this grass, as the name indicates, are shaped like a long, sharp needle with an inch or two of twisted thread through the eye. As Lewis described it, the point of the needle "is a sharp

*The sage grouse (upper left) was called "Cock of the Plains" by Captain Clark, who sketched one in his journal (left center).* (TOM ULRICH)
*The bushy-tailed woodrat (upper right) and plains pricklypear (lower right) were described by Captain Lewis near the Great Falls of the Missouri.* (JOHN JAMES AUDUBON PAINTING. LARRY THOMPSON PHOTO)
*Lewis discovered jet-black garter snakes (lower left) near present-day Townsend, where they still can be found.* (LARRY THOMPSON PHOTO)

subulate, firm point beset at it's base with little stiff bristles standing with their points in a contrary direction to the subulate point to which they answer as a barb and serve also to pres it forward when onece entered a small distance. these barbed seed penetrate our mockersons and leather legings and give us great pain untill they are removed. my poor dog suffers with them excessively, he is constantly binting and scratching himself as if in a rack of pain." (9:II,272) The design of this seed, which caused Lewis and his dog, Scannon, so much torment, is actually a marvel of adaptation. With changes in humidity brought about by rain, the shaft of the needle rotates, while the thread braces it against the earth, allowing the seed to literally drill itself into the ground.

On July 23, 1805, Lewis described a jet-black snake near present-day Townsend. Based on his description, historians assumed up to now that this was a hog-nosed snake. Actually, it was a black color phase of the common garter snake, still fairly common in the Townsend area but known nowhere else in Montana.

On August 12, 1805, Lewis, working ahead of the main party of the expedition, at last reached the Continental Divide and "tasted the water of the great Columbia River." Lewis felt that he had "accomplished one of those great objects on which my mind has unalterably fixed for many years." (9:II,335) Lewis then descended into the Salmon River Valley, where the party made its famous rendezvous with Sacagawea's people, the Shoshonis. Ten days later, the main party approached the divide, and Lewis returned to join it. Game was becoming scarce, so Lewis had his men form a bush drag to work a tributary of Horse Prairie Creek for fish. In about two hours, they caught 528 fish, most of them large trout. Among these fish may have been the first arctic grayling ever described, although Lewis's description leaves some doubt: "they are of a silvery colour except on the back and head, where they are of a bluish cast. the scales are much larger than the speckled trout, but in their form position of their fins teeth mouth &c they are precisely like them." (9:III,14) The most notable feature of the arctic grayling is its huge, rainbow-colored, fan-shaped dorsal fin; it is unusual that Lewis, careful observer and notetaker that he was, would fail to note this feature in his description.

The party proceeded over Lemhi Pass, down the Salmon River a short distance, and recrossed the divide again into the Bitterroot Valley. After a brief respite at Traveler's Rest near the mouth of Lolo Creek, it began one of the most grueling journeys ever made in North America: the 11-day climb across the Lolo Trail to the Clearwater River. Food was so scarce during this time that the men were forced to eat candles and

*Above: Lewis and Clark were the first white explorers to traverse and name the spectacular Gates of the Mountains.* (BRUCE SELYEM)

*Lewis's monkeyflower (right) and Clarkia, or ragged robin (far right), were named for their discoverers, the two captains.* (CHARLES KAY PHOTOS)

horses to survive, and the expedition almost came to a silent end deep in the wilderness. It is a tribute to the stamina of the men and the capability of the leaders that everyone lived through this ordeal and made it safely to the Pacific Ocean by November.

The Lewis and Clark Expedition spent a damp, drizzly, mildewy winter at Fort Clatsop, situated on the Pacific Ocean near the mouth of the Columbia River. In March, 1806, the explorers began their return journey, bequeathing Fort Clatsop to their Indian friend Chief Comowool. The journey back to Montana followed nearly the same route as the westward trip. The trip across the Lolo Trail went much more quickly and easily than it had the previous fall, taking only seven days. Upon reaching Lolo Hot Springs, the party celebrated with a dip in the now-famous waters, which were so hot that Lewis could only stay in for 19 minutes.

Traveller's Rest was reached on June 30, and here the expedition rested for two days. Lewis as usual spent much of his available time collecting and pressing plant specimens. Among the plants he collected here was one having a beautiful pink blossom and a large, edible root — the bitterroot, later to become the state flower of Montana. Strangely, Lewis did not mention this plant in his journals, even though it was undoubtedly abundant and was known by him to be an important source of food to the Indians. When the specimen made its way to botanist Frederick Pursh in England, Pursh named it *Lewisia rediviva* after its discoverer. This original type-specimen can be seen today at the Philadelphia Academy of Natural Sciences. Lewis also described the beautiful mountain lady's slipper, a species of orchid new to science.

While in the Bitterroot Valley, Lewis compiled another bird list, as well as a list of common shrubs. The birds he identified in the valley were "the dove the black woodpecker, the lark woodpecker, the logcock, the prarie lark, sandhill crain, prarie hen with the short and pointed tail, the robin, a speceis of brown plover, a few curloos, small black birds, ravens hawks and a variety of sparrows as well as the bee martin and the several speceis of Corvus genus." (9:V,176-7) A similar list might be made in the valley today; the species Lewis described probably included the mourning dove, Lewis's woodpecker, pileated woodpecker, horned lark, sandhill crane, sharp-tailed grouse, American robin, upland sandpiper, long-billed curlew, brown-headed cowbird, American raven, red-tailed hawk, vesper sparrow, eastern kingbird, crow, Clark's nutcracker and gray jay. The common shrubs along the valley included the "wild rose, servise berry, white berryed honeysuckle, seven bark, elder, alder aspin, choke cherry and the broad and narrow leafed

*The bitterroot (upper left), Montana's state flower, the mountain lady's slipper (lower left), Clark's nutcracker (upper right), and silver buffaloberry (lower right) were first described or collected in Montana by Meriwether Lewis.* (BITTERROOT BY PHIL FARNES, ALL OTHER PHOTOS BY LARRY THOMPSON)

*Shortly after re-entering what is now Montana in 1806, the expedition paused to take a dip in Lo Lo Hot Springs (upper left).* (PACIFIC RAILROAD SURVEY LITHOGRAPH)

*After separating from Clark, Lewis passed through the "Prairie of the knobs," a striking glacial landscape near present-day Ovando (below), and re-crossed the Continental Divide over Lewis and Clark Pass (upper right).* (LARRY THOMPSON PHOTOS)

willow." (9:V,181) At Traveller's Rest, Lewis inexplicably penned a long, detailed description of the black-tailed prairie dog, although he had not seen one alive for almost a year! Perhaps he had been working it out in his head and only here found the leisure to write it out.

On July 3, 1806, Lewis and Clark separated, Lewis heading northeast along the Blackfoot River and Clark heading southeastward toward the Missouri headwaters and eventually the Yellowstone Valley. This parting must have been an emotional one, since the two friends had no assurance they would ever see each other again. "I could not avoid feeling much concern," wrote Lewis, "although I hoped this separation was only momentary." (9:V,183) As it turned out, the two explorers were to be reunited in what is now North Dakota six weeks later.

Lewis's small party proceeded up the Little Blackfoot River through an area known today as Kleinschmidt Flats. He described this area as "an extensive high prarie rendered very uneven by a vast number of little hillucks and sink-holes...these plains I called the prarie of the knobs from a number of knobs being irregularly scattered through it." (9:V,191) This interesting area can be seen today from Montana Highway 200 about five miles west of Ovando. Geologically, it is known as a dead-ice moraine, characterized by kame-and-kettle topography — numerous hills and potholes formed by the melting in place of huge chunks of glacial ice.

Lewis noted pronghorn in this valley, one of the few places they were native west of the divide in Montana. He also prepared study skins of Columbian ground squirrels and red squirrels, collected plants, and noted passenger pigeons breeding in great numbers. His bird list included "some Curloos, bee martains wood peckers plover, robins, doves, ravens, hawks and a variety of sparrows common to the plains also some ducks." (9:V,192)

On July 7, 1806, Lewis crossed the Continental Divide at a place known today as Lewis and Clark Pass, about six miles north of Rogers Pass which is crossed by Montana Highway 200. Although this pass is quite low — 6,323 feet — its saddle supports plant species typical of the alpine tundra, a condition possibly due to the altitudinal depression of local climatic zones by wind. From this pass Lewis could see Haystack Butte near the present-day town of Augusta and the Missouri River Valley. He reached White Bear Islands just above the Great Falls only eight days after leaving Traveler's Rest; the previous summer he had taken about seven weeks to travel between the same two points. White Bear Islands and vicinity were literally swarming with bison; as Lewis described it, "I sincerely beleif that there were not less that 10 thousand buffaloe within a circle of 2 miles arround that place....it is now the season at which the buffaloe begin to coppelate and the bulls keep a tremendious roaring we could hear them for many miles and there are such numbers of them that there is one continual roar." (9:V,199)

Lewis spent a few days near the Great Falls, taking time to sketch both Rainbow Falls and the Great Falls. There, opening a cache he had buried the previous summer, he learned to his dismay that all his painstakingly prepared plant specimens, collected all the way from Fort Mandan to the Great Falls, together with some grizzly bear skins, had been destroyed by spring floods, a tremendous personal loss and a great loss to science.

On July 17, Lewis headed northward, intent upon following the Marias River to its source in the mountains. He continued, cautiously, to a point on Cut Bank Creek about 12 miles northeast of Browning, where he spent four frustrating rainy days waiting for the sky to clear so he could determine longitude. As the sky never did cooperate, he sadly named this point "camp *disappointment*," (9:V,218) and resumed his journey. The party neared starvation here, and may have come to a worse pass if not for a providential flock of passenger pigeons that selected the trees around camp as their roost.

In the distance, floating like blue islands on the sea of grassland, were the three buttes of the Sweetgrass Hills, described by Lewis as "the broken *Mountains.*" (9:V,209) Lewis was surprised to find Columbian ground squirrels this far out onto the prairie, normally the habitation of the Richardson's ground squirrel. He was also surprised to find three species of cottonwood — plains, narrow-leaved, and black — occurring in a single grove.

Lewis's caution in traveling this region was due to the fact that it was the territory of the Piegan, a tribe of Blackfeet Indians that Lewis described as "a vicious lawless and reather an abandoned set of wretches." He wished "to avoid an interview with them" (9:V,206) at any cost. Unfortunately, he was not so lucky. On July 26 he encountered a band of eight, out-runners of a much larger band only a few miles away. In the ensuing skirmish — undoubtedly the most exciting and potentially disastrous adventure of the expedition — two Indians were killed by the explorers and Lewis himself was nearly shot by a Piegan. As he described it, "being bearheaded I felt the wind of his bullet very distinctly." (9:V,225) This Indian encounter would have vast implications in events of the succeeding decades.

Lewis's party fled toward the Missouri River, fearing pursuit by the larger band of Blackfeet. It is amazing that Lewis, during this headlong flight, took the time to collect still another plant specimen new to science:

*The desert evening primrose (top) and Rocky Mountain iris (bottom) were among the many plants previously unknown to science that were first collected in Montana by Meriwether Lewis.*
(PHIL FARNES, TOP; LARRY THOMPSON, BOTTOM)

*Euphorbia emarginata*, Snow-on-the-Mountain. Lewis could not contain his joy when on the next day he met a canoe party, which had split off from Clark's detachment at the Three Forks, at the mouth of the Marias River.

Lewis and his party proceeded quickly down the Missouri River. As it was familiar territory, Lewis wrote little in the way of descriptions. Lewis reached the mouth of the Yellowstone River on August 7, and found that Clark had preceded him there and then had continued downstream to avoid the mosquitoes.

Anxious to see his friend, Lewis pressed on down the river. Before he caught up with Clark, however, he was shot in the thigh by a nearsighted member of the party, who mistook him for an elk in the willows. In "infinite pain," Lewis wrote that "wrighting in my present situation is extreemly painfull to me," and decided to "desist until I recover and leave to my friend Capt. C. the continuation of our journal. however I must notice a singular Cherry....I have never seen...in blume..." (9:V,242-44) Thus, naturalist to the end, Lewis ended his epic journal with a detailed 200-word botanical description of the pin cherry, *Prunus pennsylvanicus!*

While Lewis was making history on the high plains, Clark was doing likewise on the Yellowstone River. Taking a shortcut from the Bitterroot Valley to the Beaverhead Valley via Gibbons Pass, where a buffalo trail made for easy travel, Clark cut about 60 miles from the route the expedition had taken the previous fall. A cache containing Lewis's plant specimens collected between Great Falls and the Beaverhead River was recovered, but only one specimen, the golden currant, survives today, indicating that most of the specimens had been damaged or lost. Clark proceeded quickly and reached the Yellowstone River (he called it the "Rochejhone") near present-day Livingston on July 15.

In the absence of Lewis, Clark took the business of recording botanical and zoological observations much more seriously. He described vegetation and plant species, and noted plants that were used by Indians. His detailed descriptions of the herds of large mammals along the Yellowstone River bottom are almost unbelievable today. As he described it, "for me to mention or give an estimate of the differant Species of wild animals on this river particularly Buffalow, Elk Antelopes & Wolves would be increditable. I shall therefore be silent on the subject further." (9:V,290)

Although the party moved right along down the river —traveling as much as 80 river miles a day — Clark found the time to pen the first description known to science of the mountain sucker and the soft-shelled turtle. He also put together a species list (including "antelops, wolves, pigions, Dovs, Hawks, ravins, crows, larks, Sparrows, Eagles & bank martins &c. &c"), (9:V,279) described a fossil fish, noticed the first wild grape — an eastern species — on the river bottom, commented on the poor quality of the coal seams outcropped along the river, and described the effects of grasshoppers on the grassland ecosystem: "It may be proper to observe that the emence Sworms of *Grass hoppers* have distroyed every sprig of Grass for maney miles..." (9:V,276)

The Yellowstone River bottom land of 1806 must have looked considerably different than it does today, with its endless floodplain forests of gigantic cottonwoods. Clark and his party had to travel all the way downstream to the present site of Columbus before they could find a cottonwood big enough to make a canoe! In those days, prairie fires kept the cottonwood groves along the Yellowstone small and scattered and largely restricted to islands.

The entire expedition was reunited on August 12, safe and sound, except for Lewis, who was completely incapacitated by his severe wound. On September 21, the party reached St. Charles, Missouri, bringing to an end one of the greatest expeditions of scientific and geographical discovery of the century.

Honors were heaped upon the intrepid explorers, who had long since been given up for dead. Both men were commissioned brigadier generals; Clark was appointed Governor of Missouri Territory, and Lewis Governor of Louisiana Territory. This latter appointment proved to be a shallow honor and a grave mistake. Lewis, caught up in a demanding social life, and conscientiously devoting his energies to his new position of responsibility, was unable to find any time to work on a report of his findings on the expedition. Then, on October 11, 1809, he died under disputed circumstances of a gunshot wound at a roadside inn in Tennessee.

With Lewis gone, the only person left to write up the scientific aspects of the journey was Dr. Benjamin Barton, with whom Clark had made arrangements for preparing the scientific account. But Barton, in ill health and preoccupied with other pursuits, also failed to write the much-needed scientific account. The

### BEFORE LEWIS AND CLARK

The first white explorers to enter what is now Montana may have been two fur traders, brothers Louis-Joseph and Francois la Verendrye. In 1738, the brothers traveled with their father, the French soldier and pioneer fur trader Pierre Gaultier de Varennes, Sieur de la Verendrye, to the Mandan Indian villages near present-day Bismarck, North Dakota. In 1742, the father sent his sons on a westward expedition to search for a Northwest Passage — a water route to the Pacific Ocean. Louis-Joseph and Francois did not keep a detailed journal, and it is impossible to trace their route. Historians, however, have been fascinated with a reference in the Verendrye papers to "shining mountains," which the brothers reported seeing on New Year's Day, 1743. These may have been the Black Hills of South Dakota, the Bighorn Mountains, or simply high badlands or escarpments. It is possible that the explorers entered what is now southeastern Montana, and that the "shining mountains" were the Bighorns.

In the summer of 1805, while Lewis and Clark were toiling up the Missouri River toward its headwaters, a French fur trader named Francois Larocque was exploring the Yellowstone River Valley. Unlike the Verendryes, Larocque kept a detailed journal, which indicates that he crossed the southeastern corner of Montana, crossed the Big Horn River, descended Pryor Creek to the Yellowstone River, and followed the Yellowstone to its mouth.

Although he was by no means a naturalist, Larocque was interested in wildlife, botany, and fossils, and his journals contain many interesting observations. On July 27, 1805, Larocque described the wildlife of the Powder River Valley: "When we arrived here the plains on the western side of the river were covered with Buffaloes and the bottoms full of Elk and Jumping deers & Bears which last are mostly yellow and very fierce. It is amazing how very barren the ground is between this and the lesser [Little] Missouri, nothing can hardly be seen but those Corne de Racquettes [plains pricklypear]. Our horses are nearly starved. There is grass in the woods but none in the plains which by the by might with more propriety be called hills, for though there is very little wood it is impossible to find a level spot of one or two miles in extent except close to the River." (2:27) While camped nearby, Larocque collected some fossils of coiled cephalopods or ammonites. Although Larocque's discoveries were of limited scientific value, the importance of his explorations to the fur trade was great, and his account remains of significant historical value.

### LEWIS AND CLARK ON MOSQUITOES

"Musquetoes troublesome." Lewis, May 23, 1805
"Musquetors troublesome." Clark, May 23, 1805
"Musquetors verry troublesom." Clark, July 2, 1805
"Musquitors verry troublesom" Clark, July 18, 1805
"Misquetors verry troublesom" Clark, July 20, 1805
"Musquetoes troublesome as usual." Lewis, July 8, 1805
"Musquetoes troublesome of course." Lewis, July 1, 1805
"Musquetoes uncommonly large and reather troublesome." Lewis, July 29, 1806
"Musquetoes more than usually troublesom." Lewis, August 10, 1806
"Musquetors excessively tormenting." Clark, September 7, 1806
"Musquitors emencely noumerous & troublesom." Clark, July 10, 1805
"Musquetors excessively troublesom" Clark, August 2, 1806
"Musquetoes extreemly troublesome." Lewis, July 12, 1806

journals of the expedition were finally edited by Nathaniel Biddle but were not published until 1814. Regrettably, most of the botanical and zoological material had been left out of the Biddle edition, since Biddle understood that Barton was to have written a separate scientific report. The original journals were then lost and forgotten.

It was not until three quarters of a century later that Dr. Elliott Coues, while researching an annotation of the Biddle edition, rediscovered the long-lost original, handwritten journals at the American Philosophical Society in Philadelphia. Coues' edition of the journals, published in 1893, contained extensive scientific annotations, but it still omitted the bulk of scientific description contained in the original journals. In 1904 Reuben Gold Thwaites published the original journals verbatim in commemoration of the expedition's centennial. Thus, many of the expedition's most salient scientific findings were essentially lost to science for 100 years!

Clark resided in St. Louis after the return of the expedition, and eventually became Superintendent of Indian Affairs. In this capacity, he was to have considerable influence on later exploration, military conquest, and settlement of the Great West. He died in 1838.

Of the various plant and animal specimens collected by Lewis and Clark, few survive today. Most of Lewis's painstakingly-pressed plant specimens were lost before the expedition ever got back to St. Louis. The ones that made it were transferred to German botanist Frederick Pursh, who wrote: "A small but highly interesting collection of dried plants was put in my hands by [Lewis] ... A much more extensive one, made on their slow ascent towards the Rocky Mountains ... had unfortunately been lost .... The loss of this first collection is the more to be regretted, when I consider that the small collection communicated to me, consisting of about one hundred and fifty specimens, contained not above a dozen plants well known to me to be natives of North America, the rest being either entirely new or but little known." (8:I,x-xi) These specimens, known as the Lewis and Clark herbarium, are now housed at the Philadelphia Academy of Sciences.

Purish published in 1814 his *Flora Americanae Septentrionalis,* or "Flora of North America," which contained illustrations of 13 of the plants Lewis and Clark had brought back from the plains and mountains of the West. In acknowledgement of the contribution of the two Captains to science, Pursh named two genera — *Lewisia* and *Clarkia* — and several species in their honor.

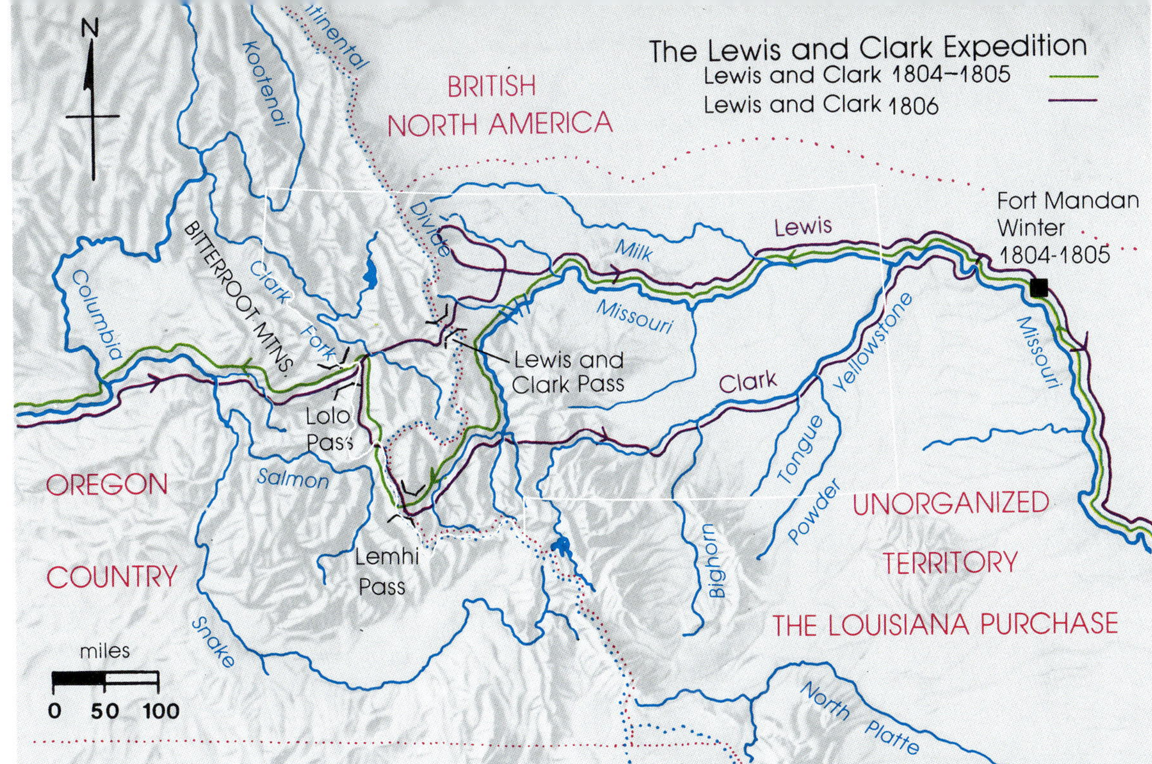


The fate of the animal specimens brought back by the expedition was less fortunate. Although various skins and skeletons — and even a living magpie and a live prairie dog —made their way to Washington, most specimens were lost or delabelled during various museum shuffles over the decades. A single specimen of Lewis's Woodpecker, collected in 1806 on the return trip, is the only surviving specimen known today from the expedition.

Nevertheless, in spite of a century's delay in publication of the journals and the loss of specimens, the Lewis and Clark Expedition is recognized today as one of the great scientific and geographical expeditions of all times. Besides discovering and describing many species of plants and animals, the explorers mapped out the geography of this hitherto-unknown region, and laid the foundations for the century of exploration that was to follow.

## Sources


1. Bakeless, J. E. *Lewis and Clark: Partners in Discovery.* New York: Morrow, 1947.
2. Brown, M. H. *The Plainsmen of the Yellowstone.* New York: G. P. Putnam's Sons, 1961.
3. Burroughs, R.D. *The Natural History of the Lewis and Clark Expedition.* East Lansing: Michigan State Univ. Press, 1961.
4. Coues, E., ed. *History of the Expedition Under the Command of Lewis and Clark.* 4 vols. New York: Francis P. Harper, 1893.
5. Cutright, P. R. *Lewis and Clark, Pioneering Naturalists.* Urbana: Univ. of Illinois Press, 1969.
6. DeVoto, B. *Journals of Lewis and Clark.* Boston: Houghton-Mifflin, 1953.
7. Eide, I. H. *American Odyssey: The Journey of Lewis and Clark.* Chicago: Rand McNally, 1969.
8. Pursh, F. Flora americae septentrionalis; *or, A Systematic Arrangement and Description of the Plants of North America; Containing, Besides What Have Been Described by Preceding Authors, Many New and Rare Species, Collected During Twelve Years Travels and Residence in That Country.* 2 vols. London: White, Cochrane & Co., 1814.
9. Thwaites, R. G., ed. *Original Journals of the Lewis and Clark Expedition, 1804-1806.* 8 vols. New York: Antiquarian Press, Ltd., 1959.
10. Walcheck, K. C. "Birds Observed by Lewis and Clark in Montana, 1805-1806." *Proceedings of the Montana Academy of Sciences* 29(1969):13-22.
11. Walcheck, K. C. "Montana Wildlife 170 Years Ago." *Montana Outdoors* 7(July-Aug. 1976): 15-30.
12. Walcheck, K. C. "With Pen and Plant in Hand." *Montana Outdoors* 13(July-Aug. 1982): 30-37.

CHAPTER 2

# David Thompson Explores Northwestern Montana

*In May of 1808, David Thompson became the first white explorer to make the arduous portage around Kootenai Falls near present-day Libby. This watercolor of the falls was painted by James Madison Alden more than half a century later.* (NATIONAL ARCHIVES)

The spring of 1807 was not an ordinary one for the Blackfeet Indians, that great Nation that roamed the high plains along the Rocky Mountain Front following the vast herds of bison. These Indians sensed, perhaps more urgently than ever before, the menace of the white man, who was slowly but inexorably penetrating western Canada and the U.S. territories — the white man, who had already driven tribe after tribe of native Americans from their homes east of the Mississippi River.

The summer before, a band of white men — namely, Meriwether Lewis and his scouting party — had penetrated Blackfeet lands deeper than had any white person before and had killed two Piegans (one of the three tribes of the Blackfeet people) near the headwaters of the Marias River. Now many Piegans had moved south from the mountains and foothills of Canada into the Missouri River country, in part seeking revenge on their brothers' murderers, who by this time were safely back in civilization.

Meanwhile, a plucky explorer, accompanied by his Indian wife and three children, quietly and unobtrusively slipped across the Canadian Rockies through the newly-vacated Indian territory. Had it not been for the Blackfeet focusing their attention southward, chances are he never would have made it through this land of hostile natives. This safe passage across the Rockies led, during the course of the next few years, to the first exploration of the land that is now northwestern Montana by an intrepid Welshman named David Thompson.

Thompson, who logged some 80,000 miles on foot, horseback and canoe during explorations that spanned six decades (1780s-1840s), was virtually unknown during his lifetime and died in poverty and obscurity. His meticulously detailed journals were kept hidden because of fur-trade-era politics, and did not see the light of day for almost a half a century.

Thompson was born in 1770 in Westminster, England to an impoverished Welsh family. His father died when he was two, and he and his brother John were raised by their mother, who sent them to a boys' charity school near Westminster Abbey. At the age of 14, David was apprenticed for seven years to the Hudson's Bay Company, one of two huge fur trading conglomerates that effectively ruled the Canadian wilds. Sailing from London in 1784, he arrived in a raw, new land where people were few; he was quickly assigned to the remote outpost of Churchill on Hudson's Bay. While at Churchill, it is believed that Thompson came across a small library of natural history books that was kept by the officers, and studied them voraciously. This period of study would be supported by the detailed and perceptive natural history observations that pervade his journals and that bespeak an insatiable curiosity coupled with a gift for observation.

Thompson traveled widely in the interior of Canada during his years with the Hudson's Bay Company (1784-1797). Toward the end of his tenure as fur trader and geographer, he learned valuable surveying skills that were to serve him well in later years. The Indians, impressed by his constant reading of the stars, called him Koo-Koo-Sint, "Star Man." When his apprenticeship was up, he became a company fur trader, and ranged farther and wider into the vast muskeg wilderness of boreal Canada. In 1797 he left the Hudson's Bay Company to join its rival, the North West Company, and as a consequence his travels shifted toward the northwestern part of Canada. In 1799 he married an Indian girl of 14 named Charlotte Small.

While Lewis and Clark were ascending the Missouri River, Thompson was exploring Lake Athabasca and the Peace River deep in the taiga of present-day northern Alberta. In 1807 he crossed the Continental Divide over Howse Pass — with a little help, however indirect, from Lewis and Clark — and became the first white person to explore the source of the Columbia River. Near present-day Canal Flats, British Columbia, where both the Columbia and the Kootenai Rivers originate, he established the trading post he called Kootenay House and there spent his first winter west of the Continental Divide.

The following spring (1808), Thompson left Kootenay House and followed the Kootenai River southward into what is now Montana. On April 26, 1808 he crossed the 49th parallel, becoming the first white man to enter Montana by this route. He stayed a while in the Tobacco Plains near present-day Rexford, an area now under the silty waters of Lake Kookanusa.

Thompson and his small crew were perpetually on the brink of starvation that spring. Game was scarce, and the fishing was abysmal. "As to fishing," wrote Thompson, "we have often angled, but never once had a bite." (9:19) Finally, one of the Indians with the party killed a mountain lion, which was summarily consumed. Before it was eaten, however, Thompson — although starving — took measurements and wrote in his journal a description of the animal. "He was three feet in height on the fore leg, from the nose to the insertion of the tail seven feet and a half, the Tail two feet ten inches; very strongly legged with sharp claws, the Back and upper part of the Tail of a Fawn color, the Belly and under part of the Tail and it's tip white, the flesh was white and good, in quantity equal to the Antelope, the Liver was rich, and the two men that eat it, for several hours had a violent headache, which passed away: The Indians say the habits of this Animal is to lie in covert, and spring upon the back of the Deer,

*Thompson traveled extensively in the Kootenai River Valley (above) and throughout northwestern Montana between 1808 and 1812. During these travels he faced Indian dangers, near-starvation, winter blizzards, and rivers "full of violent eddies, which threatened us with destruction ...."*
(TOP, ESTELLE PHOTO; BOTTOM, LARRY THOMPSON)

*Before crossing the Yaak River (top left), Thompson and his crew, on the brink of starvation, dined on mountain lion meat.* (UPPER LEFT, GEORGE WUERTHNER; UPPER RIGHT, GARY HOLMES)
*Thompson later traveled cross-country in the lower Flathead (bottom) and Little Bitterroot River valleys.* (RAY MILLER)

to which he fastens himself by his claws and directly cuts the back sinew of the neck, the Deer then becomes an easy prey." (9:20n)

On May 6, 1808 continuing down the Kootenai River, the party shot China Rapids below the current site of Libby, and presently arrived at Kootenai Falls, which Thompson called "the Lower Dalles." (5:250) Finding the falls impassable, the party was forced to portage, but found the cliffs bordering the falls were nearly as impassable as the falls themselves. "The River had steep banks of Rocks," wrote Thompson, "and was only thirty yards in width; this space was full of violent eddies, which threatened us with destruction and wherever the river contracted the case was always the same, the current was swift, yet to look at the surface the eddies make it appear to move as much backward as forward." (9:25n) Starved and exhausted after this grueling portage, the party fished at the foot of the falls, but caught "nothing as usual." (9:23) Then, the men found "part of a Chevruil, which the Eagles had more than half devoured — it smelt strongly, but as we were without Food, were glad to take what remained, altho' we would hardly bear it's Smell." (9:26) In spite of boiling the rotten deer meat, Thompson and his men got sick from this putrid fare. Finally, on May 8, the party came to a camp of Kootenai and Flat Bow Indians, from whom they obtained some native morsels: "small Carp [probably suckers] which they seine in a small River and a kind of bread made of moss from the trees." (9:27n)

One of the features of this strange and hostile western landscape that impressed Thompson was its diverse and luxuriant forests. The Kootenai River passed between primeval stands of western red cedar, western larch, Douglas fir, western hemlock, and western white pine of massive proportions, reflecting the influence of the warm, moist Pacific air masses, which unload much of their moisture here. As Thompson described these trees, "the white Cedars were from fifteen to thirty six feet girth; clean grown and tall in proportion, numbers were of the largest size, and in walking round them they appeared to have six or eight sides. The pines were from eighteen to forty two feet in girth, measured at ten feet above the ground, which the snow enabled us to do. They were finely formed, and rose full two hundred feet without a branch, and threw off very luxuriant heads .... " (9:132n)

Thompson was struck by the contrast between these magnificent groves and the tough little taiga trees of the north or the struggling pines of the east slope of the Rockies. "On the east side of the Mountains the Trees were small, a stunted growth with branches to the ground; there we were Men, but on the west side we were pigmies." (9:132-33) Thompson lamented the fact

*In David Thompson's day, entire valleys in western Montana were filled with gigantic conifers, such as these western red cedars at Ross Creek. Today only a few sites with giant cedars remain.* (JERRY PAVIA)

that all this lúmber-on-the-hoof stood languishing in these unknown wilds, "without a possibility of being brought to market" (9:20n) and being used as timber for the British Navy. "In such forests," he bewailed, "what could we do with Axes of two pounds weight!" (9:133) If only Thompson could have witnessed the dizzying rapidity with which these magnificent forests were to be stripped away a century hence. The removal of these virgin stands of rain forest by lumbermen was accomplished with such zeal and with such thoroughness that today only one small stand of the Pacific giants is left untouched in Montana. This is the Ross Creek Cedar Grove, saved by the U.S. Forest Service, which is easily accessible today from Montana Highway 56 between Troy and Noxon.

After exploring the Kootenay Lake region of British Columbia, Thompson returned to Kootenay House, where he spent his second winter in the Rockies. The following summer (1809), he repeated his descent of the Kootenai River, making the arduous portage around Kootenai Falls for the second time. There he found the berries of the kinnikinnick, or, as he called them, "small red Raisins of the Ground as at Montreal &c — they are sweet & harm less." (9:37) After spending some time in the Lake Pend Oreille region of present-day Idaho, Thompson made his first journey up the Clark Fork River into Montana. Here again he traveled though the magnificent Pacific rain forest, characterized by "much Hemlock Larch Fir Pine White & Red Cedar &c &c ... the road we have come today is mostly thro' very fine Woods, especially Cedar many of [20 to 30 feet] round & tall in proportion." (9:46-7) At Heron Rapids, he found the Indians fishing for "Herrings" (probably mountain whitefish) with a small dipping net.

Thompson left the Clark Fork River bottom somewhere near present-day Paradise and proceeded cross-country to the valley of the Little Bitterroot River. On October 16, 1809, he described the Mission Mountains, which afforded "a very wide & sublime view, they are loaded with snow as in the depth of Winter." In the Little Bitterroot Valley, Thompson observed a "plain of sterile white earth," (9:51) probably the first description of the sediments left by glacial Lake Missoula, which once filled the valleys of northwestern Montana during the Pleistocene epoch. These sediments, which may be observed today

*On February 26, 1812 Thompson climbed Mount Jumbo, the "high Knowl" at the left edge of the picture above, and looked over Mount Sentinel and the future site of the city of Missoula.* (PACIFIC RAILROAD SURVEY LITHOGRAPH)

*David Thompson wrote the first detailed description of the dipper or water ouzel (top left), which he found to be fairly common — as it is today — at Kootenai Falls.* (TOM ULRICH)

*He also described the migratory movements of waterfowl such as the pintail (middle left) and Canada goose (bottom left).* (KEN REYNOLDS, TOM ULRICH)

throughout this area, stand out from their surroundings due to their striking white coloration. The story of the origin of these sediments would not be described until a century later, and would not be believed by the scientific community for many decades after that. Thompson's party proceeded northward along the Little Bitterroot River to the vicinity of McGregor Lake and Thompson Lakes and then back to the Kootenai River, which it followed downstream into Idaho, making a third portage around Kootenai Falls.

The contrast between the abundance of game encountered in the plains of eastern Montana by Lewis and Clark and the almost total lack of game in Thompson's travels is striking. In the dense, primeval forests of northwestern Montana, about the only thing more scarce than game was fish. Thompson's journals often make reference to unsuccessful hunts and the lack of game, in stark contrast to Lewis and Clark's journals, which literally teem with elk, bison, deer, pronghorn, and bighorn sheep. "The Hills close on both Sides," wrote Thompson on the Clark Fork River, "& every where seems totally destitute of Fowl & Animals (9:47) ... we see the Tracks of no Animals nor are there Fowl of any kind (9:48) ... Huntg in every Quarter," he wrote on the Kootenai River, "but all without Success ..." (9:20) Of the Fisher River country, he wrote: "no Beaver nor Fowl, no Fish ... " (9:23)

The implications of this scarcity of game to an explorer's chances of survival are obvious. Thompson did not have the luxury that Lewis and Clark enjoyed of being able to drop a bison at a whim, and he probably had to spend a much greater proportion of his time hunting or gathering, had to rely on the Indians to a much greater degree for food, had to carry more provisions with him at all times, and probably — as his journals make painfully clear — spent a good deal of his time simply starving. That he was able to cover as much ground as he did at all seasons of the year is silent testimony to his physical and emotional stamina.

Later in the fall of 1809, after the winter snows had arrived in the Rockies, Thompson headed back up the Clark Fork River to a wide, grassy valley near the current site of Thompson Falls. Here he built the famous fur trading post he called "Saleesh House" — a sturdy cabin with timbers hewn from the gigantic fir and larch that cloaked the nearby hillsides. There, he and his small party passed the first Christmas ever spent by a white man in Montana. During the winter, Thompson made several trips to the lower Flathead

River to trade with the natives. In April, 1810, as the spring runoff was just beginning, he set off on foot back down the Clark Fork into Idaho.

As spring wore on, Thompson started up the Kootenai River, and became the first white person to travel this river upstream. On May 23, 1810, Thompson began his fourth portage around Kootenai Falls. In spite of the demands of the portage, he stopped to notice a strange little bird that actually appeared to be plunging under water to feed. There he wrote the following remarkable description, the first careful scientific account of the dipper or water ouzel, a bird that is particularly common at Kootenai Falls. "The little brown black Bird so fond of the Water & that winters along the open Waters of this Country, abt the size of a large Snow Bunting saw here today in the Brook, his Beak is abt 1 In long & pointed like a Plover his Tail short -his Eyes & a little about them of a rusty colour - all the rest of the Body is of a uniform colour of brown Black - he was in the Cascades of the Brook plunging & fishing for Worms boldly - often letting himself dive upon the foaming little Waves of the Brook & seemed always quite at his Ease his plunging was always while he kept firm foot on the bottom - the moment he lost his footing he dove down, but in an instant always brought himself up with amazing dexterity & agility - he brought for his young a small Kind of Insect out of the Water something like a very small frog - his food seemed to be in plenty, he is not in the least web footed - & with all his plunging in the little Cascades his Feathers never in the least appeared either Wet or ruffled." (9:119-20)

Thompson did not return to Montana until February of 1811, when he passed back down the Kootenai River, portaged from the Fisher River to the Clark Fork, and continued down the Clark Fork and Columbia Rivers all the way to the Pacific Ocean, again a first for a white explorer. The next fall, after surveying the entire Columbia River, he returned to Saleesh House, which he found in "ruinous condition" (9:181) after only one year's absence and which had to be completely rebuilt.

After spending his second winter there, he set off with a fairly large party to explore the area around what is now the town of Missoula. On February 26, 1812, he climbed to the top of Mount Jumbo, the impressive "high Knowl" (9:203) that overlooks the Clark's Fork and Bitterroot Valleys. From there he traced out Lewis and Clark's route, traveled just six years earlier, noting where the party had camped at Traveller's Rest and where Lewis had continued up the Blackfoot River toward the Great Falls. A few days later, Thompson ascended another "bare Knowl" (9:214) — this time the great end moraine that dams the Flathead River Valley near Polson — and became the first man to record a view of Flathead Lake: "We came smartly on trot & hard

*David Thompson's map of the West was to earn him a place as one of the greatest cartographers in the new world, but it was not released to the public until almost 30 years after his death. This section of his map shows the area around Flathead Lake, which he called "Saleesh Lake."* (COURTESY, MONTANA HISTORICAL SOCIETY)

Gallop ... When we alighted on the top of bare Knowl, commanding a very extensive View of the Lake & Country far around ... all the ranges have many hollows, swellings -& Lawns more or less sloping." (9:214-15)

Later that spring (1812), Thompson descended the Clark Fork once again to Spokane House, then headed north into Canada and re-crossed the Continental Divide heading east. This was to be his last trip across the Rocky Mountains, for later that year he retired from the North West Company and took his family to Montreal, where he set himself up in business as a surveyor. Thompson had a very large family, and he was a devoted father. He used up what might have been his retirement money rescuing his sons from business debts, and spent his last years in destitute poverty. His eyesight was failing, and eventually he was unable to continue working; he had to sell his surveying instruments and pawn his coat to feed his wife and himself. He had tried to publish the map he had prepared of the hitherto unknown regions that he had explored. Such a map could have established his international reputation as a geographer and explorer, but the North West Company — perhaps attempting to keep his valuable information out of the hands of rivals — opposed his efforts, and he never found a publisher.

During his six decades and 80,000 miles of exploration, Thompson had kept a careful journal, and while in his 70s he compiled his observations into a manuscript he called *Travels in Western North America,* (8) a chronicle of discovery that was later to be compared favorably to Darwin's *Voyage of the Beagle.* (5) Thompson had hoped to sell his manuscript to provide subsistence for himself and his wife, but again he had no luck finding a publisher, although Washington Irving had expressed an interest in the manuscript. When Thompson died in 1857, at the age of 86, his life's work remained unknown to the world.

It wasn't until the 1880s that Thompson's work was to be rediscovered. Dr. Joseph Tyrrell, a geologist working as an assistant to George M. Dawson of the Geological Survey of Canada, became curious about the amazing accuracy of the government maps of the day, and eventually tracked down Thompson's

*David Thompson's staple food during his wilderness travels was the bulb of the camas. In midsummer western Montana meadows turn into sky-blue lakes of flowers as above right.* (LARRY THOMPSON)
*He occasionally had the luck to feast on white-tailed ptarmigan, shown here in winter (top) and summer (bottom) plumage.* (TOP, TIM CHRISTIE; BOTTOM, KEN REYNOLDS)

manuscript journals and unpublished map. Elliott Coues, ornithologist and historian, published a small portion of these journals in 1897. Later, Tyrrell learned about the existence of Thompson's *Narrative*, tracked it down, and finally, in 1916, published it (8) — more than a century after Thompson had explored the wilderness that was northwestern Montana.

Thompson was more of a geographer than a naturalist, and he apparently gathered no scientific plant or animal collections and described only one new species, the dipper, while in Montana. His writings, however, are full of detailed natural history observations that reveal a rare perception and an almost mystical love of nature. While working the Clark Fork River, he kept notes on the comings and goings of waterfowl; as he describes the fall migration, "The Manito of the geese, ducks, &c. has given his orders, they collect, and form flocks of, from 40 to 60, or more; and seem to have leaders. The Manito of the aquatic fowl has now given his orders of their departure to milder climates, his prescience sees the setting in of winter, and the freezing of the ponds. The leaders of the flock have now a deep note. The order is given, and flock after flock, in innumerable numbers, rise." (5:24)

In summer, he would observe the anatomy of the "Muskitoe" through a pocket microscope while it was biting him on the hand. He did not think much of the contemporary appraisal among scientists of the role of instinct in animal behavior, believing there must be more to it than the mere mechanistic unwinding of genetically-programmed, fixed-action patterns. "I have sometimes thought Instinct," he wrote, "to be a word invented by the learned to cover their ignorance of the ways and doings of animals for their self preservation, it is a learned word and shuts up all the reasoning powers." (5:23)

The following passage, perhaps more than any other, betrays the inner feelings of this explorer-naturalist, who had faced almost daily the possibility of starvation or sudden death in the wilderness, who in his wanderings far from civilization was forced to draw his nourishment from the lives of his fellow creatures. "No dove is more meek than the white grouse [ptarmigan]. I have often taken them from under the net, and provoked them all I could without injuring them, but all was submissive meekness, rough beings as we were, sometimes of an evening we could not help wondering why such an angelic bird should be doomed to be the suffering prey of every carnivorous animal, the ways of Providence are unknown to us." (5:21)

---

According to Thompson's Montana journals, on those few evenings in Montana when the members of his exploration party were not starving they often dined on "Rice & Roots," "Flour and Roots," or "Dog & Flour with Roots." (9:57-58) "These Roots," as Thompson described them in 1847, "are about the size of a Nutmeg, they are near the surface, and are [turned] up with a pointed Stick, they are farinaceous, of a pleasant taste, easily masticated, and nutritive, they are found in the small meadows of short grass, in a rich soil, and a short exposure to the sun dries them sufficiently to keep for years. I have some by me which were dug up in 1811 and are now thirty six years old and are in good preservation. I showed them to the late Lord Metcalfe who eat two of them, and found them something like bread; but although in good preservation, they, in two years lost their fine aromatic smell." (9:57n)

These were the roots of the camas, a plant that played a central role in Native American economy in western Montana. This beautiful plant produces flowers of a deep bluish-purple, which in midsummer can make moist meadows take on the appearance of a lake. Camas bulbs formed a staple of the Indian diet in western Montana and were harvested in great quantities in the vicinities of Hot Springs, St. Ignatius, Camas Prairie (near Potomac), and the Bitterroot Valley. Camas are widespread east of the Cascades and are found as far south as Utah. In Montana, they are principally found west of the Continental Divide in the Palouse-type valleys influenced by the maritime climate. Typically, they are found in valleys that are moist in spring but dry by midsummer. The bulbs were cooked in circular pits, the remains of which can still be found on hillsides above the camas patches, then dried and powdered or formed in cakes for overwinter storage. Father De Smet referred to the camas as "the queen root of this clime," (1:488) and botanist Thomas Nuttall reported camas in such abundance as to "communicate a general blue tint to many thousands of verdant acres." (6).

---

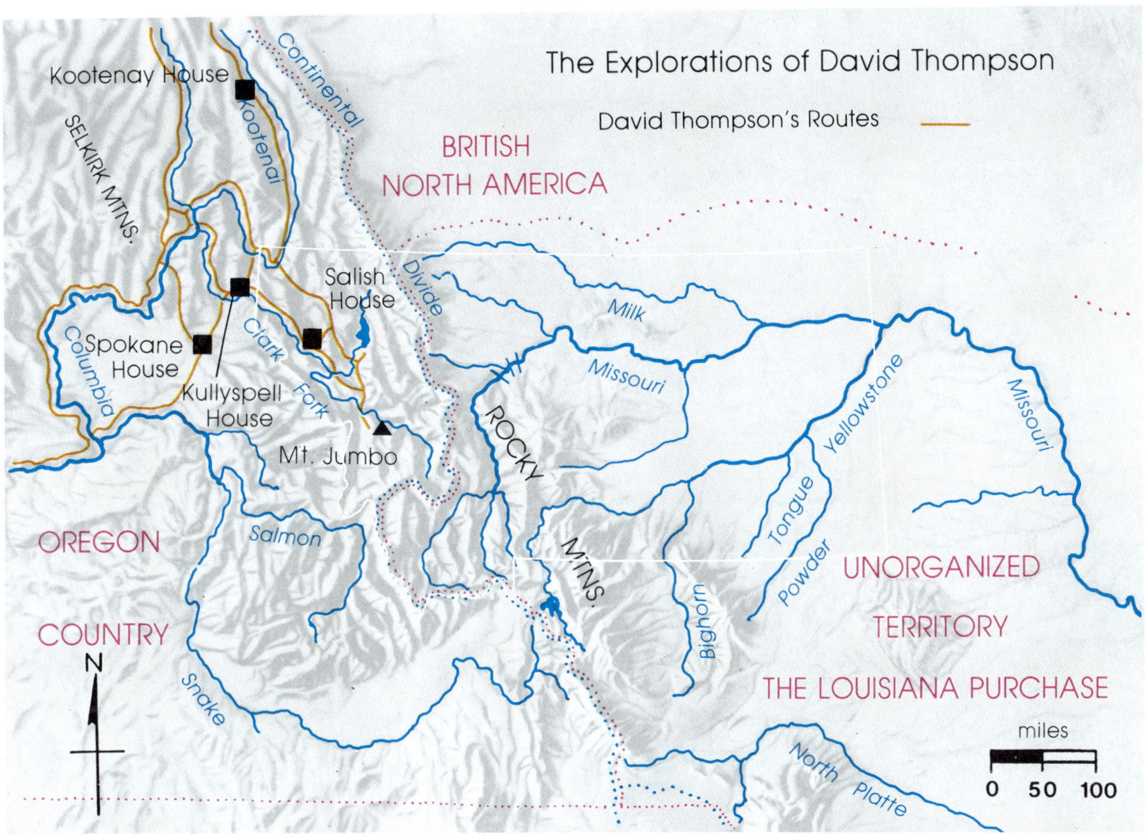


## Sources


1. Chittenden, H. M., and A. T. Richardson, eds. *The Life, Letters and Travels of Father Pierre-Jean DeSmet, S.J., 1801-1873.* New York: Francis P. Harper, 1905.
2. Coues, Elliott, ed. *New Light on the Early History of the Greater Northwest: The Manuscript Journals of Alexander Henry and of David Thompson, 1799-1814.* New York: Francis P. Harper, 1897.
3. Elliott, T. C. "David Thompson's Journeys in the Pend d'Oreille Country." *Washington Historical Quarterly* 23(1932):18-24.
4. Glover, R., ed. *David Thompson's Narrative of His Explorations in Western America, 1784-1812.* Toronto: The Champlain Society, 1962.
5. Hopwood, V. G., ed. *David Thompson's Travels in Western North America, 1784-1812.* Toronto: MacMillan, 1971.
6. Nuttall, Thomas. "A Catalogue of a Collection of Plants Made Chiefly in the Valleys of the Rocky Mountains or Northern Andes, Towards the Source of the Columbia River, by Mr. Nathaniel B. Wyeth, and Described by T. Nuttall." *Journal of the Academy of Natural Sciences of Philadelphia* 7(1834): 1-60.
7. Thompson, David. "Narrative of the Expedition to the Kootenae and Flat Bow Indian Countries on the Sources of the Columbia River." *Oregon Historical Quarterly* 26(1925):23-49.
8. Tyrrell, J. B., ed. *David Thompson's Narrative of His Explorations in Western America, 1784-1812.* Toronto: Publications of the Champlain Society, XII, 1916.
9. White, M. C., ed. *David Thompson's Journals Relating to Montana and Adjacent Regions, 1808-1812.* Missoula: Montana State Univ. Press, 1950.

CHAPTER 3

# Prince Paul of Wurttemberg

*Prince Paul of Wurttemberg ascended the Missouri River to the Three Forks and descended the Yellowstone River in 1830, a time when elk and bison were still abundant on the Great Plains. Prince Paul's account of his Montana travels was in the hands of a publisher when he died in 1860 and has since been lost or destroyed.* (LEFT, TOM DIETRICH; RIGHT, TOM ULRICH)

The annals of the exploration of Montana are strewn with the wreckage of lost discoveries such as Lewis's cached plant specimens, destroyed by the spring floods. As important as those specimens might have been to posterity, their loss fades compared to those that befell two scientific expeditions in Montana. One was the nearly total loss of three years' grueling and painstaking study through a mountainous wilderness; the other the nearly total loss of a life's work in natural history. In both cases those losses pitched those involved from certain fame to obscurity. They are especially poignant because the information so painfully gathered was lost not on a raging river nor during a furious Indian raid, but only after the collections had been safely transported back home. This, then, is the sad tale of one of these ill-fated, forgotten expeditions. We shall meet the other in a later chapter.

Friederich Paul Wilhelm, Prince of Wurttemberg, was the first bona fide scientist to set foot in Montana. Three years before Prince Maximilian and 13 years before John James Audubon he combed the Montana plains and Rockies collecting everything from wildflowers to wood ticks, discovering and naming species by the dozen. Yet today his name is known to but a handful of Montanans, and none of the species he collected and studied bears his name.

Prince Paul, born in Karlsruhe in Silesia in 1797, was related to or knew many of the reigning royal figures of Europe. Queen Victoria of England was his second cousin; Tsar Paul I of Russia his uncle, and Nicholas I and Alexander I his devoted cousins. Emperor Napoleon III of France and Emperor Franz I of Austria were likewise close relatives. King Friedrich I, first king of Wurttemberg, was his uncle, and for 44 years, during the reigns of Paul's cousin King Wilhelm I and second cousin Karl I, the Prince was second in the line of succession to the crown. In the royal court, he was held of equal rank and in equal esteem with the crowned heads. His education at the Stuttgart Gymnasium was the best his country could offer; he studied botany and zoology and longed to follow the example of the famous naturalist Baron von Humboldt. The young Prince was no idle pupil; he was a member of numerous scientific societies throughout Europe, and eventually received doctorate degrees in philosophy, medicine, and anatomy.

At an early age, it became clear that neither the court life nor the military life — the usual destiny of young men of his position — was for Prince Paul. He longed for the life of the Humboldtean explorer-naturalist, and, like so many young men of the European ruling classes and aristocracy, he was drawn to the lure of adventure in the wildernesses of the remaining unexplored continents. In 1817 he resigned a commission as a major general in the Prussian army under Frederick II to devote himself exclusively to natural history pursuits. He was soon exploring in the Near East, Algeria, Russia, and the Caribbean, and he began the rudiments of the natural history collections that would soon grow to become the most extensive private collection in all of Europe.

Prince Paul made four expeditions to the United States: 1822-24; 1829-31; 1849-51; and 1857. He visited what is now Montana on the second of these.

In 1822 he embarked on what was to be the first of these four major expeditions to the North American continent. In May of 1823, he wrote to General William Clark of the Lewis and Clark Expedition (then Superintendent of Indian Affairs) at St. Louis asking permission to travel deep into the Indian territory of the upper Missouri River. "Wishing ... to be considered only as a traveler in pursuit of scientific knowledge," he wrote, "my intension in coming to the United States [has] for its sole object ... the improvement of botany and natural history." (1:268) Traveling under the alias of "Baron von Hohenberg," he met General Clark at St. Louis shortly thereafter, and continued up the Missouri River with his eye on the Yellowstone River country so vividly described by Clark. He made it nearly as far north as present-day Pierre, South Dakota, but unfortunately was forced to cancel his plans to explore the Yellowstone River in Montana because of the Indian danger.

During his first Missouri River expedition, Prince Paul assiduously collected everything that ran, flew, slithered, crawled, or blossomed. He made it back to Stuttgart in 1824 laden with specimens of plants, frogs, turtles, birds, shells, insects, and mammals, including the skin and antlers of a mule deer.

In addition he brought back to Germany Sacajawea's son Baptiste Charbonneau ("Pompey" to Lewis and Clark), whom he had met on the Missouri River. Charbonneau not only traveled with the Prince, he stayed with the Prince in Germany for ten years and joined him on some of his later expeditions.

Prince Paul was, at least at the time, a believer that it was the duty of an explorer-naturalist to quickly publish the findings of his explorations, so that the scientific world might benefit from his discoveries. Therefore, he quickly set to work cataloging, arranging, and writing. In preparing the manuscript for a book on his first North American journey, he quarried volumes and volumes of painstakingly handwritten notes and sketches (the Prince was an accomplished sketch artist) and pored over his rapidly growing collections.

But the writing seemed to progress painfully slowly, and events got in the way. He was married in 1827 to Princess Sophie Dorothea Caroline von Thurn und Taxis, and a year later became the father of a baby boy

*In 1830, Prince Paul became the first in a long and distinguished parade of international nobility to visit Fort Union, the fur-trading post at the mouth of the Yellowstone. The former site is now a National Historic Site.* (PACIFIC RAILROAD SURVEY LITHOGRAPH; LARRY THOMPSON PHOTO)

*Prince Paul undoubtedly passed many a scene similar to this during his ascent of the Missouri.* (PAINTING BY KARL BODMER, COURTESY INTERNORTH ART FOUNDATION, JOSLYN ART MUSEUM, OMAHA, NEBRASKA)

*Pompey's Pillar, named for Sacajawea's son who would be Prince Paul's friend and traveling companion.* (TOM DIETRICH)

— his only child, Maximilian. In 1828 the first version of Prince Paul's account of his first journey to America was prepared for printing, but it never reached the public. Only one copy of this book (probably a printer's proof) was ever printed.

By this time the call of the American wilderness became too strong for the Prince to resist, and in 1829 he set sail again for the New World, hoping to realize his frustrated goal of exploring the Yellowstone River country he had heard so much about from General Clark. This journey was to last three years. From Santo Domingo, he sailed to New Orleans and traveled to St. Louis, where he spent the winter. In the spring of 1830, he began his second ascent of the Missouri River, and by May he had arrived at Fort Union (situated just upstream of the junction of the Missouri and Yellowstone Rivers near the present-day Montana-North Dakota border). Prince Paul was the first in a long and distinguished parade of international nobility to travel to this Wild West fur-trade post.

One of the few remaining records of Prince Paul's Montana explorations is the register of his purchases made while at Fort Union. Between May 17 and August 2, 1830, the Prince ran up a bill of $714.75 for supplies and services. This was a substantial sum of money in those days, even for a prince, and although he paid his tab at Fort Union in full, he was in debt to the fur-trade company of Pratte, Chouteau, and Co. when he finally returned to Europe.

From Fort Union, the Prince continued up the Missouri River into what is now Montana. He filled notebooks with natural-history observations and sketches, but all that is known today of his itinerary is that he traveled to the "foot of the Rocky Mountains" at the "Headwater region of the Missouri," (1:333,472) studied the Blackfeet and Assiniboines, and returned down the Yellowstone River with voluminous collections of plant and animal specimens.

After a brief return to Fort Union, Prince Paul descended the Missouri River and spent three months with the Sioux Indians at Ft. Tecumseh (later Ft. Pierre). That fall and winter he headed south to Mexico, and then toured the northeastern United States. In 1831 he returned to Europe.

Almost immediately upon his return, Prince Paul began converting the Castle of Bad Mergentheim, which he and his wife had received as a wedding gift, into one of the most complete private scientific museums in Europe. Work on his North American specimens undoubtedly took up a great deal of his time, for it was not before 1834 that he made any scientific report of the findings of his North American expeditions in the form of a brief paper presented *in absentia* at a convocation of German naturalists in Stuttgart. He probably started work on a book describing his second journey about this time, but he still had to face the nagging fact that his first book was not yet published.

So he accepted his duty to science and dusted off the unpublished account of his first journey, which he had written some eight years earlier. The Prince revised this 1828 version extensively and here and there added footnotes alluding to his more recent Montana travels. Prince Paul's book on his first journey (1822-1824) was finally published in 1835, 11 years after his return; in it, he promised that his observations made in Montana on the second journey (1829-31) would be "reported in due time... On the basis of my collections, I intend to publish in separate treatises the geographic and natural historical observations of my two trans-Atlantic journeys." (1:8,333) In the 1840s, the Prince commissioned an artist named Rosshirt to paint 90 watercolors based on his field sketches and on the specimens of plant and animals that he had brought back from America.

Some of the natural history descriptions that appeared in this edition undoubtedly were influenced by observations made on his little-known second journey. He described the white-tailed jackrabbit, a common resident of the Montana plains: "In the winter this hare is snowwhite down to the toes and lower part of the paws, which are yellowish. The tips of the ears are dark black, shading into a light brown color. This is a very large hare. In the summer it is light brown except the belly, which is entirely white." (1:383) Of the Canada goose, he wrote: "the Canadian goose is incorrectly named, since it is the most widely distributed variety in North America. It might be called much more appropriately Anser nigricollis ("black-necked goose")." (1:344) The Prince was struck by the close similarity between the northern Great Plains and the grasslands of South America. "Strikingly peculiar and manifestly unique is the geographic distribution of plants which show the greatest analogy to the temperate volcanic plateaus of Mexico and Peru, and which seem to have been transferred, as if by magic, from the regions of the Andes into the midst of the prairie country of the central part of the United States." (1:382)

Prince Paul's account of his first journey contains the following account of the prairie rattlesnake, which he undoubtedly encountered many times in Montana:

"On account of their clumsiness it is a rare occurrence that rattlesnakes attack or pursue a person. They are really less dangerous than is usually assumed. Their rattling and their rigid stare reveal more the feeling of fear than that of anger. There is scarcely a case on record in which these snakes had injured a sleeping person. It is true that their love for warmth often brings these unwelcome guests into the neighborhood of night camps of travelers, indeed even under their blankets. ...The art of charming snakes especially rattlesnakes by Whistling and the use of superstitious ceremonies is one of the tricks with which Indian jugglers have long worked upon the credulity of weakminded persons. In order to gain superiority over their fellow-men some creoles succeeded in gaining possession of the secret, and they know how to lend this business all the mystical dignity which constitutes the customary formula of such meaningless actions, whose purpose is the deception of the simple. With great and solemn earnestness an old Frenchman maintained, when I had come back to the river bank, that he possessed this art, and requested me to follow him into the forest after the completion of my meal. Tho I was very tired I could not resist this invitation, since I, in a way, flattered myself that I should be able to see thru the deception. In this I succeeded beyond all expectation. After he had conducted me to a decaying tree the trickster began to

*Prince Paul traveled to the headwaters of the Missouri River (above) and descended the Yellowstone River, shown here with the Absaroka Mountains in the background.* (PENCIL SKETCH BY A. E. MATHEWS, COURTESY MONTANA HISTORICAL SOCIETY; TOM DIETRICH PHOTO)

*Prince Paul suggested that the name of the Canada goose be changed to "black-necked goose," since the bird is by no means restricted to Canada. He also described how the Indians charmed rattlesnakes by whistling.* (TOM ULRICH; RIGHT, ALLEN WIEDENRICH)

whistle, after he previously had conjured the good and evil spirits with all sorts of incantations. As I had foreseen, several perfectly tame rattlesnakes, accustomed to his well known call, crawled forth and approached the would-be-magician, who with commanding voice admonished me to go away from the poisonous reptiles. I did not find it necessary to obey this order, and soon convinced myself, to the great chagrin of my companion, that the poison fangs had been drawn from the mouths of the snakes. It does not seem improbable to me that one can attract the snakes to him during the mating season by imitating their peculiar whistling sound. It is said that snakes then approach the whistling person, but upon looking sharply they flee hastily. This the snake-charmers take advantage of and maintain, that because of their peculiar power the snakes could do them no harm. At the same time I am convinced that the smell of many objects, especially smoked leather and the decoctions of many leaves and roots are repulsive to snakes, that they, as it were, become stupefied by them and unable to hit. Indians and creoles generally use gunpowder internally and externally as a remedy for the bite of the rattlesnake. I myself have convinced myself of the effectiveness of this simple remedy, and believe that I am justified in recommending it, especially since every traveler in the wilderness has his powder horn with him. The Indians, however, also have other antidotes, and never undertake a distant journey without them. They maintain, however, with the greatest assurance that without magic no remedy would be effective." (1:264-6)

After a number of other collecting trips to various parts of the globe, Prince Paul returned to North America for the third time in 1849. On this trip he was accompanied by a renowned German novelist, the Baron von Moellhausen. The two traveled extensively in the West, but did not make it back into Montana, although Prince Paul met up with his "beloved and reverend old friend," Pierre Jean De Smet. The Baron gives in his accounts of the trip some insights into the personality of the Prince: "The duke is a man of an intellectuality far beyond ordinary comprehension," he wrote, "But his weak point is impulsiveness. His courage is so boundless that it often approaches downright madness itself." (2:206,217) The Prince disappeared on a trip to Fort Laramie, and was given up for lost. When he finally turned up alive after a miraculous escape from death in a blizzard, the news was heard around the country, for by that time Prince Paul's name was almost a household word in the United States and Europe.

In 1860 Prince Paul finally buckled down to some serious, long-postponed writing and to the job of describing his western collections. Unfortunately, he died that year, leaving behind a massive legacy including more than a hundred hand-written journals, a thousand sketches and maps, and untold specimens, which were heaped to the ceiling in the Castle-Museum of Bad Mergentheim. Among this material were the Montana journals and specimens.

At the time of his death, the Prince was nearly in poverty, and the extensive natural history collections at Mergentheim Castle, over which he had labored for so many years, were auctioned to pay debts and thus scattered back to the four winds. As one authority later wrote, "Only those who work intimately with the skins of birds and animals and the dried specimens of ... plants can know the proportions of this loss to the natural history of a young America and an old world." (3:xxviii) Fortunately, however, Prince Paul's son Maximilian had the foresight to deposit the precious manuscripts and journals in the Royal State Library archives at Stuttgart for safekeeping.

The book-length manuscript describing the natural-history results of the second journey, including the Montana material (which the Prince had finally prepared for publication), was inexplicably not among these papers. No one knows today what happened to this priceless volume, or where, or if, it exists. In all probability it was in the hands of a publisher awaiting the perfectionist Prince's painful revisions when the Prince died. Also missing were the journals of the second journey.

As the 19th Century wore on, Europe and America gradually came to forget about the colorful prince who at the time of his death had seen more of the Old West than any other European explorer. The published record of his first journey did not make much of a hit —it was eclipsed by the brilliant and lavishly illustrated book published by Prince Maximilian of Neuwied (not to be confused with Prince Paul's son Maximilian) in 1839 — and was also soon forgotten. Then in 1928, an archivist named Friedrich Bauser pried open the lid of a mysterious trunk that had lain forgotten in a corner of the Royal State Library archives for more than half a century.

The discovery of this trunkful of Prince Paul's unpublished writings was a momentous event, and Bauser knew he had stumbled onto a treasure. From the manuscripts in the trunk, Bauser was able to assemble a biography of the Prince, and in the late 1930s Bauser was negotiating for the publication rights to Prince Paul's writings. Sadly the priceless journals, which today would no doubt rank with those of Maximilian and Lewis and Clark as classics of Montana exploration, were destroyed in a bombing raid on Stuttgart during World War II, wiping out almost all traces of the Prince's life-work.

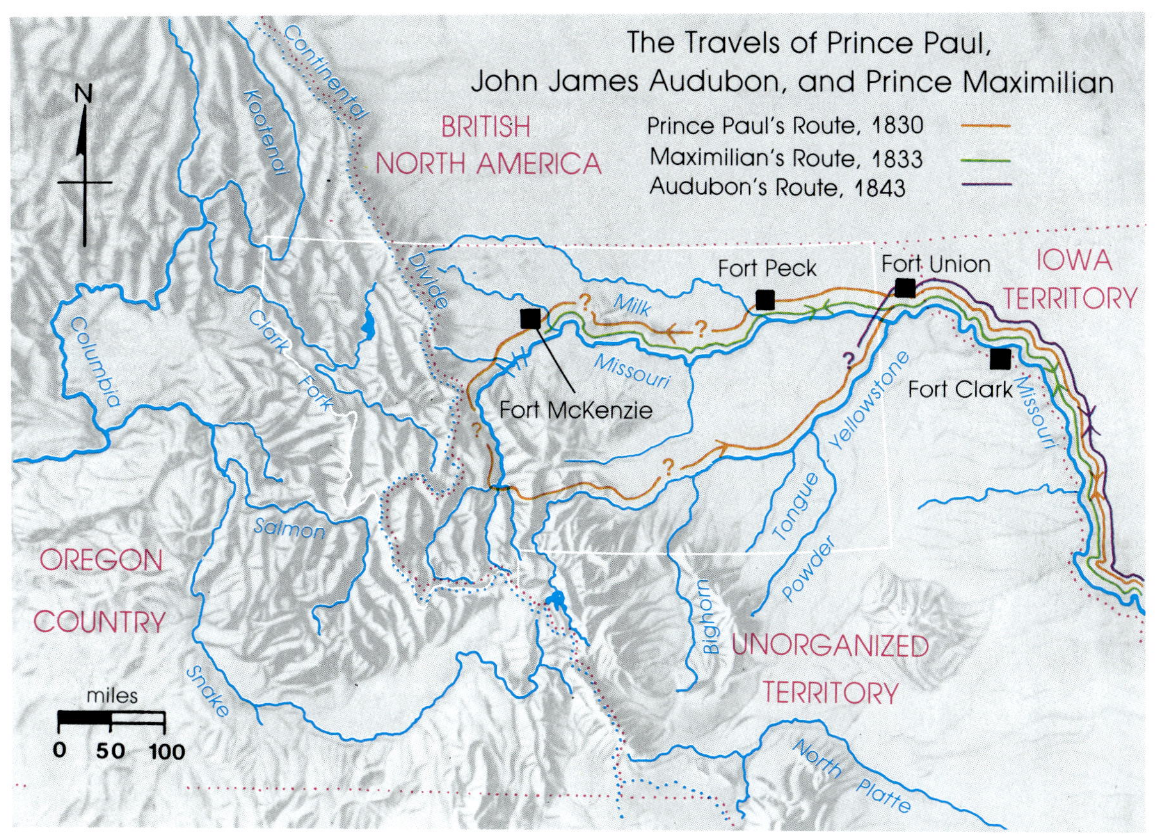


## Sources


1. Bek, W. G., trans. "First Journey to North America in the Years 1822 to 1824, by Paul, Prince of Wurttemberg." *South Dakota Historical Collections.* Vol. 19. Pierre: South Dakota Historical Society, 1941.

2. Butscher, L. C., ed. "An Account of Adventures in the Great American Desert by His Royal Highness, Duke Paul Wilhelm von Wurttemberg." *New Mexico Historical Review.* 17(1942): 181-225, 294-344.

3. Nitske, W. R., and S. Lottinville, eds. *Travels in North America, 1822-1844.* Norman: Univ. of Oklahoma Press, 1973.

4. Speich, V. M. "A Royal Voyager on the Ohio and Mississippi Rivers, 1822-1823." M.S. Thesis, Univ. of Wyoming, Laramie, 1939.

CHAPTER 4

# The Early Plant Collectors: Wyeth, Geyer, and Burke

*Nathaniel J. Wyeth called the Flathead River Valley, with the Mission Mountains in the background, "the most romantic place imaginable ... it is really a scene for a poet."* (PACIFIC RAILROAD SURVEY LITHOGRAPH)

Captains Lewis and Clark were the first to collect plant specimens from the wilds of what is now Montana, but they were by no means botanists as we think of the term today. Early 19th-century America had but a handful of people who had both the academic training and the good fortune to be able to pursue botany as a full-time profession. As the universities in the new United States were not yet ready to begin producing trained botanists, most of the world's botanical specialists were Europeans. The allure of the unexplored regions of North America was too much for these European scientists to resist. Because the greatest European botanists of the day, tied as they were to their university chairs, could not always get away to collect for themselves, they arranged for others to do the footwork for them — collecting by remote control, if you will. Here we will trace the adventures in Montana of three of these field agents: a Yankee entrepreneur, a German gardener, and a hard-working but unfortunate Englishman.

## Nathaniel J. Wyeth

Nathaniel J. Wyeth was a New Englander and a businessman. He was born in Cambridge, Massachusetts, in 1802, and revolutionized the New England ice-cutting industry by inventing a technique for cutting ice into blocks. He was soon swept up in the romance of the fur trade and decided to head out to the Oregon country to become a trader and, perhaps, to start businesses raising tobacco and selling salmon in this new frontier.

In New England, Wyeth had made the acquaintance of one of the country's most famous botanists, Thomas Nuttall. An Englishman by birth, Nuttall had come to America in 1807 and accepted a position at Harvard. Three years later, he traveled with John Bradbury, another English botanist, up the Missouri River almost as far west as the present-day Montana border, collecting many plant species new to science. Nuttall was noted even then as something of an eccentric. He would get so wrapped up in his plant collecting that he would forget to eat and would wander off and become lost. He later became a recluse and equipped his office with a trap door through which he could escape to avoid any and all visitors. Before Wyeth embarked on his Oregon adventure, Nuttall asked him to take the time to bring back a few plant specimens from the unknown frontiers he would be passing through.

In the spring of 1832, Wyeth traveled overland to Fort Vancouver on the Pacific Ocean, passing well to the south of Montana en route. The journey was not an easy one. Seven of the party, including his cousin John B. Wyeth, got fed up with the hardships and deserted the expedition at Pierre's Hole in eastern Idaho. The remaining 11 members of the party barely survived a skirmish with the Blackfeet Indians nearby. Nevertheless, Wyeth still found the time to "collect some flowers for friend Nuttall." (5:191) Unfortunately, these plant specimens, so painstakingly collected and pressed, suffered the same fate as many another early western collection — lost in shipment.

Wyeth wintered at Fort Vancouver, and when spring (1833) returned, began the long march back to Boston. His return route took him to Spokane House and up the Clark's Fork River into Montana, which he entered in early April. He soon arrived at Flathead Post, a fur trading post near the site of David Thompson's Saleesh House, and stayed over a few days to rest up and to collect some early spring plants. He was quite impressed with the scenery of the area, and wrote the following description (probably of the area near present-day Dixon): "This valley is the most romantic place imaginable ... a level plain of two miles long by 1 wide ... on the N a range of rocky and snow clad Mts. ... on the S. the Flathead river a rapid current and plenty of good fishing running at the immediate base of another lofty Snowy and Rocky range of Mts. Above and below the valley the mountains of each range close upon the river so as apparently to afford no outlet either way ... it is really a scene for a poet." The valley, wrote Wyeth, "abounds with the finest Kamas [camas] I have yet seen ... as provisions are scarce in camp the women dug much of it." (5:189-90)

Wyeth's party proceeded to the Bitterroot Valley in the vicinity of present-day Missoula, where they found an encampment of about 1,000 Flathead Indians. Wyeth collected more plants here, then continued up the Bitterroot River, crossed Gibbons Pass into the Big Hole Valley, and followed the Big Hole River to its headwaters. Near the head of the Big Hole River Wyeth noted that "there is a visible change in the appearance ... vegetation is not so forward the trees appear stinted and small the land poorer and covered with Sedge ...." The weather began to deteriorate, and the party was hit with "a double portion of the usual weather viz. rain Hail snow wind rain and Thunder into the bargain ... we are so near where they make weather that they send it as if [it] cost nothing." (5:196-7) One of the party killed a sage grouse, and Wyeth penned a long and detailed description of this animal in order to settle an argument with the famous botanist David Douglas, whom Wyeth had met on the Columbia River the previous year. Wyeth then recrossed the Continental Divide into Idaho near present-day Salmon, Idaho. The party continued to join the fur rendezvous at Fort Bonneville near Jackson Hole, Wyoming, then headed northward toward Montana.

Wyeth's exact return route into Montana is uncertain. It is likely that he followed the Bighorn

*Wyeth collected plants in the Bitterroot River Valley, as had Captain Meriwether Lewis a quarter of a century earlier.* (TOM DIETRICH)

*Wyeth also explored and collected in the Missoula Valley, shown here today.* (TOM DIETRICH)

River, but his journals contain no mention of the spectacular cliffs and canyons that this river cuts between the Pryor and Bighorn Mountains. On August 12 the party stopped along the Bighorn River to hunt some bison bulls from which to manufacture "bull boats," unlikely craft made of bison hides stretched over flimsy willow frames. Wyeth noted seeing three "grisly bears" in the area and complained of the mosquitoes, which he said "affect me almost as bad as a rattle snake." On August 16, Wyeth set out in the bull boat he had made, which was to serve him well all the way to Fort Union at the mouth of the Yellowstone. He found his craft "to answer the purpose well — large enough — runs well — leaks a little ... rapid shoals at places." He had to stop after three miles, however, on account of "too much liquor to proceed, therefore stopped." Later on, the entire party suffered from this "severe bout of drinking," (5:209-10) and it is hard to imagine anyone with a horrible hangover negotiating the dangerous rapids of Bighorn Canyon in a boat made of buffalo hides.

The next day the party miraculously made it all the way to the mouth of the Bighorn River and only a week later arrived at Fort Union at the mouth of the Yellowstone River. Wyeth continued down the Missouri River and back home to Boston.

Upon his return, Wyeth shipped a package of plant specimens, which had somehow survived the trip, on to his friend Nuttall. Wyeth was fairly apologetic about the collection, and wrote to Nuttall that "I am afraid they will be of little value to you. The rain has been so constant ... that they have lost their color in some cases." (5:67) Wyeth had also prepared some skins of birds to send Nuttall, but all had rotted from the moisture and the warmth. Unfortunately none made it back to civilization.

*Wyethia, or mule's ears, found in wet meadows of southwestern Montana, was named for its discoverer, Nathaniel Wyeth.* (CHARLES KAY)

Nuttall did not share Wyeth's low opinion of the collection, however. He described the plants in the *Journal of The Academy of Natural Sciences of Philadelphia* as follows: "Besides their number, there being many duplicates, they are the finest specimens, probably, that were ever brought from the distant and perilous regions of the West by any American collector." (4) Nuttall named one of the 113 species *Wyethia* in honor of his friend.

So impressed was Nuttall with the strange new plants brought back by Wyeth and with Wyeth's descriptions of the largely unexplored interior of the continent, that the following year (1834) Nuttall himself (along with an ornithologist named John Kirk Townsend) accompanied Wyeth on his second expedition to the West. Nuttall, who had been refused a leave of absence from his university post, had to resign to make the journey. The account of this journey is one of the great classics of scientific discovery, but unfortunately this time the path of the expedition never crossed the Montana Border.

## Charles Andreas Geyer

The next serious botanical collecting in Montana was not begun until a decade after Wyeth's journey and was conducted by European collectors. The mastermind behind these collecting expeditions was Sir William Jackson Hooker, England's most eminent and respected botanical figure and author of the *Flora Boreali-Americana*, the definitive work on North American flora, which was published 1833-1840. Hooker was one of the very few people whom Charles Darwin took into his confidence prior to publication of *On The Origin of Species*. Hooker supervised a network of enthusiastic plant collectors who scoured many remote corners of the world, including the New World, to find new plants for him to describe.

One of the many botanical enthusiasts influenced by Hooker was a German gardener's son named Charles Andreas Geyer. Geyer was born in Dresden in 1809 and spent his youth as a gardener in Zabelitz and Dresden. Geyer corresponded with Hooker for years, and it was probably at Hooker's suggestion that he voyaged to the United States in 1834 to collect plants in unknown regions of the continent. In 1835 Geyer traveled from New York to the lower Platte River, and later collected over a vast region between the Missouri and Mississippi rivers. In spite of many hardships — one plant collection "suffered much by the filling of a canoe," (2:IV,480) another was lost entirely — Geyer gained the attention of the great American botanists of the day, including John Torrey, Asa Gray, and George Engelmann. In the 1840s, Geyer shrewdly began to capitalize on the fact that attractively pressed specimens of plants from the American hinterlands were becoming a marketable commodity in Europe. He thus began to collect plants for sale to the botanical public as well as for the sake of science.

In 1843, the same year John James Audubon traveled to Fort Union, Geyer headed west with one of the most luxurious dude efforts in the history of the country — the expedition to the Wind River region of what is now Wyoming organized by Sir William Drummond Stewart of Murthly Castle, Scotland. Sir William had just sold an estate for about a million dollars and had decided that there would be no better use for the money than to travel to the then-legendary wonderland of the American frontier for a little hunting and fishing — and to do it in style. Sir William's entourage included Geyer and two other European botanists, Professor Karl Frederick Mersch of Luxemburg, and Alexander Gordon of Scotland. Geyer parted with Stewart once they arrived at the Wind River Mountains, and he joined a caravan of Jesuit missionaries bound for Father De Smet's new Montana mission, St. Mary's, in the Bitterroot Valley.

Geyer, like many other early naturalists, could not have made the journey on his own resources. He owed a great debt to the larger parties, which he joined in his travels. "It must, no doubt, be gratifying to the lovers of natural history that such assistance is rendered the scientific travellers; not only since it would be impracticable, even with all the means to traverse the different Indian tribes unmolested, or without considerable difficulties, but it also shows that the necessity for extending our knowledge of the productions of nature is felt and cheerfully aided, even in the recesses of that vast western wilderness. May future explorers, for whom there is yet enough in store, meet with the same reception under those hospitable roofs!" (2:IV,483)

Geyer's exact route through Montana is difficult to trace, but it appears that he first entered the state near Targhee Pass, descended the Madison River, crossed over the divide near present-day Virginia City into the Beaverhead Valley, then crossed the Big Hole Valley and Gibbons Pass to the Bitterroot Valley. In describing the biological regions and sub-regions that he saw during his travels, Geyer described the Beaverhead country as the "Green Desert, cold and inhospitable, though less so than the great tracts of sandy desert lower east." (2:V,24) He was greatly impressed with the Bitterroot Mountains, the "Green Mountains" (2:V,200) as he called them, and the verdant Bitterroot Valley. "Highly picturesque scenery, a healthy climate of the first order, a serene sky which heightens the beauty of its clear waters, render this country of evergreens peculiarly pleasant. Though the waters are snowy and bright, the cold is remarkably moderate. The rivers are scarcely ever frozen, which may be owing in a degree to their swift currents. The summers are warm and sunny, and a beaming morning in the month of June and July displays endless charms for the admirer of natural beauty. The luxuriant green of the mountains in the background, the lakes, the rivers with their falls, the gigantic pine-forests, separated by meadows into parklike groups, with the highly coloured flower-carpet, figured beautifully by dense masses which appear conglomerated together of each sort, far more exclusively than on the eastern side of the Rocky mountains, form a charming coup-d'oeil." (2:V,202)

Geyer was especially impressed with the gigantic conifers that appeared as he progressed westward. "The bulk of the woods," he wrote, "consists of the majestic and valuable *Pinus ponderosa* [ponderosa pine], attaining an average height of 150 feet, and not seldom a trunk from 4 to 8 feet [in] diameter, beautifully rounded and clothed with reddish-brown bark

... The leaves are long and thick, clustering together at the ends of the branchlets; the cones also appear often in bunches of 3-5, they are ovate, with a short recurved spine on the scales ... Far more sombre and dense trees than *P. ponderosa* fill with perfect darkness the deep defiles in the Green Mountains, and principally the majestic *Thuja gigantea* [western red-cedar] of Nuttall. Its average height is 200 feet, and the diameter of the trunk 10-12 feet; one very large specimen, which I measured with my horse-line, came up to about 47 feet circumference." (2:V,204-5)

Geyer was one of the first to notice the phenomenon of forest succession. "It is a curious fact," he wrote, "that while the forests are left undisturbed, the remains are always composed of such or such kinds in almost unchanged proportion. Not so when fire has swept over, and has destroyed the pristine race of trees; then others spring up, which were before either not at all there, or in the minority. So where *Pinus ponderosa* is removed by fire, *Abies rubra* [probably Douglas fir] will fill that space to suffocation; if after a few years it is burnt again, another tree takes the place." (2:V,206)

Geyer's notes provide historians with one of the richest sources of ethnobotanical lore, as he provided abundant descriptions of aboriginal food sources. Of the bitterroot, he wrote that "The Indians, especially the Flathead tribes, value this root highly, and it is with them prepared with the marrow of the bison, the most dainty dish. It has also acquired fame among Europeans, and travellers generally use it in those regions as a very wholesome food, and it is prized in spite of its strong bitter taste, which resembles the bitter of the China-bark. The root is dug during flower-time, when the cuticle is easily removed; by that it acquires a white colour, is brittle, and by transportation broken to small pieces. Before boiling, it is steeped in water, which makes it swell, and after boiling it becomes five to six times larger in size; resembling a jelly like substance. As it is so small a root, it requires much labour to gather a sack, which commands generally the price of a good horse. Indians from the lower regions trade in these roots by handfuls, paying a high price. This plant was first collected by the great pioneer, Captain Meriwether Lewis, whose attention was probably directed to it by the Indians ...." (2:V,307-8) Geyer noted that the bitterroot was very abundant in the upper reaches of the Bitterroot and Clark Fork rivers.

Together with the Bitterroot, the camas — called "Gamass" by Geyer — provided the primary winter staple of the Salish Indian tribes.

"The digging of the Gamass bulb," wrote Geyer, "is a feast for old and young amongst the Indians; a sort of picnic which is spoken of throughout the whole year. The different neighbouring tribes meet on the same plain and mostly at the same time, at the same spot where their forefathers met. Here the old men talk over their long tales of olden times, the young relate hunting adventures of the last winter, and pass most of their time in play and gaming; while on the women alone, young and old, rests the whole labour of gathering that indispensable food. They, especially the young women, vie with each other in collecting the greatest possible quantity and best quality of Gamass, because their fame for future good wives will depend much on the activity and industry they show here; the young men will not overlook these merits, and many a marriage is closed after the Gamass are brought home....

*Charles Geyer, a German who collected plants in Montana in 1843 and 1844, found magnificent climax ponderosa pine forests in western Montana, "not seldom a trunk from 4 to 8 feet [in] diameter, beautifully rounded and clothed with reddish-brown bark."* (RON GLOVAN)

"The digging of the Gamass takes place as soon as the lower half of the flowers on the raceme begin to fade, or better, when the time of flowering is entirely passed. For that purpose, the Indian women use a stick two feet long, curved like a sabre, of hawthorn wood, which is provided with a cross piece of elk-horn on the top, serving as a handle. This instrument they use with astonishing dexterity, so that they very seldom strike the point twice after the same bulb. Four or five sacks of raw bulbs is a common day's labour, which dwindle to about two after baking and drying.... As soon as they have gathered a sufficient quantity of bulbs, they

*Geyer wrote a detailed account of the preparation and use of the tasty bulbs of the camas, the overwinter staple food of the Salish Indians. He also wrote of the use by some tribes of the black tree lichen, a last-ditch survival food, the taste of which, Geyer thought, "would reduce a living man to a mummy."* (RIGHT, G. R. HIGBEE; ALL OTHERS, LARRY AND SUE THOMPSON)

prepare for baking. For that purpose, they dig or scrape a hole in the ground of three or four feet in depth, make a fire and throw in a good layer of red hot stones, then a layer of clean grass over those, and now a layer of Gamass, the latter having before been cleaned from the adhering soil. This is repeated until the hole is level with the ground above. The fire is now moved on the top of the pit, and kept burning for about twenty-four hours or longer.

"The raw Gamass bulb resembles in its substance, the common Squill. By baking, it acquires a sweet taste, and when boiled the taste is not unlike the syrup of Squills, but not so sweet. Those accustomed to that food, like the Indians, remain strong and fleshy; but a European falls off very soon if he has nothing else. Eating a great quantity produces flatulence, as has been observed by travellers before. (2:V,299-300)

Geyer also made note of some of the more unlikely foodstuffs partaken of by the Indians. The Indians ate ponderosa pine seeds, even though "they are insipid, even when roasted." They even used the cambium layer (inner bark) of the lodgepole pine, which "they scrape off with a knife, after removing the bark. It is a very cooling and by no means unpleasant article of food," Geyer wrote, speaking, no doubt, from first-hand experience. (2:V,204-5) Even pincushion cacti were edible, reported Geyer; they "afford quite a seasonable refreshment in the Missouri Plains; though only during the time of growth when the fibres are tender. In taste they resemble raw cucumbers ...." (2:V,26)

When times grew tough, the Indians would resort to the last-ditch wild food supplies. When the "Gamass" and bitterroot supplies run low in February and March, the Indians "are compelled to fell trees, to gather the long moss from the pines, which they bake .... This composition is of greenish-brown colour ... and has a wild acrid taste, like tan, so that one would think it would reduce a living man to a mummy." (2:V,301)

The Bannock Indians, who sometimes visited the upper Beaverhead country traversed by Geyer, "live the most wretched life of any Indians in the West ... oftentimes, when they can get neither game nor roots to live on, they eat grasshoppers; ... very large and fat, of every shade of brown and black, wherewith these deserts abound. For this purpose they are caught in large quantities, boiled alive without ceremony and eaten like craw-fish. It is said that the soup of them is very sweet and a favourite drink .... In case of scarcity of such grasshoppers, the Bannaks make soup of a large species of ants ...." (2:V,30)

Geyer's observations of animals were also a valuable contribution to scientific knowledge. He described the commensal relationship between the black-tailed prairie dog, or "Prairie Marmot" (2:V,490) as he called it, and the burrowing owl, and described the characteristic vegetation that grows around the mounds. He described the food preferences of bears, and the flavor of the sage grouse, or "Sage-cock; as grey as the Artemisia [sagebrush] itself, and the flesh of it as bitter too." (2:V,29) He also described a "curious meeting between the grizzly bear and antelope," (2:V,36) where three pronghorn appeared to be flirting with death at the claws of a pair of grizzlies.

The following account of a rattlesnake den, however, leaves one wondering whether the weeks in the wilderness, the full moon, and the diet of strange roots might have colored Geyer's perception somewhat. While examining a specimen of clover-fern, Geyer reports, "I was attacked by a large rattlesnake, which I despatched instantly ... after having done, I took up my tin cup to go to drink at the river, the moon shining bright. A noise seemed close to me, resembling the sound produced by dragging sticks over hard ground at a distance. As soon as I had traversed the small grassy prairie and stood at the bank, but 3 or 4 feet above the gravelly, stony water's edge, I, to my astonishment, beheld countless numbers of rattlesnakes, dashing and whirling on the gravelly space below. The moon shone clear, and I could distinctly see that they were crawling under and above each other, especially near the rounded granite boulders, which lay here and there. Around these they kept rattling incessantly, the greater number beating their rattles against the stones. The noise was increased by the rustling of their scaly bodies on the gravel. The stench on the spot was very disgusting. Struck by fear, I retreated to my camp-fire, wrapped myself in my blanket, and watched, fearing these guests should take it in their heads to come to my fire, and find me asleep." Sensing perhaps that someone might someday suspect that this tale was a bit of a tall one, Geyer wrote the following disclaimer. "To tell marvellous tales of snakes and hunting-stories has been so common in America, that every one must be careful to relate a true adventure, lest he excites suspicion at the mere mentioning of what he is going to say, that it will be a hoax." (2:IV,512-13)

*Geyer claimed to have spent a night camped near a rattlesnake den, surrounded by "countless numbers of rattlesnakes, dashing and whirling ..."* (KRISTI DuBOIS)

Geyer left St. Mary's Mission in the middle of winter and headed west. He ended up getting lost, "wandering alone in the mountains and woods for 13 days, where the snow was two and three feet deep." He finally arrived in the Spokane area "almost exhausted by want of food." (2:IV,483) Such hardships, however, Geyer accepted as part of the package of exploring new remote wilderness, part of the price one must pay for the glory of discovering hitherto undescribed rarities. Among the "great inconveniences to which the traveler is exposed" in these wild and rugged mountains, foremost are "the incessant rains during the months of May and June, which fall so heavy, that the water runs an inch deep upon the ground, accompanied too with violent winds. Next are the mosquitoes during calm nights, and swarms of blood-thirsty horse-flies by day, plaguing alike man and beast incessantly. Not less annoying are the night watches, necessary here to guard the animals from the marauding Pawnees, especially after a hard journey and in bad weather." Geyer concluded that it was all worth it in the end: "After weary day and sleepless night are past, when once the morning sun makes its appearance, all troubles are over and almost forgotten. Every one is engaged in breaking up camp, talking about the most probable adventures of the coming day." (2:IV,491-2)

In spite of the hardships, Geyer's expedition was highly successful, and he assembled a collection of between 10,000 and 20,000 plant specimens. In Geyer's report of his expedition, published in the *London Journal of Botany*, (2) he offered sets of mounted specimens, consisting of from 200 to 600 different species, for sale "to Botanists at the rate of 2 pounds the 100 species, all expenses included." (2:IV,482) Geyer's friend Hooker later published a full catalogue of Geyer's collections. Today, botanists are reminded of this assiduous German collector by at least a dozen plant species that bear his name.

Geyer returned to Dresden in the fall of 1845, and went forthwith to Murthly Castle. His purpose was to see if Sir William Stewart had been serious when he mentioned one day in the Wind River Mountains that he might have a job for Geyer as castle gardener. He had not. Geyer then bought some land near Berlin and started a nursery, teaching English and botany as a sideline. He died in 1853.

*In 1845, Joseph Burke botanized in the vicinity of the Centennial Mountains and traveled as far east as the Musselshell River.* (GEORGE WUERTHNER)

## Joseph Burke

Geyer's botanical sojourn in Montana was soon followed by another by a European also under the guidance of Hooker. Joseph Burke, an Englishman, worked a vast area of the continent, including much previously unexplored country in Montana. Burke's explorations, however, remain virtually unknown today because of a succession of unfortunate accidents.

Burke had collected in South Africa between 1839 and 1842, and his work there was so successful that his sponsor, Edward Smith Stanley, 13th Earl of Derby, president of the Linnaean Society and of the Zoological Society, commissioned him to collect in North America. Hooker was also involved in getting this promising young botanist into the New World and successfully sought funding for the endeavor from the Hudson's Bay Company.

In June of 1843, Burke left England and traveled by ship to York Factory on Hudson's Bay. He was to have spent the following summer collecting around Edmonton House and Jasper House; the only problem was that the year 1844 did not have a summer. It was so cold that many plants did not flower, and so damp that Burke's fungi, bird, and mammal specimens rotted.

*Charles Geyer referred to the Beaverhead and Big Hole (above) Valleys as the "Green Desert, cold and inhospitable," and the Bitterroot Mountains (left) as the "Green Mountains."* (MARK THOMPSON PHOTOS)

In the fall of 1844 Burke traveled down the Columbia River to Fort Walla Walla. There, he met "Mr. Geyer the collector — I had the pleasure of his company but a short time, as he left the same day by the boats that I came in." (3:798) Burke then traveled to Fort Hall on the Snake River, following a portion of the Oregon Trail. There a mishap wiped out months of painstaking collecting. "On ascending the bank which was very steep & rocky & about a hundred yards high — when nearly at the top a horse [bit] another that was before him. he kicked until he throwed his load which although on the ground was still attached to the saddle — he then took fright & ran down towards [the] river, dashing his load from rock to rock — when at the bottom [he] fell & layed there until he was taken — It chanced to [be] my luggage — It was quite distressing to examine it — My insects & bottles filled with spirits of wine were all broken to pieces — Other tin boxes that I had were beaten out of all shape — In short I have nothing left that it was possible to destroy by dashing against rocks." (3:800)

As if this were not torture enough, the horrible weather continued, the food ran out, and most of the party got sick from eating too many wild onions. The Indian danger was still severe; as Burke wrote, "The whole country is quite in a ferment — We hear of nothing but fights & murders ...." And to top things off, Burke was subjected to that perennial plague of explorers: "I am stung out of all patience by the Moschettos." (3:803)

So late was the spring of 1845 that the countryside did not begin to turn green until late June. At that time, Burke left Fort Hall with a buffalo-hunting party and on July 5 entered Montana, probably crossing at an unnamed pass near the Lima Peaks. There Burke's party "encamped in a beautyful spot amongst the hills, sloaping from the Mountains was quite a flower garden." Among the flowers was one that swept Burke off his feet: "In that place I found a most beautyful Columbine, I did not see it before, & have not seen it since — It was growing at the foot of a hill, in a rich loamy soil — The flower stems are about ten inches in hight — flowers very large & beautyfully white, with varieties shaded a clear light blue — In my opinion It is not only the Queen of Columbines, but the most beautyful of all herbaceous plants — I never felt so much pleasure in finding a plant before ...." (3:804) This was the Colorado columbine, *Aquilegia coerulea.*

Burke's party then dropped into the Beaverhead Valley and followed the river downstream to near present-day Twin Bridges. There they came upon a Nez Perce camp with 50 lodges and several thousand horses. On July 23, they crossed into the Madison drainage, then continued to the Three Forks and up Sixteenmile Creek to the headwaters of the South Fork of the Musselshell River near present-day Ringling. The party descended the Musselshell River, then proceeded cross-country to meet the Yellowstone River near the mouth of the Bighorn River. When the buffalo hunt was over, the party returned via Bozeman Pass, the Madison River, and Raynolds Pass. Here, Burke mentions hearing of nearby "boiling & Sulphur springs. One of them I am told, throws the water to the hight of one hundred feet. It was too far out of my way to visit them." (3:806) This is probably one of the earliest references to Old Faithful Geyser.

Once back in the Snake River country, on August 21 Burke decided that he had to go back to the Lima Peaks and collect some seeds of his "Queen of the Columbines," (3:804) since the flowers had not yet produced enough seeds at the time of this first visit. So he separated from the main party and climbed back up to the pass, alone in wild Indian country, to seek his

*Joseph Burke discovered the Colorado Columbine, which he called the "Queen of the Columbines," along the Montana-Idaho border.* (JAN WASSINK)

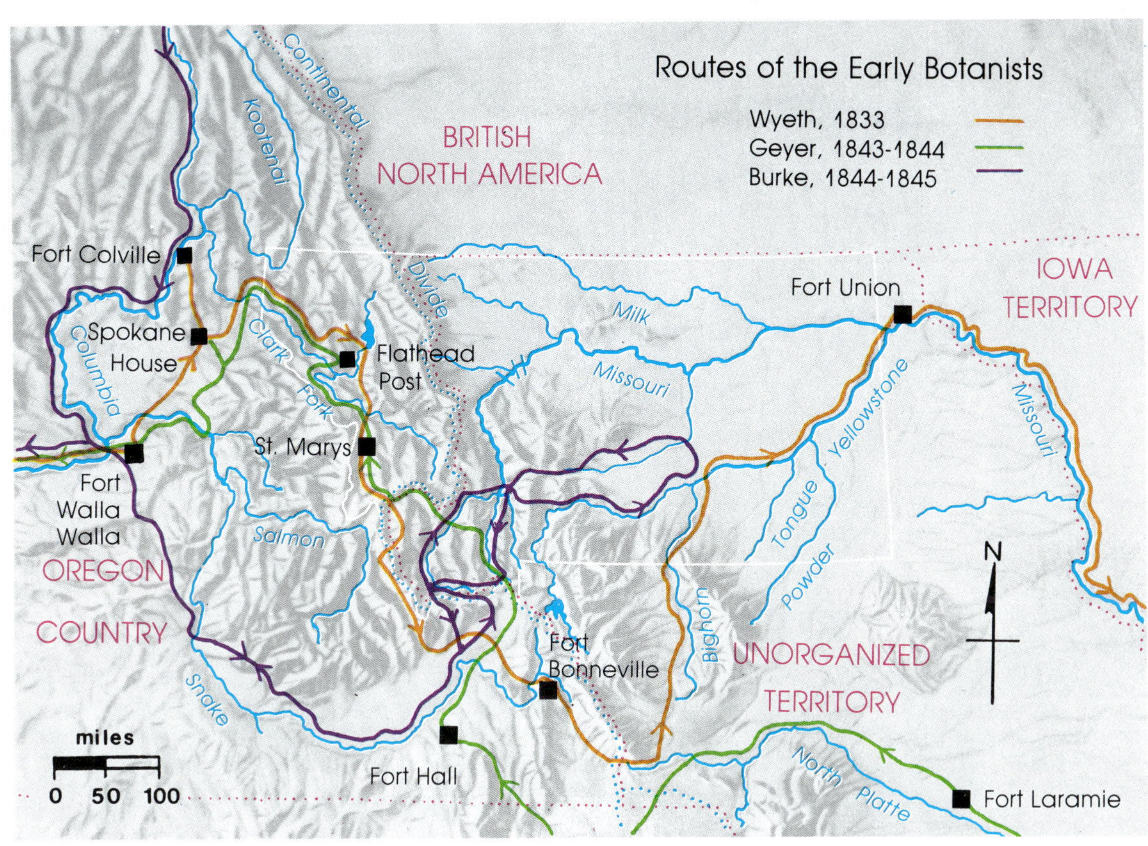


prize specimen! Burke wintered at Fort Hall, then continued westward the following spring to Oregon and Northern California.

Although he collected in North America for more than three years, Burke's collections were never written up or deposited and described as a unit, and we will never know what rarities or exciting new discoveries he made in Montana. At any rate, one can only speculate how many Montana species would today be named "burkeii" had this dedicated botanist been spared misfortune!

This trio of early collectors — Wyeth, Geyer, and Burke — succeeded in bringing back only only plant specimens but also descriptions of the new country, the Indians and their ways, the productivity of the land, and the geography of a hitherto unknown *terra incognita*.

## Sources


1. Biedleman, R. J. "Nathaniel Wyeth's Fort Hall." *Oregon Historical Quarterly* 58(1957):197-250.
2. Geyer, C. A. "Notes on the Vegetation and General Character of the Missouri and Oregon Territories, Made During a Botanical Journey from the State of Missouri, Across the South-Pass of the Rocky Mountains, to the Pacific, During the Years 1843 and 1844." *London Journal of Botany* IV(1895):479-92, 653-62; V:22-41, 198-208, 285-310, 509-24.
3. McKelvey, S. D. *Botanical Explorations of the Trans-Mississippi West, 1790-1850.* Jamaica Plain, Mass.: Arnold Arboretum of Harvard University, 1955.
4. Nuttall, T. "A Catalogue of a Collection of Plants Made Chiefly in the Valleys of the Rocky Mountains or Northern Andes, Towards the Source of the Columbia River, by Mr. Nathaniel B. Wyeth, and Described by T. Nuttall." *Journal of the Academy of Natural Sciences of Philadelphia* 7(1834)1-60.
5. Young, F. G., ed. "The Correspondence and Journals of Captain Nathaniel J. Wyeth, 1831-36. A Record of Two Expeditions for the Occupation of the Oregon Country." *Sources of the History of Oregon* I: parts 3-6. Eugene: Oregon Historical Society, 1899.

CHAPTER 5

# Prince Maximilian Explores the Upper Missouri

*Prince Maxmilian (wearing black coat) and artist Karl Bodmer (at far right) are introduced to Minatarree chiefs at Fort Clark during their 1833 ascent of the Missouri River.* (AQUATINT AFTER KARL BODMER, COURTESY INTERNORTH ART FOUNDATION, JOSLYN ART MUSEUM, OMAHA, NEBRASKA)

Prince Maximilian, a highly-educated and well-respected naturalist, was the second trained scientist since Meriwether Lewis to traverse the eastern Montana wilderness (Prince Paul being the first). The Prince hailed from the Prussian principality of Wied, located at Neuwied near Coblenz on the east bank of the Rhine. He was born in 1782 to a large family, and showed as a child a natural aptitude for science, which his family encouraged and nurtured. He was fortunate to have as a friend and mentor none other than Alexander von Humboldt, one of the most eminent European scientists of his day.

Maximilian fought in the Napoleonic Wars as an officer in the Prussian Army. He was captured in battle and, upon his eventual exchange, awarded the Iron Cross and promoted to major-general. When the wars were over, Maximilian joined two other scientists for a two-year scientific expedition into the jungles of Brazil. The report of this expedition, published in 1820-21, instantly established for Maximilian an international reputation as an explorer-naturalist of considerable ability.

Maximilian was a trained and capable geologist, botanist, and zoologist, but his special love was the study of primitive peoples and their way of life. While in Brazil, he had recorded careful descriptions of the native tribes and their ecology, descriptions that today remain classics in the field. It was probably through the published journals of Lewis and Clark that Maximilian first learned of the aboriginal cultures of the Great Plains, a rich and largely undescribed field for the student of primitive cultures. The inevitability of the demise of these native peoples must have been very apparent to Maximilian, for in 1831 he began planning another major scientific expedition, this time to the wild interior of the North American continent.

On July 4, 1832, Maximilian landed in Boston Harbor, accompanied by the talented young artist named Karl Bodmer and by a trusted friend and retainer from his Brazilian days named David Dreidoppel. The Prince spent the remainder of that summer learning woodcraft and hunting skills in the forests of Pennsylvania, then traveled to a remarkable community in Indiana called New Harmony. New Harmony was a commune of idealistic intellectuals that had been founded by the cotton magnate Robert Owen. It was to be a model community where it could be proven that scholarship and cooperation could solve all the ills of society. New Harmony was an intellectual Mecca for naturalists, and even diverted some of the limelight from Philadelphia, which had long been the center of scientific endeavor in the new United States. Maximilian therefore had the opportunity to spend the long winter (1832-1833) learning natural history from such authorities as Charles LeSueur, the French ichthyologist who doubled as the colony's artist-in-residence.

One of the principals of this Utopian village at the time of Maximilian's visit was the brilliant entomologist and ornithologist Thomas Say, with whom Maximilian had corresponded before setting out from Germany. Say had traveled to the Rocky Mountains 13 years earlier with Major Stephen H. Long's Yellowstone Expedition (which, unfortunately, never made it to the Yellowstone River). And the long winter nights at New Harmony were undoubtedly filled with Say's tales of exploration.

In the spring, Maximilian traveled to St. Louis, where he met with a warm reception from the aging General William Clark of the Lewis and Clark Expedition. Maximilian stayed with Clark for several days and undoubtedly heard many firsthand descriptions of Clark's experiences in the still mostly unexplored terrain he was about to enter. Clark gave him a hand-copied facsimile of the map that he and Lewis had prepared during their journey of discovery; this was one of the best maps available at that time. Like Prince Paul of Wurttemberg, Maximilian traveled under an alias: "Baron von Brausenburg." (2:93)

On April 10, 1833 Maximilian and crew set off as passengers on the American Fur Company's steamboat *Yellowstone*, which was leaving on its second annual trip up the Missouri to Fort Union. Of the approximately one hundred passengers on the craft, perhaps the oddest was Maximilian, described by one authority as a "squat, splenetic German aristocrat." (4:16) Lieut. James H. Bradley wrote the following first-hand description: "In this year an interesting character in the person of Prince Maximilian, from Coblentz on the Rhine, made his first appearance in the Upper Missouri. The prince was at that time [fifty] years of age, but well preserved, and able to endure considerable fatigue. He was a man of medium-height, rather slender, sans teeth, passionately fond of his pipe, unostentatious, and speaking very broken English. His favorite dress was a white slouch hat, a black velvet coat, rather rusty from long service, and probably the greasiest pair of trousers that ever encased princely legs. The prince was a bachelor and a man of science, and it was in this latter capacity that he had roamed so far from his ancestral home on the Rhine." According to Bradley, Bodmer and Dreidoppel both "seemed gifted to a high degree with the faculty of putting their princely employer into a frequent passion, till there is hardly a bluff or valley on the whole upper Missouri that has not repeated in an angry tone, and with a strong Teutonic accent, the names of [Bodmer and Dreidoppel.]" (1:206-7)

The *Yellowstone* landed at Fort Union on June 24, 1833, and the Prince and his small retinue received as cordial a welcome as the wilderness had to offer. Fort Union at that time was pretty much the civilized hub of the Upper Missouri, and boasted such amenities as imported wines, dairy products, and — when the steamer landed once a year — the latest fashions from St. Louis. It was also the principal trading post over an area of hundreds of square miles, and drew great crowds of Assiniboine and Cree Indians during the trading season. Maximilian wasted no time in beginning his ethnological studies of these tribes, and immediately set Bodmer to work painting portraits of the natives and the landscapes in which they lived.

*Karl Bodmer's* Landscape with Herd of Buffalo on the Upper Missouri *was painted near the mouth of Little Porcupine Creek, about 15 miles above present-day Wolf Point, on July 14, 1833. Note the white wolf in lower left.* (PAINTING BY KARL BODMER, COURTESY INTERNORTH ART FOUNDATION, JOSLYN ART MUSEUM, OMAHA, NEBRASKA)

*On July 25, 1833, Maximilian and his party came upon the White Castles of the Missouri River, which "so perfectly resembled buildings ... that we were deceived by them, till we were assured of our error."*

*These spectacular formations were inundated by the waters of Fort Peck Reservoir.* (PAINTING BY KARL BODMER, COURTESY INTERNORTH ART FOUNDATION, JOSLYN ART MUSEUM, OMAHA, NEBRASKA)

Since the continuous stream of Indians provided such a phenomenal opportunity for the study of aboriginal ways of life, and since few wild animals, with the exception of gray wolves and coyotes, dared set foot near the Fort, Maximilian recorded little in the way of wildlife observations during his stay at Fort Union, concentrating instead on his studies of the Indians.

That all changed, however, on July 6, when Maximilian and his party set off up the Missouri on a keelboat named the *Flora*, bound for Fort McKenzie, another outpost of the American Fur Company located at the mouth of the Marias River. During this trip, which took a little over a month, Maximilian was dazzled by the geological formations along the river, the same ones which had so impressed Lewis and Clark. First came the "White Castles" stretch of the river, just above the present site of Fort Peck Dam, where cliffs and blocks of white sandstone so closely resembled stone buildings that the explorers could not believe they were not man-made.

Next came the *Mauvaises Terres*, or bad lands, where Maximilian observed "we seemed to be suddenly transported to the mountains of Switzerland." (5:XXIII,55) Then the river cut through the "Stone Walls" section, known today as the White Cliffs, where the party of explorers was so transfixed they could not leave the deck all morning. Bodmer painted and sketched feverishly the whole time, and his exquisitely detailed drawings and paintings are our only record of some of these inspiring formations, which are now buried forever at the muddy bottom of Fort Peck Reservoir.

Like Lewis and Clark, Maximilian was particularly impressed by the intrusive dikes that cut through the sandstones of the White Cliffs area and that bear such a remarkable resemblance to man-made masonry. These formations, wrote Maximilian, "traverse the mountains in narrow perpendicular strata, like regularly built walls. These walls consist of a blackish-brown rock, in the mass of which large olive-green crystals are disseminated. They run in a perfectly straight line from the summits of the mountains to the foot, appearing to form the outworks of the old castles. The surface is divided by rents or furrows into pretty regular cubic figures like bricks, which renders their similarity to a work of art still more complete." (5:XXIII,79) Lewis and Clark called this rock conglomerate, but Maximilian correctly disagreed with this identification. The dikes are actually porphyry and were formed when the immense glob of molten rock that forms the core of the adjacent laccoliths flowed into cracks in the surrounding sedimentary strata. These dikes radiate like spokes of a wheel in all directions from the Highwood Mountains, but are most visible here along the river banks where exposed by erosion.

During his month-long trip up the wild Missouri, Maximilian not only kept Bodmer busy sketching and painting, and Dreidoppel hunting, he also busied himself on shore collecting plants, birds, mammals, fossils, and butterflies, and on deck preparing skins and skeletons of animals. On July 26, he caught a "pretty striped squirrel," (5:XXIII,65) a least chipmunk, and decided to keep it as a pet. The skins and partly-cleaned skulls of other less fortunate specimens were stretched out on the deck to dry; they created such a bad odor as they baked in the July sun that the crew members would pitch them into the river in the night, infuriating the irascible prince.

The banks of the Missouri River still supported herds of big game animals, although Maximilian found

that the fur trade had reduced the populations substantially since Lewis and Clark's day. "The vast prairie scarcely offers a living creature," wrote the Prince, "except now and then herds of buffaloes and antelopes, or a few deer or wolves." (5:XXIII,42) Grizzly bears were frequently seen by the crew, and bands of 30 to 50 mountain sheep clambered over the *Mauvaises Terres* and Stone Walls. Maximilian discovered the famous Elkhorn Prairie, where stood a pile of elk antlers 18 feet high and 15 feet in diameter which the Indians had erected as a medicine sign. "These plains," wrote Maximilian, "which are dry in summer, and frozen in winter, have certainly much resemblance, in many of their features, with the African deserts." Nevertheless, he noted, "Various plants, interesting to the botanist, are everywhere to be found." (5:XXIII,42)

Maximilian was impressed with the dense stands of cottonwoods that lined the bank of the river. "These trees," he observed, "probably do not form, in any part of the globe, such fine and lofty forests as they do here." (5:XXIII,60-61) Among the birds he encountered in these riparian forests were magpies, great horned owls, and yellow-breasted chats. However, he was not greatly impressed with the diversity of bird life here, and wrote

*Maximilian reached the White Cliffs section of the Missouri River on August 6, 1833. In the distance of this painting by Bodmer is the "Gate of the Stone Walls," an "apparently narrow gate, the white walls in the two banks approaching so near to each other, that the river seemed to be very contracted in breadth ..."* (PAINTING BY KARL BODMER, COURTESY INTERNORTH ART FOUNDATION, JOSLYN ART MUSEUM, OMAHA, NEBRASKA)

*Karl Bodmer (1809-1893) of Zurich, Switzerland, was perhaps the greatest artist ever to work the wild Missouri. On September 18, 1833, near the mouth of the Judith River, Bodmer painted these herds of elk and bison along the shores of the Missouri River.* (PAINTING BY KARL BODMER, COURTESY INTERNORTH ART FOUNDATION, JOSLYN ART MUSEUM, OMAHA, NEBRASKA)

"I could not help making comparisons with my journeys on the Brazilian rivers. There, where nature is so infinitely rich and grand, I heard from the lofty, thick, primeval forests on the banks of the rivers, the varied voices of the parrots, the macaws, and many other birds, as well as of the monkeys, and other creatures; while here, the silence of the bare, dead, lonely wilderness is but seldom interrupted by the howling of the wolves, the bellowing of the buffaloes, or the screaming of the crows." (5:XXIII,42)

At the time Maximilian left Fort Union, the peak of the bird breeding season had passed, and bird activity, especially singing, had declined sharply. It is unfortunate that the Prince could not have traveled this stretch of the river in early June, when, although the diversity would certainly not approach that of the tropical jungles, he would have found the "lofty, thick primeval forests on the banks of the rivers" to be resounding with a cacophony of bird songs, many of which probably belonged to the same species of birds he had heard in Brazil!

Maximilian's journal reveals that he was an astute observer and a careful notetaker. He noticed that the bark of many of the cottonwoods along the Missouri riverbank had been scraped or rubbed off at a height of 15 feet above the water surface and he correctly

"*Fort McKenzie at the Mouth of the Marias River.*"
(PAINTING BY KARL BODMER, COURTESY INTERNORTH ART FOUNDATION, JOSLYN ART MUSEUM, OMAHA, NEBRASKA)

deduced that this damage had been caused by ice scouring in early spring when the river runs at flood stage.

He noticed a "black and white finch, which appeared to me to be a new species, and in its mode of life greatly resembles the rice bird." (5:XXIII,35) This was the lark bunting, a common bird along the upper Missouri. He recognized a gigantic tooth, brought to camp by a Cree beaver hunter from the high, wild reaches of the Milk River that was said to have come from the skeleton of a colossal serpent, to be the molar of a fossil mammoth. He noticed that the Richardson's ground squirrels disappeared in late summer, and correctly deduced that they must go into hibernation. He quickly learned to identify the major species of trees and shrubs along the river, although they were totally foreign to him (and there were, of course, no field guides available in those days).

*Karl Bodmer's exquisite wildlife paintings, such as this portrait of a pronghorn, corroborated Prince Maximilian's detailed narrative.* (PAINTING BY KARL BODMER, COURTESY INTERNORTH ART FOUNDATION, JOSLYN ART MUSEUM, OMAHA, NEBRASKA)

He was able to sort out many fur-trade era myths from fact — for example, the widely held belief that rattlesnakes were so mean that they bit themselves. He correctly predicted that several new species of chipmunks and ground squirrels would eventually be described from this region, and that the bison would eventually disappear and with it the Indian cultures. He realized that geological features are the result of long, slow processes that are at work every day and that produce an ever-changing landscape, a view that was quite radical in his day.

But perhaps more importantly, he penned a detailed and accurate description of Indian ecology, recording as a true ecologist and ethnologist the interplay of their habit, resources, culture, and beliefs.

When the *Flora* finally arrived at Fort McKenzie on August 9, Maximilian's attention was once again focused upon the Indians who had come to the fort to trade. A large camp of Blackfeet occupied the grounds around the fort, and the Prince set Bodmer to work at once painting portraits while the Prince himself sought out information on customs, habits, and ways of life. He described in detail the wild plants used by the Indians for dyes, decorations, food, medicine, and stimulants. Maximilian himself got caught up in the trading fever; he swapped some whiskey for a female grizzly cub, and was soon presented with a companion grizzly — a young male — by the fort supervisor. Maximilian's fondness for pets earned him still another gift, a young swift fox, which became quite tame and which he found to be a "capital mouser." (5:XXIII,125)

While at Fort McKenzie, Maximilian had the rare opportunity to view firsthand an Indian war. At daybreak on August 28, the fort was awakened by the sounds of musket fire, and Maximilian jumped up to find "the whole prairie covered with Indians on foot and on horseback, who were firing at the fort." (5:XXIII,146) The attacking band numbered about 600 Assiniboines and Crees, a force which could have easily overwhelmed the fort and all its occupants. Prepared to fight to the end, Maximilian grabbed his gun and headed for the battle. The attack, however, was directed not at the whites who occupied the fort but at a nearby encampment of about 20 tents full of drunken Blackfeet, who had been carousing and singing until the early morning hours. The battle raged all morning, and soon more Blackfeet arrived at the scene from their main encampment 8 or 10 miles away. When the smoke cleared the casualties were found to be astonishingly small — about 14 Blackfeet and six Assiniboines had been killed. A dead Assiniboine warrior had fallen near the fort and had been scalped by the Blackfeet; Maximilian was very much interested in this unfortunate Indian, since he wanted to add his

*Bodmer's* View of the Bear Paw Mountains from Fort McKenzie, *the trading post located just above the mouth of the Marias River, was painted on September 11, 1833.* (PAINTING BY KARL BODMER, COURTESY INTERNORTH ART FOUNDATION, JOSLYN ART MUSEUM, OMAHA, NEBRASKA)

*Prince Maximilian was very much interested in the cultures of the Indian tribes whose territories he traversed, and he directed artist Bodmer to paint many Indian portraits, including this one of* Ihkas-Kinne, Siksika Blackfeet Chief *wearing a heavily-ornamented otter-fur garment.* (PAINTING BY KARL BODMER, COURTESY INTERNORTH ART FOUNDATION, JOSLYN ART MUSEUM, OMAHA, NEBRASKA)

skull to his collection of specimens. Unfortunately, a group of Blackfeet "were engaged in venting their rage on the dead body," and "before I could obtain my wish, not a trace of the head was to be seen." (5:XXIII,149)

Maximilian had intended from the start to continue up the Missouri River and to pass the winter in the Rocky Mountains, where unknown plants and animals surely existed in abundance. However, the Indian situation made this impossible. Large bands of hostile Indians were gathered near the Great Falls, and the Assiniboine-Blackfeet war was clearly not over. The Blackfeet were not to be trusted, and a small party of white men found alone in the wilderness would be quickly dispatched. Also, the Assiniboines were not likely to forgive the whites for what they perceived as unfair support of the Blackfeet during the Fort McKenzie battle. So it was that the Prince made a reluctant decision to head back down the Missouri and spend the winter elsewhere. A crew was hastily assembled to build a small boat for Maximilian and his crew.

On September 14, the three Europeans, a helmsman, and three Canadian engages piled into the small craft, which was already almost full with Maximilian's gear and specimens. In the center of the boat, huge cages containing the young grizzlies were lashed on top of the cargo, an arrangement that made it impossible to travel from one end of the boat to another. Worst of all, there was no room to sleep aboard, which meant that the boat would have to put in to shore each night, leaving the party wide open for attack by Indians. As Maximilian put it, "As we had reason to be on our guard against the Indians, we regretted that my two bears were unusually dissatisfied with their confinement, and manifested their feelings by moaning and growling, which might very easily have attracted some hostile visitors." (5:XXIII,169) But winter was coming on, and there was no choice but to take things as they came. Bidding adieu to Fort McKenzie forever, the small party pushed off.

By the next morning, disaster had struck. Maximilian awoke to find that the boat had leaked and taken on large amounts of water. The damage this caused to Maximilian's collections, made with such care and over so many months, was incalculable. All of the party's clothes, instruments, and books were soaked. "I discovered, to my great regret," he wrote, "that the pretty striped squirrel, which I had hoped to bring alive to Europe, was drowned in its cage." (5:XXIII,170) Many of the animal skins, as well as some prized Indian leather dresses, were soaked and already beginning to mildew. Everyone was numb with cold from spending the night on shore in a downpour, which had prevented them from sleeping. To make matters worse, a "bleak wind" (5:XXIII,170) came up and chilled the travelers to the bone. The greatest disappointment came when the party had proceeded a distance downstream and built a fire. "What afflicted me the most," wrote Maximilian, "was my fine botanical collection of the Upper Missouri, made with labour and expense of time, which I could not now put into dry paper, and which therefore, was, for the most part, lost." Only a fellow scientist could fully appreciate the seriousness of this loss to a conscientious scientist like Maximilian, whose collections undoubtedly contained many species unknown to science. Maximilian tried to dry the papers on which the plants had been mounted, but the wind sent them careening across the prairie. "My extensive herbarium had to be laid, on account of the wind, under the shelter of the eminences of a small lateral ravine, which took me the whole day, and yet all the plants became black and mouldy." (5:XXIII,171)

After salvaging what they could from their soaked gear, the men continued downstream. The rutting season for elk and bison was under way, and the riverbanks were teeming with large animals, a striking contrast to the conditions of the upstream float. Flocks of whooping cranes, waterfowl, hawks, and songbirds filled the river valley. Maximilian eventually recovered, although only temporarily, from the loss of his collections, and was moved to eloquence by the exquisite fall scenery: "A solemn silence prevailed in the vast solitary wilderness, where Nature, in all her savage grandeur, reigned supreme. Not a breath of air was stirring; buffaloes were quietly grazing on the sides of the hills, and even my bears lay still, after a fresh bed of poplar branches had been made for them." (5:XXIII,182) The little crew finally pulled into Fort Union two weeks after it had left Fort McKenzie; not a single person had been seen during the return trip.

Near the mouth of the Marias River, Maximilian had collected a specimen of a strange steel-blue bird which bore some resemblance to a jay. He named this bird *Gymnorhinus cyano-cephalus*. This strange new bird was indeed a new discovery for science; although Lewis and Clark had observed it at least twice during their journey, it had not been scientifically described and named until Maximilian. This bird was the pinyon jay, which for decades was known among ornithologists as "Maximilian's jay."

Maximilian's second sojourn at Fort Union was less eventful than his first; all the Indians had departed, save a lone half-breed Blackfeet whose tepee was pitched near the fort. The Prince took advantage of the opportunity to participate in a bison hunt, and helped bring down a bull. As more Indians began passing through camp, Bodmer resumed his portraiture, although eventually it became so cold that his paints froze. The first snowstorm hit on October 27, and three days later the party left Montana to proceed downstream to Fort Clark, this time taking a somewhat larger boat than the one that had carried them from Fort McKenzie to Fort Union.

Maximilian and his crew spent the winter (1833-34) among the Mandan Indians at Fort Clark, literally following in the path of Lewis and Clark. Over the winter Maximilian developed scurvy, which was eventually cured when wild onions and fresh milk were obtained as spring approached. That summer, the expedition traveled from St. Louis to New York, and on August 8, 1834, Maximilian left for Europe. The two bears not only survived the winter, they lived to arrive in Europe.

The following summer, disaster again struck Maximilian's ill-fated collections. Most of the bulky materials, including skins, skulls, Indian artifacts, and probably much salvaged botanical material, had been left behind at Fort Union, awaiting the next steamer to the outpost. These were picked up by the steamer *Assiniboine*, and had made it most of the way down the Missouri when the ship wrecked and burned. The cases containing Maximilian's specimens were not insured, and therefore no great effort was made to save them from the burning ship. "When the steamer caught fire," wrote Maximilian, "the people thought rather of saving the foods than my cases, the contents of which were, probably, not considered to be of much value, and so they were all burnt." (5:XXII,28) This loss affected the eager scientist much more than the loss of the plant specimens. He bitterly refers to it again and again in his narrative.

Back in Germany, the Prince quickly set to work analyzing what precious little was left of his collections and preparing his narrative. The project took longer than he had planned. In 1839 the first installments of the journals first rolled off the press. Unbound sections of text were shipped to subscribers as they were printed (it took three years to print the entire narrative) as were the exquisite, hand-colored aquatint engravings made under Bodmer's direction from paintings he had made on the expedition. The German text was 300,000 words long, condensed from a field journal of probably half a million words. An English translation was published in London in 1843. Maximilian put an immense amount of his own resources into publication of the work, and certainly did not swell the family fortunes with the proceeds. But the book was widely read in Europe, and influenced many a future aristocratic European explorer to make the toilsome pilgrimage to the Upper Missouri. As a document of scientific exploration in the American West, Maximilian's *Travels* are second in importance only to the journals of Lewis and Clark.

*On October 6, 1833, hunters brought this whooping crane, today an endangered species, to Maximilian at Fort Union. Bodmer promptly executed this water color sketch.* (PAINTING BY KARL BODMER, COURTESY INTERNORTH ART FOUNDATION, JOSLYN ART MUSEUM, OMAHA, NEBRASKA)

History recognizes Maximilian primarily as an ethnographer who described the Plains Indians in their final days of glory, before disease and the white man's devastating influence erased their native cultures forever, and as the sponsor of artist Karl Bodmer. But Maximilian's journals stand as solid proof that the Prince was the most capable and highly trained naturalist to describe the Upper Missouri before 1850. His narrative tries to replace the irretrievable loss of the bulk of the scientific collections with detailed descriptions based on memory or field notes. One can only guess what new species from the *terra incognita* might have been described based on the Prince's lost collections, or what wonders he would have discovered had he continued to winter in the Montana Rockies.

## Sources


1. Bradley, J. H. *Affairs at Fort Benton from 1831 to 1869.* Boston: J. S. Canner and Co., 1966.
2. Brown, M. H. *The Plainsmen of the Yellowstone.* New York: G. P. Putnam's Sons, 1961.
3. Goetzmann, W. H., D. C. Hunt, M. V. Gallagher, and W. J. Orr. *Karl Bodmer's America.* Lincoln: Univ. of Nebraska Press, 1984.
4. Thomas, D., and K. Ronnefeldt, eds. *People of the First Man: Life Among the Plains Indians in Their Final Days of Glory; The First Hand Account of Prince Maximilian's Expedition up the Missouri River, 1833-34.* New York: Promontory Press, 1982.
5. Thwaites, R. G., ed. *Early Western Travels, 1748-1846.* Cleveland: The Arthur H. Clark Company, 1904-07.

# CHAPTER 6

# Father Pierre Jean DeSmet

*In 1841 Father Pierre Jean DeSmet, S. J., founded St. Mary's Mission in the Bitterroot Valley, near the present location of the Lee Metcalf National Wildlife Refuge.* (TOM DIETRICH)

"I have been for years a wanderer in the desert. I was three years without receiving a letter from any quarter. I was two years in the mountains, without tasting bread, salt, coffee, tea, sugar. I was for years without a roof, without a bed. I have been six months without a shirt on my back, and often have I passed whole days and nights without a morsel of anything to eat." (1:57) So wrote Father Pierre Jean DeSmet, S. J., consummate wilderness wanderer, a man who traveled some 180,000 miles in his lifetime, mostly on foot or horseback, and who crossed the Atlantic no fewer than 19 times.

Father DeSmet was a Jesuit priest, not a scientist. He had no academic training in biology, no large university to sponsor his scientific exploits, and no government grants or salary to finance research. No new species were discovered by or named after him. He was usually seen in his simple black robe, perhaps leading a mule; he was never known to stuff a bird skin nor to pop a hellgramite into a vial of alcohol. Yet he was intensely aware of the natural world, and felt an exhilarating love of nature that drew him back year after year to the uncharted wilds of Montana. "Lovely nature, sublime nature, terrible nature — the plains, the valleys, the hills, the mountains hiding their snowy summits among clouds — nature in all her forms ... " filled Father DeSmet with awe and reverence, and roused his spirit to "a thousand reflections, each more philosophic than the rest." (1:1486)

DeSmet was a careful observer, and wrote extensively of the strange and terrible landscapes of the West and of their furred and feathered inhabitants. Many of DeSmet's 180,000 miles were logged in Montana, and in fact DeSmet's tireless criss-crossing of the state over a period of three decades certainly earns him the distinction of the most well-traveled of the early Montana explorer-naturalists.

DeSmet was born in the quaint Flemish town of Termonde in Belgium in the year 1801. At the age of 20 he joined a band of missionaries headed for the New World. Without family support, he had to pawn all his possessions to pay for his passage. Eventually he arrived in Phildelphia, and after six years at the Jesuit novitiate there he was ordained a priest. He then moved to St. Louis, where he helped found the first Jesuit novitiate west of the Mississippi River. He soon became director of the departments of language, history and philosophy at the newly-founded St. Louis University. Ill health — probably exacerbated by overwork — then forced the young priest to return to Europe for several years. Upon his return, he founded a mission among the Potawatomi Indians near present-day Council Bluffs, Iowa, and traveled up the Missouri River on a peace mission to the Sioux.

To DeSmet, the interior of the continent was swarming with the souls of countless savages desperately in need of saving. DeSmet's life work was clearly laid before him: to reclaim and salvage as many of these lost souls as was possible for one man to do in a lifetime. When the call came for volunteers to bring salvation to the Salish Tribe deep in the unexplored wilderness that was to become Montana DeSmet jumped at the opportunity. This decision was one that was to bring him into his first contact with the Indians of the Rockies and one that was to change his life. It was also to change the course of Montana history.

DeSmet joined with the American Fur Company's annual expedition to the mountains in the spring of 1840. The party followed the Oregon Trail into what is now eastern Idaho. DeSmet split off from the main party and entered Montana by crossing the Continental Divide from Henry's Lake to Red Rock Lakes. Somewhere near Alder Gulch, DeSmet discovered a stream whose bed appeared to be composed almost entirely of gold sand. Fearing the impact of a gold rush, he kept his find a secret for more than 20 years.

The party descended the Jefferson River to the Three Forks, then followed Captain William Clark's route over Bozeman Pass to the Yellowstone River. The Yellowstone, to DeSmet's horror, was still "the range of the grizzly bear, the most terrible animal of this desert; at every step we came upon their terrifying tracks." A dead bear brought into camp had paws 13 inches long and fitted with seven-inch claws. "The strength of this animal is surprising," he wrote. "An Indian has assured me that with a single blow of his paw he has seen one of these bears tear away four ribs from a buffalo, which fell dead at his feet." (1:235) DeSmet had a first-hand demonstration of the grizzly's power when he saw a sow charge from a willow thicket and knock over a Salish Indian horse — with the Indian still on it.

The grizzly and other unfriendly wildlife, however, were not the greatest of the hazards of the Yellowstone. "Right here I will remark that in these solitudes, though the howling of wolves, the hissing of venomous serpents and the roaring of the tiger [mountain lion] and grizzly bear are capable of freezing one with terror, this fear is nothing in comparison with that which fresh tracks of men and horses can arouse in the soul of a traveler, or the columns of smoke that he sees rising about him." (1:236) The travelers, luckily, made it to Fort Union without a brush with the hostile Blackfeet Indians to whom he referred. From there, DeSmet returned down the Missouri River to civilization, ending the first of his many whirlwind tours of Montana.

*Father DeSmet logged some 180,000 miles in his lifetime, many of them in Montana.*

In the fall of the following year (1841), DeSmet returned to Montana with the intent of founding a mission among the Flathead Indians. He again entered the state from the Snake River Plains of Idaho, but this time he took a direct route north to the Deer Lodge Valley and traveled along the Clark's Fork River to its confluence with the Bitterroot River near present-day Missoula. A few miles south, in the lush Bitterroot Valley near present-day Stevensville, DeSmet established the famous St. Mary's Mission, the first permanent white settlement in the state. Situated in one of Montana's richest wildlife areas on what is now the Lee Metcalf National Wildlife Refuge, St. Mary's Mission offered a fine array of nature's creations for the scrutiny of the inquisitive naturalist-priest.

In November DeSmet braved the winter snows and traveled to Fort Colville, Washington, to obtain badly-needed supplies for the brand-new mission. DeSmet's exact route cannot be retraced, but it seems he may have crossed the Rattlesnake Mountains near Evaro Hill northwest of Missoula. On the way he took a side trip to Flathead Lake. "The lake is highly romantic," he wrote, "and is from forty to fifty miles long. Mountainous and rocky islands of all sizes are scattered over its bosom, which present an enchanting prospect. These islands are filled with wild horses. Lofty mountains surround the lake and rise from its very brink." (1:373) Despite this detour, he was able to return before the end of the year with a load of tools and supplies.

Of the high mountains surrounding St. Mary's, DeSmet wrote that "they abound in bucks [elk], buffalo, and sheep, whose wool is as white as snow and as fine as silk [mountain goat], also in all kinds of bears, wolves, panthers [mountain lion] and Carcajou [wolverine] ... There are also found tiger cats [Canada lynx], wild cats [bobcats] and whistlers, a species of mountain rat [yellow-bellied marmot]. The moose is found here, but is seldom caught, on account of its extraordinary vigilance, for on the slightest rustling of a branch it leaves off eating, and will not return to its food for a long time afterward ... Amongst the most remarkable birds we distinguished the Nun's eagle [bald eagle] (so called by travelers on account of the color of its head, which is white, whilst the other parts of the body are black), the black eagle [golden eagle or turkey vulture], buzzard [red-tailed hawk], waterfowl, heron, crane, pheasant [probably blue grouse] and quail [probably grouse]." (1:344-5)

In April of 1842, DeSmet left St. Mary's and traveled westward along the Columbia River to Fort Vancouver, again making a side trip to Flathead Lake. Like David Thompson and Thomas Blakiston — indeed, like all of the early explorers — DeSmet was greatly impressed by the giant cedars of the lower Clark Fork River. This forest, wrote DeSmet, "is certainly a wonder of its kind; there is probably nothing similar to it in America. The savages speak of it as the finest in Oregon [Territory], and really every tree which it contains is enormous in its kind. The birch, elm and beach [sic], generally small elsewhere, like the toad of La Fontaine, that aimed at being as large as the ox, swell out here to twice their size.... Cedars of four and five fathoms in circumference are here very common; we saw some six, and I measured one forty-two feet in circumference. A cedar of four fathoms, lying on the ground, measured more than 200 feet in length." (1:349-50)

DeSmet proceeded westward to Fort Vancouver on the Lower Columbia River. At one point on the journey five boatmen in his party were killed in a treacherous

*St. Mary's Mission (left) was the first permanent white settlement in Montana. DeSmet later founded a second mission at St. Ignatius (right).* (TOM DIETRICH PHOTOS)

rapids on the Columbia, and DeSmet himself narrowly escaped drowning. DeSmet returned to St. Mary's in the fall, remained briefly, then ascended the Bitterroot Valley to its head and crossed over into the Big Hole drainage. From there he descended the river to the Three Forks, then followed his route of two years earlier down the Yellowstone to Fort Union and back to St. Louis.

The next two years were spent by DeSmet in St. Louis, Boston, Ireland, and Italy raising funds for his new missions. In 1843 he published a book describing his travels entitled *Letters and Sketches; With a Narrative of a Year's Residence Among the Indian Tribes of the Rocky Mountains.* (2) In 1844 he sailed around Cape Horn to Astoria on the Oregon Coast, then traveled to the eastern part of what is now Washington State, where he founded a new mission he called St. Ignatius. The next spring (1845) he returned briefly to St. Mary's for provisions, then commenced an epic journey over the Canadian Rockies in an attempt to establish contact with the Blackfeet Indians of the northern Canadian Plains.

Intending to travel cross-country to the Kootenai River valley from the Clark's Fork River, DeSmet hacked a tortuous trail through a jungle of vegetation along the present Idaho-Montana border. The path, which David Thompson had called "The Great Road of the Flatheads," was "much obstructed by fallen trees, morasses, frightful sloughs, from which the poor horses with much difficulty extricate themselves ..." (1:487) Axe in hand, DeSmet was forced to cut his way through these somber forests, where "hosts of trees ... has been levelled by the autumnal blasts and storms." (1:491) Some of the forests were so dense that the light of day was excluded altogether, and DeSmet could not see his guide only twelve feet away. He saw strange plants such as wild ginger at the bases of the giant cedars. Here DeSmet was subject to "the gloomy and harrowing thoughts which imagination conjures up in these dismal regions. The most fearful apprehensions dismay the bravest heart and cause an involuntary shudder, as some dire apparition of a bear or panther stalks in fancy before the mind, whilst groping our way amidst these dark and frightful haunts, from which there is no egress." (9:XXIX,201)

Finally, having surmounted all these obstacles, DeSmet arrived at "a smiling and accessible valley ... where the [Kootenai] river winds in such fantastic beauty, that it serves to make the weary traveler not only forget his past dangers, but amply compensates him for the fatigues of a long and tiresome journey." (1:487)

In the Kootenai River Valley near present-day Troy, DeSmet found that the Indians had learned to exploit a recurrent natural phenomenon in obtaining food. For most of the year, the river is slow and tranquil, until "aroused from its inertness by the universal thaw; it then descends with such astounding impetuosity that it destroys the banks, and in its furious course, uproots and bears along trees, fragments of rocks, &c., which vainly oppose its passage. In a few days the entire valley is overflowed, and it presents to view immense lakes and morasses, separated by borders of trees." The lakes and morasses thus formed "are filled with fish; they remain there inclosed as in natural reservoirs, for the use of the inhabitants. The fish swarm in such abundance that the Indians have no other labor than to take them from the water and prepare them for the boiler." (1:487-8)

A strange species of sturgeon, "which measures from six to ten and sometimes twelve feet in length," (1:490) was speared by the Indians from the waters of the Kootenai. The white sturgeon, found in Montana only in this stretch of the Kootenai River, is today nearly extinct in the state.

The Kootenai Indians, who inhabited this appealing valley, were often forced to subsist on moss when the stores of camas, fish, and dried bison meat ran out. DeSmet's view of this fare was no more favorable than David Thompson's. "It is a parasite of the pine, a tree common in these latitudes, and hangs from its boughs in great quantities; it appears more suitable for mattresses than for the sustenance of human life. When [the Indians] have procured a great quantity, they pick out all heterogeneous substance, and prepare it as they do the camas; it becomes compact, and is, in my opinion, a most miserable food, which in a brief space reduces those who live on it to a pitiable state of emaciation." (1:489)

The charm of the Kootenai River Valley quickly wore off as DeSmet continued upstream toward the site of present-day Libby and began the painful, eight-mile portage around Kootenai Falls. Here, among "precipitous and frightful rocks, ... the traveler is compelled ... to risk his life at every step, and brave obstacles that appear, at first sight, insuperable.

*DeSmet traveled along the "fearful and unfathomable chasms" of Kootenai Falls (far left), and described many species of Montana wildlife during his travels, including the moose, the pika or "diminutive mountain hare" (above right), and the "industrious beaver."* (FROM LEFT: GEORGE WUERTHNER; CONRAD ROWE; TOP, RON GLOVAN; BOTTOM, TOM ULRICH)

Whatever can be imagined appalling seems here combined to terrify the heart — livid gashes of ravines and precipices, giant peaks and ridges of varied hue, inaccessible pinnacles, fearful and unfathomable chasms filled with the sound of ever-precipitating waters, long, sloping and narrow banks, which must be alternately ascended, and many times have I been obliged to take the attitude of a quadruped and walk upon my hands ... Amid these stern, heaven-built walls of rock, the water has forced its way in varied forms, and we find cataracts and whirlpools engulfing crags and trees, beneath their angry sway. Whilst the eye rests with pleasure on the rich and russet hues of distant slopes, upland turf and rock-hung flower — the ear is stunned by the confused sounds of murmuring rills, rushing streams, impetuous falls, and roaring torrents." (1:491-2)

Finally arriving on level ground in the vicinity of present-day Libby, DeSmet noted the presence of coal seams and lead and silver ore and thought the valley an ideal site for a future community. "What," he wondered, "would this now solitary and desolate land become, under the fostering hand of civilization?" (1:493)

DeSmet proceeded north to the Kootenai Indian encampment on the Tobacco Plains near the current site of Eureka. Of the wildlife of these wild mountains and canyons, he wrote the following: "The ordinary music of the desert is, the shrill cry of the panther [mountain lion], and the howling of the wolf. The diminutive mountain hare, six inches high, and whose biography has not yet found a place in natural history [pika], amuses itself amidst the stony rubbish, and exhibits wonderful activity; whilst his neighbor, the lubberly porcupine, clambers up, seats himself upon a branching cypress and gnaws the bark. He views the eager huntsman with a careless and indifferent air, unconscious that his tender flesh is regarded as a most delicious morsel. The industrious beaver, like a wary sentinel, warns his family of man's approach by striking the water with its tail. The muskrat, or musquash, plunges immediately into the water. The otter quits his sports and slides upon his belly among the reeds — the timid squirrel leaps from bough to bough, until it reaches the topmost shade of the cypress; the marten jumps from tree to tree, and buries itself in the foliage — the whistler [marmot] and weasel repair to their respective domiciles: — a precipitous flight alone saves the fox his rich silvery pelisse — the badger, or the ground hog, too remote from his dwelling, digs the sandy soil, and buries himself alive, to avoid pursuit ... it requires the joint efforts of two men to force him from his hiding place ... " Even DeSmet's old friend the grizzly bear was found here, a beast who "is not content with growling and menacing the intrepid adventurer, who dares infringe on his cavernous domains, but grinds his teeth, expressive of his rage." (9:XXIX,214)

From the Tobacco Plains, DeSmet continued northward to the headwaters of the Kootenai River and crossed the Continental Divide to the buffalo plains of the Saskatchewan River Valley. He visited Rocky Mountain House, Fort Edmonton, and Fort

*These lithographs, made by DeSmet's friend and fellow priest Nicholas Point, appeared in DeSmet's books. At left is St. Mary's Mission near present-day Stevensville; at right is a bison-hunting scene sketched in the "Muscle-Shell mountains" while traveling across central Montana on a peace mission.* (COURTESY, MONTANA HISTORICAL SOCIETY)

Assiniboine, but he was unable to make the contact with the Blackfeet he so desired. He did, however, meet the Mountain Assiniboines, a destitute tribe that he found to be "filthy beyond conception ... devoured by vermin, which they, in turn, consume." Among them DeSmet enjoyed what he called the "choice ragout of the Rocky Mountains," a dish that was made by boiling pre-chewed meat in blood, followed by a dessert "composed of pulverized ants, grass-hoppers and locusts, that have been dried in the sun." (1:510-11) The next spring (1846) DeSmet recrossed the Divide across the Columbia icefields to the headwaters of the Columbia River and followed that river all the way downstream to Fort Walla Walla.

In the summer of 1846, DeSmet returned to St. Mary's Mission, then struck eastward in a second attempt to make contact with the feared and warlike Blackfeet. He was accompanied by Father Nicholas Point, an amateur artist, who made sketches of the regions traversed during this journey. A band of Salish, traditional enemies of the Blackfeet, followed in an entourage that stretched almost a mile behind the two priests. The party descended the Yellowstone to a point near present-day Big Timber, then headed northward toward Judith Gap, passing "through a broken and undulating, dry and woodless country, destitute of any water fit to drink — stagnant pools of brackish water being the only kind found here to satiate the thirst." Their course took them past the "Muscle-shell Mountains" (probably the Crazy Mountains), whose peaks "rise abruptly from the plain around, resembling broken, elevated islands in the midst of the ocean, and their tops tufted with a heavy growth of cedar and pine." (1:584-7)

Finally, as it neared the Judith River Breaks, the party was met by a Blackfeet war party. The news was good, however: "Their tribe", wrote DeSmet, "will be delighted to receive a visit from us ... our persons are considered sacred among them." (9:XXIX) The two priests finally met a large Blackfeet encampment near present-day Fort Benton, and spent three weeks preaching to the assembled tribes. The results of the encounter were more successful than DeSmet could ever have dreamed. Not only had he succeeded in establishing an alliance between the warring Salish and Blackfeet tribes, but he also was able to reconcile the Bloods and Piegans, two divisions of the Blackfeet Nation that had recently been at war.

Unfortunately, DeSmet had to return to St. Louis, and did not return to Montana for five years. During this time, the alliances he had forged weakened and finally broke down, and animosity between Indian and white grew steadily.

Upon his return to civilization in 1846, DeSmet began work on a book describing his travels, which he entitled *Oregon Missions and Travels over the Rocky Mountains in 1845-6.* (3) As an appendix to this book, which was published in 1847, DeSmet included a list of "plants of the Rocky Mountains in flower in August and September." Among the flowers he listed were such familiar Montana species as yellow stonecrop, coneflower, springbeauty, harebell, columbine, and avens.

DeSmet's reputation as a peacemaker eventually attracted the U. S. Government. DeSmet was, in the mid-1800s, one of the few white men who could enter Sioux and Blackfoot country in relative safety. He therefore spent much of his later life on peace missions to the warring tribes. In 1851 he crossed eastern Montana overland from Ft. Union to Rosebud Creek, traversing the Terry Badlands en route, and proceeded to the Great Peace Council at Fort Laramie in what is now Wyoming. He later traveled up the Missouri River to Fort Benton many times, and in 1866 he declined a nomination as Catholic Bishop of Montana. In perhaps his greatest peace mission, he traveled overland in 1868 westward to the Powder River country, near present-day Miles City, for a peace council with the hostile Sioux who "had declared war to the death with the white race." (9:XXIX) Eight years later, three years after Father DeSmet's death, this hatred was to culminate at the Battle of the Little Big Horn.

What kind of man was this great peacemaker whom the Indians respected and feared as a holy man? As a fellow pioneer described him, "He was genial, of fine presence, and one of the saintliest men I have ever known, and I cannot wonder that the Indians were

*DeSmet's travels took him from Flathead Lake (left), where he noted "mountainous and rocky islands of all sizes ... filled with wild horses," to the arid badlands of southeastern Montana (right).* (PACIFIC RAILROAD SURVEY LITHOGRAPH; KRISTI DuBOIS PHOTO)

made to believe him divinely protected. He was a man of great kindness and great affability under all circumstances; nothing seemed to disturb his temper." (1:114) Perhaps more revealing is the following verbal self-portrait, penned by DeSmet in a letter to his niece: "... a man of medium size, with gray hair, tending to white. The center of his wide face (a foot, or near it), is occupied by a nose with which a Greek or a Roman would not find much fault. Its nearest neighbor is a mouth of ordinary size, which hardly ever opens save to laugh or to make others laugh." On account of his size (he weighed 210 pounds at the time), he advised his niece that "if you ever build a new house, give the door to my chamber six inches extra width ..." (1:1473-4)

DeSmet's writings abound in natural history descriptions and grandiloquent statements about natural wonders and scenic vistas. Some are surprisingly accurate and perceptive; others tend to affirm commonly-held superstitions, many of which stemmed from Indian legends, about the lives of wild animals. For example, he wrote that hibernating bears purge themselves and load up on dry seeds before crawling into their cave, then spend the winter sucking fat from their paw, turning over precisely four times during the course of the winter. He soberly describes a rattlesnake which was "basking in the sun, surrounded by eight or ten little ones. As soon as she perceived me, she gave the rattle, opened her throat wide, and in an instant the whole brood descended. I withdrew some seconds, and then returned; the young ones had come forth from their living tomb, to which my presence quickly obliged them to seek refuge anew." (1:622)

For the most part, though, DeSmet's writings portray an accurate and genuine early account of the plants, animals, and natural wonders of the Montana wilderness. His writings on ethnobotany, Indian uses of edible wild plants, are particularly valuable to today's anthropologist studying the habits of Native Americans prior to extensive European contact. The diet of the Kootenai Indians, he wrote, included not only such delectibles as rose hips, chokecherries, black caps, serviceberries, raspberries, currants, gooseberries, hawthornes, balsamroot, bitterroot, biscuit-root, camas, arrowroot, wild onion, and Sego lily, but also "a number of detestible fruits and roots which serve as nutriment for the Indians, but at which a *civilized* stomach would revolt and nauseate," (1:488) including black tree moss and conifer bark. The prairie Indians had a vastly different diet that was based on bison meat but that also included wild plums, silver buffaloberries, and Indian bread-root.

DeSmet's writings contain one of the earliest detailed descriptions of the sulphurous nether-region known today as Yellowstone National Park. DeSmet, in all his travels through the Rockies, never actually made it into this region, but he heard tales about it from the Indians and from Jim Bridger. DeSmet believed that "the most extraordinary spot ... and perhaps the most marvelous of all the northern half of this continent, is in the very heart of the Rocky Mountains (1:1377) ... This locality is often agitated with subterranean fires. The sulphurous gases which escape in great volumes from the burning soil infect the atmosphere for several miles, and render the earth so barren that even the wild wormwood cannot grow on it ... Bituminous, sulphurous and boiling springs are very numerous in it. The hot springs contain a large quantity of calcareous matter, and form hills more or less elevated ... The earth is thrown up very high, and the influence of the elements causes it to take the most varied and the most fantastic shapes. Gas, vapor and smoke are continually escaping by a thousand openings, from the base to the summit of the volcanic pile; the noise at times resembles the steam let off by a boat ... The hunters and the Indians speak of it with a superstitious fear, and consider it the abode of evil spirits, that is to say, a kind of hell. Indians seldom approach it without offering some sacrifice, or at least without presenting the calumet of peace to the turbulent spirits, that they may be propitious. They declare that the subterranean noises proceed from the forging of warlike weapons: each eruption of earth is, in their eyes, the result of a combat between the infernal spirits, and becomes the monument of a new victory or calamity." (1:660-1)

DeSmet called the Missouri River "My river," on account of his many ascents and descents. "Let us descend the Missouri together," he invited the reader

*DeSmet believed that the Great Falls of the Missouri were second only to Niagara in terms of beauty and grandeur. Today Ryan Dam stands at the head of the falls.* (PACIFIC RAILROAD SURVEY LITHOGRAPH)

in one of his books. "You shall admire with me the length of its course, its breadth, its marvels, and its dangers ... I have drunk the limpid waters of its sources, and the muddy waters at its mouth, distant more than three thousand miles from each other ... Whenever I crossed this magnificent river the sensations which I experienced bordered on the sublime, and my imagination transported me through the world of prairies which it fertilises, to the colossal mountains whence it issues." (1:1355-65)

The Great Falls of the Missouri, according to DeSmet, "are not as sublime as those of the Niagara, but they may hold second place for grandeur among all the waterfalls of this vast continent ... (1:1363) The water, the rocks slightly covered with a veil of foam, the lofty cliffs which frame it all, that succession of rapid currents, the deafening noise of the fall and the cataract, spreading into the distance, the column of vapor rising and presenting to the sun all the vivid colors of the rainbow, make the scene very beautiful and very wild at the same time." (1:1368)

Beginning about a hundred miles below the Great Falls are the White Cliffs and *Mauvaises Terres* described so eloquently by Meriwether Lewis. DeSmet too was enthusiastic in his description of these natural wonders, and felt that it was "the wonder of all travelers" and "the most remarkable place in the vast territory of the United States (1:851) ... Viewed at a distance, these lands exhibit the appearance of extensive villages and ancient castles, but under forms so extraordinary, and so capricious a style of architecture, that we might consider them as appertaining to some new world, or ages far remote. Here a majestic gothic tower, surrounded with turrets, rises in noble grandeur, and there enormous and lofty columns seem reared to support the vault of heaven. Further on you may descry a fort beaten by the tempest and surrounded by mantellated walls ... Cupolas of colossal proportions, and pyramids which recall the gigantic labors of ancient Egypt, rise around ... It is like the entrance to an immense monumental cemetery, with its statues, busts, obelisks, columns, vases and urns, tables, entablatures, mortuary frescoes and monuments of every sort ... There follows a succession of ancient manors and convents, castles, cathedrals, bastions and forts, surmounted by towers and parapets and surrounded by sentinels motionless at their posts ... The Bad Lands of the Missouri will some day take their place among the great wonders of the American hemisphere." (1:624,1369-70) All this from a man who had traveled some 180,000 miles around the globe!

The great treeless plains cut through by the Missouri River reminded DeSmet of an ocean of grass, and he referred to it as "the Prairie Ocean." Petrified tree trunks found in the badlands convinced DeSmet that the region was once thickly forested. "Why," he asked, "are not these lands wooded as they must have been in former times? ... Some observers attribute it to the action of frequent fires which have passed over these localities; others to the change undergone in the climate, or to the natural sterility of the soil; and there are some who pretend that some operation or convulsion of nature has destroyed the forests which formerly existed here, and has reduced them to their present condition." (1:659) DeSmet noticed that the interior regions of the great continents — the steppes of Asia, the pampas of South America, and the Great Plains of the U. S. — all share a common aspect, that of treelessness and aridity. Climbing over the badlands, DeSmet was amazed to find "enormous heaps of shells of the testaceous kind and of the genus muscula [molluscs], which I found a few feet from the summits of the loftiest hills," and was convinced by them that "this portion of land has undergone changes as great as they are amazing." (1:659) In this he was anticipating the findings of Ferdinand Hayden, Edward Drinker Cope, George Bird Grinnell, and later paleontologists, who confirmed DeSmet's then-heretical image of a changing planet.

DeSmet loved to send descriptions of prairie animals to associates in St. Louis and Belgium. A selection of his finest writings on various animal subjects follows.

**On prairie dogs and burrowing owls:** "The prairie dog, in shape, color, and agility, more resembles the squirrel than the animal from which it has taken its name. They live together in separate lodges, to the number of several thousands.... The grass which springs up in the neighborhood of their dwellings they tear up by the roots; but their vandalism has its exceptions. They seem to respect and spare certain flowers which generally surround their little abodes, and give them a much more agreeable look.... They pile up the earth around their dwellings about two feet above the surface of the soil, thus protecting themselves against the inundations which, in the rainy season or at the melting of the snows, would engulf them and their little hopes ... It is said too that they live only on the dew and grass roots, a remark founded upon the position of their village, which is always found where the ground is waterless and barren ... A kind of small owl and the rattlesnake appear to entertain amicable relations with the prairie-dog, and are commonly found at the entrance of their lodges, and in the general fight the three seek safety in the same asylum. The motives and nature of this singular sympathy are unknown." (1:622,1395)

**On mosquitoes:** "And what shall I say of mosquitoes? I have suffered so much from them, that I cannot leave them unnoticed. In the middle of the day they do not trouble the traveler, if he keep aloof from

*DeSmet mistakenly believed that prairie dogs, burrowing owls and rattlesnakes lived together peacefully in the same burrows. He accurately described how the plains Indians were able to capture up to 200 antelope by means of a simple but ingenious trap.* (ABOVE LEFT, PHIL FARNES; RIGHT, ROBERT GILDART; BOTTOM, TOM ULRICH)

the shade and walk in the burning sun. But at nightfall they light on him, and hang on him till morning, like leeches sucking his blood. There is no defense against their darts, but to hide under a buffalo skin, or wrap one's self up in some stuff which they cannot pierce, and run the risk of being smothered. — When green or rotten wood can be procured, they may be driven away by smoke, but in such case the traveler himself is smoked, and in spite of all he can do his eyes are filled with tears. As soon as the smoke ceases, they return to the charge till other wood is provided and thrown on the fire, so that the traveler's sleep is frequently interrupted, which proves very annoying after the fatigue of a troublesome journey." (1:1392)

**On the beaver:** "Some of the Indian tribes believe that beavers are a degraded race of human beings, whose vices and crimes have induced the Great Spirit to punish them by changing them into their present form; and they think, after the lapse of a number of years, their punishment will cease, and they will be restored to their original shape. They even believe that these animals use a kind of language to communicate their thoughts to each other, to consult, deliberate, pass sentence on delinquents, etc.... The flesh of the beaver is fat and savory. The feet are deemed the most dainty parts. The tail affords a substitute for butter ..." (1:1393-4)

**On the pronghorn:** "The Cabri (antelope) resembles the deer in form and size; the antlers are smaller and have but two branches ... When startled or shot at and missed, he darts forward with incredible swiftness, but curiosity induces him to halt and look back. The hunter tries to amuse his curiosity, by holding up and waving some bright-colored object: the animal approaches, and curiosity becomes the cause of his death ... The antelope hunt is a favorite sport with the Indians. They choose a spot of ground from fifty to eighty feet square, and inclose it with posts and boughs, leaving a small opening or entrance, two or three feet wide. From this entrance they construct two wings or hedges, which they extend for several miles. — After this they form a large semicircle, and drive the antelopes before them till they enter between the hedges, where they press so hard upon them that they force them into the square inclosure, in which they kill them with clubs. I have been told that the number of antelopes thus driven into the inclosure, often amounts to more than 200." (1:1396)

**On the bison:** "The Indians say that the buffaloes live together as the bees, under the direction of a queen, and that when the queen is wounded, all the others surround and deplore her. If this were the case, the hunter who had the good fortune to kill the queen, would have fine sport in dispatching the rest." (1:1398)

**On the porcupine:** "The American porcupine, the *Hystrix dorsata*, is called by modern Zoologists, the *Prickly Beaver*. In fact there is great similarity between the two species in size and form, and both inhabit the same region. The porcupine, like the beaver, has a double peltry or fur; the first is long and soft; the second, is still softer, and greatly resembles down or felt. They both have two long sharp, strong tusks, at the extremity of the jaw-bone. The Flat-heads affirm that the porcupine and beaver are brothers, and relate that anciently they abode together ..." (1:512)

**On the wolf and coyote:** "Of wolves we have seen four varieties, the grey, the white, the black and the bluish. The grey seems to be the most common, as they are the most frequently seen. — The black wolves are large and ferocious animals. They sometimes mingle with a herd of buffaloes, and at first appear quite harmless, but when they find a young calf strayed from its dam, or an old cow on the brink of a precipice, they are sure to attack and kill the former, and to harass the latter till they succeed in pushing it down the precipice. The wolves are very numerous in these regions. The plains are full of holes, which are generally deep, and into which they retire when hunger does not compel them

## THE DEMISE OF ELKHORN PRAIRIE

On July 11, 1833, near present-day Wolf Point, Prince Maximilian came onto the most striking Indian monument on the northern Plains: "About 800 paces from the river, the hunting or war parties of the Blackfoot Indians have gradually piled up a quantity of elk's horns till they have formed a pyramid 16 or 18 feet high, and 12 or 15 feet in diameter. Every Indian who passes by makes a point of contributing his part ... and often the strength of the hunting party is marked, with red strokes, on the horns they have added to the heap. All these horns, of which there are certainly more than 1,000, are piled up, confusedly mixed together, and so wedged in, that we found some trouble in extricating, from the pyramid, a large one, with fourteen antlers, which we brought away with us.... The prairie ... is called Prairie a la Corne de Cerf [Elk Horn Prairie] ...." (9:II,34-5)

Bodmer made an on-the-spot sketch of this remarkable edifice. De Smet also made note of the Elk Horn Prairie when he traveled past in October of 1846. He described it as the "Monumental Elkhorn Prairie," and noted that "So far as I know, it is the only place in all this part of the country which has possessed a true monument, erected by the hands of the Indians. A tower had been constructed here, composed exclusively of elks' antlers; it was of remarkable height. Its base formed a great square. After every campaign against the elk and deer, so abundant in this region, the Indians would come here to deposit religiously the trophies of their hunt, that is, the skulls of the animals surmounted by their antlers. The most ancient of the Assiniboins ... could not give me any account, either of the epoch nor of the circumstances which gave rise to the erection of this unique monument." (I:1371:2)

*The Elkhorn Pyramid on the Upper Missouri.* (AQUATINT AFTER KARL BODMER, COURTESY INTERNORTH ART FOUNDATION, JOSLYN ART MUSEUM, OMAHA, NEBRASKA)

On June 18, 1850, during his ascent of the Missouri River in the *El Paso*, naturalist Thaddeus Culbertson came upon Elk Horn Prairie, and saw a "distant view of it ... like a white monument several miles off." He found it to be about 15 feet high and 20 or 25 feet in circumference and composed exclusively of elk horns, not skulls. He believed that, since there were no heads, they were probably all horns that had been shed. "What a great number of Elk must have been there," wrote Culbertson, "to have furnished such a number of horns. As to its origin no certain information can be gained. Old traders say it has been there to their knowledge twenty years and how much longer they can't tell as old Indians say they are ignorant of the time or the occasion of its being made." (6:109)

Culbertson collected a number of plant specimens "as mementoes of Elk Horn Prairie" (6:110); these included penstemon, yarrow, downy painted-cup and silvery bladderpod. (7) Culbertson, however, became that day an unwilling participant in the inexcusable if inevitable vandalism of the Indians' sacred ancient monument. One of the traders on the *El Paso*, Mr. Picotte, had gotten the idea that he wanted to transport the entire elkhorn pyramid back to St. Louis with him. "All on board," wrote Culbertson, "excepting the old gentleman himself, would prefer to leave it untouched, especially as the horns are not in a good state of preservation." (6:115) Nonetheless, most of the crew participated with gusto in this earliest act of vandalism. As soon as the boat stopped, about 30 men including Picotte and Culbertson jumped off and ran toward the pile of horns. By the time Culbertson got there, one man had already climbed the pile and was tossing down antlers. On the return trip three days later the crew finished off the job, and soon "this noted, and almost revered land mark [was] on the hurricane deck of the *El Paso*." (6:115) News of this outrageous act eventually reached De Smet, who wrote, "The cupidity of a modern vandal has caused the demolition of this strange, savage structure, which had resisted all the tempests, windstorms, stern winters and other vagaries of the atmosphere of this strange region. He took his capture to St. Louis and sold it, and there the antlers were transformed into handles for knives, forks and daggers." (1:1372) to prowl about, or when they are pursued by the huntsman. There is a small sized wolf [coyote], called the medicine wolf, regarded by the Indians as a sort of manitou. They watch its yelpings during the night, and the superstitious conjurers pretend to understand and interpret them. According to the loudness, frequency and other modifications of these yelpings, they interpret that either friends or foes approach the camp, etc., and if it happens that on some occasion they conjecture right, the prediction is never forgotten, and the conjurers take care to mention it on every emergency." (1:1399)

"Wolf Point ... deserves a small notice. Here is the rendezvous *par excellence* of the wolves, those animals so cruel, but timid and cowardly at sight of man. They will attack together a calf or a cow, which they have managed to separate from the herd; they watch for buffalo to cross the river and try to climb steep and difficult places; the poor animals get mired in the mud, and often entire herds perish. The wolves throw themselves on them and devour them. On these occasions, these rivals of the jackals and hyenas express their joy in their own manner, in a kind of concert of terrifying howlings, as if a pandemonium had been convoked. I have several times found myself close to these carnivorous animals in cases of this kind. To prevent being kept awake all night, we had to fire a few shots from time to time, which reduced the frightened wolves to silence." (1:1372)

In 1847 DeSmet speculated on the fate of the mountain and prairie wilderness in which his beloved savages eked out their precarious existence. "Are these vast and innumerable fields of hay forever destined to be consumed by fire, or perish in the autumnal snows? How long shall these superb forests be the haunts of wild beasts? And these inexhaustible quarries, these abundant mines of coal, lead, sulphur, iron, copper, and saltpetre — can it be that they are doomed to remain for ever inactive? Not so — the day will come when some laboring hand will give them value: a strong, active, and enterprising people are destined to fill this spacious void. — The wild beasts will, ere long, give place to our domestic animals; flocks and herds will graze in the beautiful meadows that border the numberless mountains, hills, valleys, and plains of this extensive region." (1:529)

DeSmet's last trip to Montana was in 1870, three years before his death. At that time, regular steamboat traffic was plying the Missouri and Yellowstone, and Bannack was already a ghost town. Communities were springing up at Helena, Bozeman, Fort Benton and Virginia City. Father DeSmet, the peacemaker, naturalist, and chronicler of the wilderness, lived to see his beloved wilderness irrevocably tamed.

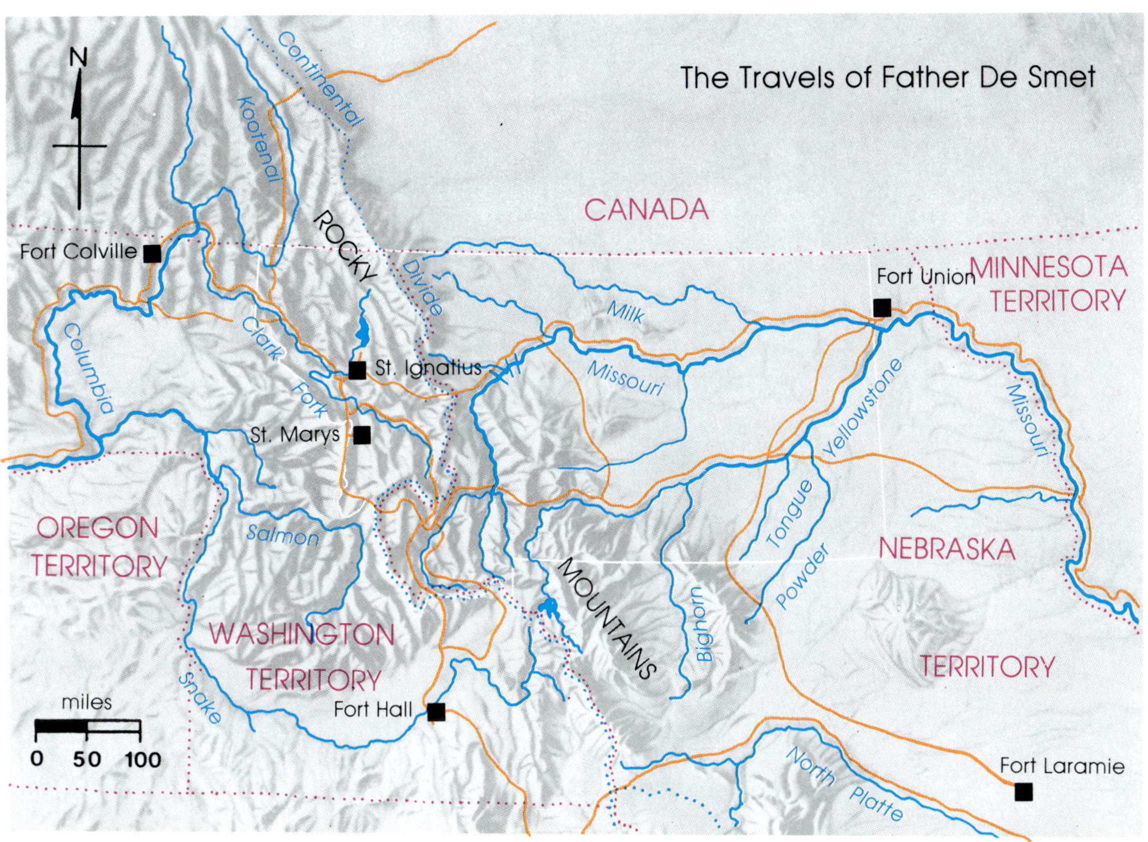


## Sources

1. Chittenden, H. M., and A. T. Richardson, eds. *The Life, Letters and Travels of Father Pierre-Jean DeSmet, S.J., 1801-1873.* New York: Francis P. Harper, 1905.
2. DeSmet, P. J. *Letters and Sketches: With a Narrative of a Year's Residence Among the Indian Tribes of the Rocky Mountains.* Philadelphia: M. Fithian, 1843.
3. DeSmet, P. J. *Oregon Missions and Travels over the Rocky Mountains in 1845-46.* New York: Edward Dunigan, 1847.
4. DeSmet, P. J. *Western Missions and Missionaries: A Series of Letters.* New York: Kirker and Dunigan, 1863.
5. Magaret, H. *Father DeSmet, Pioneer Priest of the Rockies.* New York: Farrar and Rinehart, 1940.
6. McDermott, J. F., ed. "Journal of an Expedition to the *Mauvaises Terres* and the Upper Missouri in 1850, by Thaddeus Culbertson," *Smithsonian Institution Bulletin on American Ethnology* 147(1950):1-145.
7. Porter, T. C. "List of Plants Collected by Mr. Culbertson." *Fifth Annual Report.* Washington, D.C.: Smithsonian Institution, 1851: 133-36.
8. Terrell, J. *Black Robe: The Life of Pierre-Jean DeSmet, Missionary, Explorer, and Pioneer.* New York: Doubleday, 1967.
9. Thwaites, R. G., ed. *Early Western Travels, 1748-1846.* Cleveland: The Arthur H. Clark Company, 1904-07.
10. Thwaites, R. G., ed. *Original Journals of the Lewis and Clark Expedition, 1804-1806.* 8 vols. New York: Antiquarian Press, Ltd., 1959.

CHAPTER 7

# Audubon's Missouri River Adventure

*In June of 1843 John James Audubon and his party discovered a new species of bird in what is now Montana. Audubon named it "Sprague's Missouri Skylark" in honor of his friend and companion, Isaac Sprague. It is now called Sprague's pipit.* (JOHN JAMES AUDUBON)

"Vivid and ardent was his genius, matchless he was both with pen and pencil in giving life and spirit to the beautiful objects he delineated with passionate love.... Of his work the magical beauties of form and color and movement are all his; his page is redolent with Nature's fragrance." (7:7) With these words, ornithologist Elliott Coues described one of the most famous wildlife artists and naturalists the world has ever produced: John James Audubon.

Born in Santo Domingo in 1785, Jean-Jacques Audubon, as he was originally christened, was the illegitimate son of a French sea captain and his Creole mistress. The young Audubon was raised and educated in France, and came to the United States in 1803, the year of the Louisiana Purchase, to escape being drafted into Napoleon's army. At the age of 28 he married an English girl named Lucy Bakewell, who had developed a love of natural history from discussions with her family doctor, Erasmus Darwin, grandfather of Sir Charles. Lucy, more than any other person, was responsible for focusing Audubon's natural talent as an artist and naturalist and for helping him become one of the great figures of his century.

Although Audubon had always loved to paint and study birds, he did not get started seriously on his life's work until he reached his late 30s, when his business ventures failed and he went bankrupt. He developed a technique for painting birds that allowed him to infuse his paintings with more life and realism than had any previous artist. He worked from freshly-killed birds, which he propped up into lifelike poses by means of wires. Unfortunately, this technique required prodigious numbers of specimens, and Audubon killed countless birds on his travels.

In 1827, after years of work and the accidental loss of hundreds of paintings, Audubon published the first installment of his immortal *Birds of America,* (3) a colossal work including the "elephant folio" of 435 full-color bird portraits reproduced at the unheard-of size of 39½" x 29½." Publication of the entire work was to take 11 years. He later republished this work in a smaller-sized edition, which was an outstanding financial success and brought him international recognition as well as financial security. He also published his famous *Ornithological Biography,* (2) a 3,000-page compendium of life-history data for all the birds listed in his earlier books.

Audubon's goal, however, was only half completed. He had great plans to paint every animal in North America, and no sooner had he completed his work on birds than he began work on a sequel, to be called by the impressive title *The Viviparous Quadrupeds of North America* (4) (Viviparous quadrupeds was a stilted 19th-century term meaning, literally, four-legged creatures that bear live young — in a word,

*These four mammals, for which Audubon used the rather ponderous term viviparous quadrupeds in the title of his book, were common sights. Today all are rare, threatened or endangered. Audubon's son, John Woodhouse Audubon, painted the gray wolf (upper left), black-footed ferret (upper right), and grizzly bear (lower left). Audubon himself painted the wolverine.*

*Red fox (top), thirteen-lined ground squirrel (bottom left), and black-tailed prairie dog painted by John James Audubon.*

mammals.) His collaborators in this work would be his two sons, John Woodhouse and Victor, and the Reverend John Bachman. Bachman was a very close family friend, and in fact two of his daughters were married to Audubon's two sons. He was recognized as one of the nation's experts on mammals, and agreed to prepare the text of the work without pay, Audubon, of course, doing all the plates. Audubon, starry-eyed with enthusiasm and undaunted by the monumental task he had laid out for himself — to illustrate every known mammal in the United States, working from real specimens, living or dead — estimated in 1840 that it would take him only two years to do the illustrations and Bachman another year to complete the text. As it turned out, the last volume was not to reach print until 1854, three years after the naturalist's death.

So it was that in the year 1843 Audubon decided that it would be necessary for him to head west into the wild frontier to observe firsthand the marvelous creatures of which he had read so much: the herds of bison, the prairie dogs, the pronghorn, the swift fox, the dizzying diversity of rodents. To help him collect specimens from which to work, Audubon brought along four friends and fellow naturalists: John Bell, a taxidermist whose New York shop was a gathering place for local naturalists; Isaac Sprague, a noted artist whose specialty was plant illustrations; Edward Harris, an amateur geologist and patron of scientific men; and Lewis Squires, a neighbor's son who served as Audubon's secretary.

On April 25, 1843, Audubon and his party left St. Louis on an American Fur Company steamer, the *Omega*. They were accompanied on the journey by about 100 drunken *engages* (trappers) and a number of Indians. The trip upstream was the quickest on record, 48 days from St. Louis to Fort Union, and the *Omega* pulled up near the famous fur trading post of Fort Union on June 12. Audubon and crew were ushered to the very room that had served Prince Maximilian and his entourage a decade earlier. Audubon found the room "small, dark, and dirty, and crammed with our effects, [so that] it would have been difficult to draw, write, and work in." (5:II,34) Alexander Culbertson, sensing the artist's dissatisfaction, graciously offered the party quarters in his own house. Culbertson, the principal factor at the Fort, staged a gala welcome for the arrivals, with music (featuring Culbertson himself on the fiddle) and dancing until 1:00 the next morning.

Audubon stayed at Fort Union for a little more than two months. This was to be the last adventure for the artist, who was nearing 60 and complaining that he could no longer paint for 15 hours nonstop as he used to do. "I am, as years go, an old man," wrote Audubon, "but I do not feel old, and there is so much of interest here that I forget oftentimes that I am not ... young ...." (5:II,126) Understandably, the artist enjoyed himself while out West, and spent a great deal of his time participating in the chief amusements of the frontier, bison hunting (both real and sham) and wolf-chasing. Horsemanship was a fine art at Fort Union, and Culbertson dazzled the newcomers with a display of his proficiency, first at a mock bison hunt, where a prize of a new suit was offered to the person who could fire the most shots and reload while galloping at full speed, and then at a wolf chase, where Culbertson shot a wolf and picked it up, wounded but still alive, without dismounting from his horse.

Audubon would ride along on many of the hunts but tended to stay on the periphery of the action. Nevertheless, he nearly was killed in one close call. Culbertson had taken Audubon on a two-day hunt along the Yellowstone River in what is now Montana. They were hunting wolves at the time, but someone saw a bison bull and the party decided to go after it. The bull was wounded by several shots, and the group drew up close to finish the animal. As Audubon described the ensuing encounter, "I came very near to being finished off by him through my own folly. I stood directly in his path as he advanced, fired at his head, then ran in front of him instead of veering to one side, not thinking that he could overtake me. As I ran I glanced back and was horrified to see Mr. Bull within three feet of me, ready to give me a taste of his horns. I turned off sharply. The Buffalo was unable to wheel quickly enough to follow. Bell took the gun ... and shot the bull directly behind the shoulder blade. He tottered, fell forward on his horns, rolled on his side, and soon was dead." (8:257)

At the time of Audubon's visit, bison were still numerous on the prairies. Audubon reported that one of the fur company officers "passed through herds of Buffalo for six days in succession," and saw the prairie "almost blackened by these animals, which covered the plain to the hills that bounded the view in all directions." (4:II,47) "In fact," wrote Audubon, "it is *impossible to describe or even conceive* the vast multitudes of these animals that ... feed on these ocean-like prairies." (5:II,146)

But Audubon could see the pending doom for the bison. Fort Union alone required 600 to 800 bison each year to feed personnel and guests, and many more were killed just for sport or amusement. Winter weather also took its toll. "Buffaloes become so very poor during hard winters, when the snows cover the ground to the depth of two or three feet, that they lose their hair, become covered with scabs, on which the Magpies feed, and the poor beasts die by the hundreds. One can hardly conceive how it happens, notwithstanding these many deaths and the immense numbers that are

*John Woodhouse Audubon was very much his father's rival as an artist. Above is the son's coyote. The senior Audubon painted the summer (left) and winter (right) color phases of the snowshoe hare.*

*The northern grasshopper mouse, discovered by Prince Maximilian at Fort Union in 1833, is a most unusual rodent that howls like a miniature wolf and attacks and kills other mammals like a weasel. Audubon too encountered it at Fort Union. Painting by John Woodhouse Audubon.*

murdered almost daily on these boundless wastes called prairies, besides the hosts that are drowned in the freshets, and the hundreds of young calves who die in early spring, so many are yet to be found. Daily we see so many that we hardly notice them more than the cattle in our pastures about our homes. But this cannot last; even now there is a perceptible difference in the size of the herds, and before many years the Buffalo, like the Great Auk, will have disappeared; surely this should not be permitted." (8:257)

Audubon was literally swept away by the romance of buffalo-hunting, which was pretty much a legend back east, and his letters and journals read like a hunting chronicle. Bachman, plugging away at the text of *Viviparous Quadrupeds* back home, sensed that Audubon was having entirely too much fun, and prodded him to get back on track and not neglect the small rodents (in which Bachman was especially interested). Audubon got the message and began devoting more attention to his real task of collecting and painting the strange new quadrupeds that surrounded him. In all, Audubon brought back from his Missouri River adventure 11 new bird species and a handful of new mammals. Although the artist kept a very poor travel itinerary, and it is often impossible to tell from his journals exactly where he traveled and where his specimens were taken, it seems likely that two of these species were first discovered by Audubon in Montana: Spragues's pipit and Baird's sparrow. Audubon rediscovered the northern grasshopper mouse, an extremely unusual carnivorous rodent.

Audubon's party fell into a pattern after a while: Harris and Bell would spend the day hunting far and wide around the Fort and would bring the specimens they obtained back to Audubon and Sprague, who spent most of their time indoors painting and drawing. Bell and Sprague would take care of preparing skins, and Sprague would collect and paint specimens of plants so that Audubon's animals could later be depicted accurately in their natural habitat.

One rainy June day, Harris and Bell were out hunting while Audubon and Sprague were working indoors in the Fort. When the two hunters returned, Audubon saw to his "delight and utter astonishment" that they had brought back two spanking new species of birds: one was "a Lark, small and beautiful," (5:II,41) which Audubon later named Sprague's Missouri Skylark in honor of his friend; the other was a hybrid between a red- and a yellow-shafted flicker. On July 26, Bell killed another new species which Audubon named Baird's sparrow in honor of Spencer Fullerton Baird, his young friend and protege in the East who was to become one of the central figures in American natural history in later decades. This was the first bird dedicated to Baird, but it was the last one to be named, described, and illustrated by Audubon.

Audubon's Missouri River journals, which weren't made public until 1896, contain a wealth of information about wildlife in the Fort Union area. Although the focus of his interest was mammals, he nevertheless recorded and described dozens of species of prairie birds. He caught catfish, sturgeon, and spiny soft-shelled turtles in the Yellowstone and Missouri Rivers. He looked for snakes, but was surprised to find them scarce. He recorded one of the few sightings of the sedge wren from Montana. Wolves, he noted, "not only eat their own kind, but are the most mischievous animals in the country; they eat the young Buffalo calves, the young Antelopes, and the young of the Bighorn on all occasions, besides Hares of different sorts, etc." (5:II,49)

Shortly after his arrival at Fort Union, Audubon purchased a live badger from an Indian squaw. He tried to keep it in his room, but he found it "so mischievous, pulling about and tearing to pieces every article within its reach and trying to dig up the hearth stones," that he had to move it into an adjacent room. There, it quickly dug itself under the hearth stones, and Audubon had to drag it out by brute force whenever he wanted to examine it. "It was provoked at the near approach of anyone and growled continuously at all intruders. It was not, however, very vicious and would suffer one or two of our companions to handle and play with it at times." (4:I,363-4) Audubon succeeded in bringing this unusual pet back to New York alive, along with a mule deer and a swift fox.

*Left: Lifelike painting of a red squirrel, one of Audubon's finest works. Above: The aging Audubon was painted in frontier dress by his son at about the time of his Missouri River Expedition.*(COURTESY OF THE AMERICAN MUSEUM OF NATURAL HISTORY)

Audubon fell in love with the pronghorn, thinking it one of the most beautiful creatures of the prairie. "Hurrah for the prairies and the swift Antelopes as they flee from the hunter like flashes or meteors, seen but for an instant," he wrote. (4:II,195-6) Decades before Audubon's visit, Captain William Clark reported that "antelopes are curious and will approach any thing which appears in motion." (15:I,354) Audubon decided to test out this tale, and approaching a herd to within about 300 yards, he lay on his back and began kicking his heels in the air. True to the legend, one of the curious animals approached within 60 yards to see what in the world was going on. Audubon shot —and missed. 40 years later, Teddy Roosevelt was to report that "nowadays there are very few localities indeed in which they are sufficiently unsophisticated to make it worth while trying these time-honored tricks of the long-vanished trappers and hunters." (13:106) Nevertheless, Montana pronghorn are still as curious as ever, and will walk right up to a hunter or photographer engaged in any similarly bizarre behavior!

While painting the head of a pronghorn buck, Audubon noticed that the horns seemed shiny and new, and he wondered whether or not the horns were shed. This was an important point, because if the horns were shed it would mean that the animals were not closely related to the Old World antelopes at all. "I am quite amazed at the differences of opinion respecting the shedding —or not shedding — of the horns of the Antelope; and this must be looked to with the greatest severity, for if these animals *do* shed their horns, they are no longer *Antelopes*." (5:II,41-2) The pronghorn does, indeed, shed its horns, but this fact was not established until 1858. At that time, the discovery led to the classification of the American pronghorn in its own separate family, the Antilocapridae, quite distinct from the Old World antelopes, which along with the American bison belong to the family Bovidae.

Like Maximilian, Audubon had hoped to continue upstream to the headwaters of the Missouri River and perhaps into the foothills of the Rockies themselves. However, it was wisely decided not to proceed into "Black feet Country, for reasons which are suficiently great to prevent us from paying our regards to these treacherous Rascals." (11:114)

Near the end of his stay, however, Audubon, acting against the advice of his friends, went on a side trip to the *Mauvaises Terres* or badlands, possibly near present-day Glendive or Fort Peck. There he found a wonderland of strange formations carved by millenia of erosion into the siltstones and mudstones of the Hell Creek formation. "The only idea I can give in *writing* of what are called the 'Mauvaises Terres' would be to place some thousands of loaves of sugar of different sizes, from quite small and low, to large and high, all irregularly truncated at top, and placed somewhat apart from each other.... The tops of some of these hills, and in some cases whole hills about thirty feet high, are

*Bison, painted by John James Audubon from sketches made at Fort Union.*

BISON GASTRONOMY

The bison was the mainstay of Indian and white alike on the prairie, and it is not surprising that a gourmet tradition evolved around bison cookery. Lewis and Clark enjoyed a type of bison sausage, dubbed *Poudingue blanc* or "white pudding" by Toussaint Charbonneau, its cook, which, Lewis wrote, "we all esteem one of the greatest delicacies of the forrest." Lewis thought it worthwhile to record the exact recipe for its preparation for posterity. "About 6 feet of the lower extremity of the large gut of the Buffaloe is the first morsel that the cook makes love to," he wrote. "This he holds fast at one end with the right hand, while with the forefinger and thumb of the left he gently compresses it, and discharges what he says *is not good to eat*, but of which in the sequel we get a moderate portion." The cook then prepares a filling of bison tenderloin, kidney fat, flour, pepper, and salt, and fills the gut with it, pushing out a little more of what would otherwise have soon become buffalo chips. The sausage is tied off, and "is then baptised in the missouri with two dips and a flirt, and bobbed into the kettle; from whence after it be well boiled it is taken and fryed with bears oil untill it becomes brown, when it is ready to esswage the pangs of a keen appetite or such as travelers in the wilderness are seldom at a loss for." (15:II,15-16)

Audubon missed the opportunity to partake of this white pudding while at Fort Union, but he witnessed some even more highly developed gourmet delights there. The aging Audubon's teeth were mostly gone, and his normal diet usually consisted of biscuits and molasses. However he did partake of some boiled dog meat at the Fort and found it excellent eating. The Indians, in fact, considered a feast of fatted dog as one of the highest honors they could bestow upon a guest.

At Fort Union, according to Audubon, a successful party of white hunters would immediately begin feasting on a bison almost from the moment it hit the ground. Culbertson would "break in the skull of the bull, and with bloody fingers draw out the hot brains and swallow them with peculiar zest." (5:II,141) Even Culbertson's wife, the Blackfeet princess, would partake of this delicacy. "The very sight of this turned my stomach," reported Audubon, "but I am told that were I to hunt Buffalo one year, I should like it even better than dog meat." (5:II,104) When the brains had been eaten, the feast continued: "another has now reached the liver, and is gobbling down enormous pieces of it; whilst, perhaps, a third, who has come to the paunch, is feeding luxuriously on some — to me — disgusting-looking offal." (5:II,141) Tongues were among the first items removed from the carcass; in later years, hunters would take only the tongue, leaving the remainder of the animal to rot on the prairies. Indians successful in killing a nursing cow bison would "cut out the milk bag of the cow and eat it fresh and raw in pieces the size of a hen's egg." (8:254) According to Sprague, "the Indians eat ... the inner coat of the nostrils raw! and consider them as great delicacies." (14) Even the stomachs were eaten; as Audubon describes it, "one of the stomachs was partly washed in a bucket of water; an Indian swallowed a large piece; one of the crew ate the rest of it uncleaned." Audubon, "no meat eater except when there is nothing else on hand," (8:254) found the whole idea repulsive but finally gave in and tried a bite. To his utter astonishment he found it delicious.

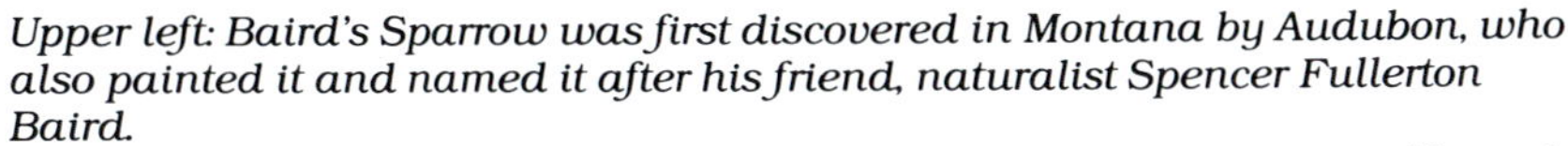

*Upper left: Baird's Sparrow was first discovered in Montana by Audubon, who also painted it and named it after his friend, naturalist Spencer Fullerton Baird.*
*Upper right: Audubon purchased a pet badger while at Fort Union and brought it back alive to New York. This painting is by John James Audubon.*
*Lower left: White-tailed jackrabbit by John James Audubon.*
*Lower right: Pronghorn by John Woodhouse Audubon.*

## AUDUBON'S BIGHORN SHEEP

The "Grosse Corne," the "bighorned Anamals" first described in Montana by Lewis and Clark, belonged to a race now extinct, *Ovis canadensis audubonii*, Audubon's bighorn sheep. These animals were very similar in appearance to the race of Rocky Mountain bighorns that inhabit western Montana today, having nearly identical horns but differing in the shape of some of the bones of the skull. The major difference between the races, however, was in habitat and diet. The western Montana race inhabits high mountains in summer and cliffs and grassy hillsides in winter. Their diet consists primarily of bunchgrasses, serviceberry, chokecherry,and Rocky Mountain maple.

In contrast, Audubon's bighorn inhabited the eroded river breaks, badlands, escarpments, and Mauvaises Terres of eastern Montana. They probably fed, as Lewis surmised, on the sparse grasses and "arromatic Herbs" that grow on these desolate wastes of gumbo, clinker, and sandstone — Nuttall's saltbrush, big sagebrush, winterfat, and skunkbrush sumac. Steep escape terrain is an essential feature of the habitat for both races of bighorn. Steep mountain cliffs fill this need in western Montana, and breaks serve the same purpose in the plains.

Audubon's bighorn probably differentiated from the main Rocky Mountain stock after the close of the latest glacial episode about 10,000 years ago. Populations could have followed steep terrain along the breaks of the Missouri and other major rivers to colonize the newly-eroded badlands scattered throughout eastern Montana. By the time of Lewis and Clark's visit, Audubon's bighorns were widely distributed in eastern Montana, North Dakota, South Dakota, and Wyoming, inhabiting breaks and badlands along the lower Missouri and Yellowstone Rivers as well as the isolated mountain ranges such as the Sweetgrass Hills and Bear Paw Mountains.

The extinction of this race followed inevitably upon the heels of the explorers, settlers, and stockmen. The animals were easy prey for riflemen shooting from riverboats, as the sheep probably felt secure atop the inaccessible knobs and pinnacles. Competition with sheep and cattle undoubtedly contributed to the demise of Audubon's bighorn, since estimates are that Montana may have supported as many as 600,000 cattle and 500,000 sheep by the 1880s.

Probably the most significant factor contributing to the extinction of Audubon's race was disease brought to the badlands by domestic stock. Edward L. Munson, a surgeon with the U. S. Army, wrote to George Bird Grinnell that bighorns were abundant in the Bear Paw Mountains as late as 1885 but were gone by 1897 due to an Anthrax epidemic contracted from domestic sheep. It is not known when the last Audubon's bighorn passed from the scene; small herds probably held on in remote places such as the Sweetgrass Hills as late as the 1920s.

*Audubon's bighorn sheep, painted by John Woodhouse Audubon from sketches and specimens taken by his father.*

Attempts to introduce Rocky Mountain bighorns to the eastern badlands habitats, left vacant by the disappearance of the Audubon's race, have met with limited success. This indicates that there may have been at least some genetic adaptation of Audubon's sheep to the breaks environment. In 1947, 16 Rocky Mountain bighorns from Colorado were released in the Missouri Breaks; the population increased to the 50s by 1951, but disappeared by 1963, due largely to disease. In the late 1950s, 43 more sheep were released in the Two Calf Creek area of the Missouri Breaks; a few dozen still hang on there. The greatest success has been in the Blue Mountains area of southeastern Montana, where transplants of 11 sheep in 1958 and 25 sheep in 1976 have increased to more than 100 animals. It is probable that the Rocky Mountain race will never flourish in the breaks and badlands as did the well-adapted Audubon's bighorn.

Mounted specimens of Audubon's bighorn sheep are extremely rare, with only a few remaining in the world. However, three full mounts are on public display in Montana: one in the Science building at Northern Montana College in Havre, one in the Miles City regional office of the Montana Department of Fish, Wildlife, and Parks, and one in the Valley County Pioneer Museum in Glasgow. (16)

*The yellow-rumped warbler once was called Audubon's warbler.* (TOM ULRICH)

composed of a conglomerated mass of stones, sand, and clay, with earth of various sorts, fused together, and having a brick-like appearance. In this mass pumice-stone of various shapes and sizes is to be found.... In wet weather, no man can climb any of them, and at such times they are greasy, muddy, sliding grounds.... The strata are of different colored clays, coal, etc., and an earth impregnated with a salt which appears to have been formed by internal fire or heat ... lava, sulphur, salts of various kinds, oxides and sulphates of iron; and in the sand at the tops of some of the highest hills I have found marine shells, but so soft and crumbling as to fall apart the instant they were exposed to the air .... In the valleys between the hills and ravines, some of which are not more than ten or fifteen feet wide, while their depth is beyond the reach of the eye. Others vary in depth from ten to fifty feet, while some make one giddy to look in ...." (5:II,148-9) The water in the *Mauvaises Terres* was so brackish and foul that the party had to mix it with whiskey in order to make it drinkable.

While in the Badlands, Audubon encountered an animal, now extinct, that today bears his name: the Audubon's bighorn sheep. Audubon's description of the habitat use and habits of this animal to this day are the most complete and detailed ever written. "The Mauvaises Terres are mostly formed of grayish white clay, very sparsely covered with small patches of thin grass, on which the bighorns feed, but which, to all appearance, is a very scanty supply, and there, and there only, they feed, as not one has ever been seen on the bottom or prairie land further than the foot of these most extraordinary hills. The places where they are most frequently found are barren, and without the least vestige of vegetation.... On the sides of the hills, at various heights, are shelves of rock or stone projecting out from two to six, eight, or even ten feet, and generally square, or nearly so; these are the favorite resorts of the Bighorns during the heat of the day, and either here or on the tops of the hills they are to be found.... here they lie, but are aroused instantly upon the least appearance of danger, and, as soon as they have discovered the cause of alarm, away they go, over hills and ravine, occasionally stopping to look round, and when ascending the steepest hill, there is no apparent diminution of their speed. They will ascend and descend places, when thus alarmed, so inaccessible that it is almost impossible to conceive how, and where, they find a foothold.... When not found on these shelves, they are seen on the tops of the most inaccessible and highest hills, looking down on the hunters, apparently conscious of their security, or else lying down tranquilly in some sunny spot quite out of reach." (5:II,148-53)

Audubon noted that many of the rams had deformed horns; legend had it that this came about as a result of the sheep flinging themselves off the cliffs and landing on their horns, as John Palliser believed. Audubon found this hard to believe, and correctly surmised that the damage must be due to the butting of heads of the rams during the rut.

Audubon's experience in the badlands was one of the most difficult, yet one of the most memorable, adventures on this last great expedition. The trip was "one constant time of toil, anxiety, fatigue, and danger." Yet he concluded, "Such the country! Such the animal! Such the hunting!" (5:II,154)

Among all the adventures and hunting escapades, Audubon and Sprague did find time to produce paintings in abundance. Some of the Indians were so impressed with the realism the two artists could give to their work that they would run away in fear. The Indians regarded the two artists as medicine men with magical powers. Culbertson's Blackfeet wife, the Princess Natawista Iksana (which means "Medicine Snake Woman" in Blackfeet) held Audubon in highest esteem, and frequently presented the artist with gifts and mementoes. On one occasion, she swam into the Missouri River and caught six mallard ducklings, bringing them to the artist for him to sketch.

As summer drew to a close, the artist's great wilderness adventure neared its end, and on August 16 the party left Fort Union in a Mackinaw barge named the *Union*. The return to St. Louis went more slowly than the ascent, and the party did not arrive there until October 19.

Audubon immediately returned to work on the illustrations for the *Quadrupeds*, working feverishly alongside his sons and the Reverend Bachman. Things were progressing well until one day in 1846. The aging artist stood before his easel, but could not focus his eyes upon the painting before him. He realized his painting days were through. The loss of his sight was such a blow to the great artist that his mind retreated into a distant, childlike revery. "Alas, my poor friend Audubon!" wrote Bachman upon seeing what had happened to his associate of so many years. "The outlines of his beautiful face and form are there, but his noble mind is all in ruins. It is incredibly sad." (1:467)

So Bachman and John's sons took over the monumental job of completing the *Quadrupeds*. Son John Woodhouse finished nearly half of the plates that appeared in the final publication. Comparison of his work with his father's will reveal that he was very nearly his father's equal in talent and ability. The senior Audubon died in 1851 following a stroke, and never lived to see his last two volumes come off the press.

## Sources


1. Adams, A. B. *John James Audubon: A Biography*. New York: G. P. Putnam's Sons, 1966.
2. Audubon, J. J. *Ornithological Biography*. 5 vols. Edinburgh: A. Black, 1831-1839.
3. Audubon, J. J. *Birds of America*. 7 vols. Edinburgh: Lizars, and London: Havell, 1826-1838.
4. Audubon, J. J., and J. Bachman. *The Viviparous Quadrupeds of North America*. 3 vols. New York: V. G. Audubon, 1845-1854.
5. Audubon, M., ed. *Audubon and His Journals, with Zoological and Other Notes by Elliott Coues*. 2 vols. New York: Charles Scribner's Sons, 1897.
6. Durant, M., and M. Harwood. *On the Road with John James Audubon*. New York: Dodd, Mead & Co., 1980.
7. Ford, A., ed. *Audubon's Animals: The Quadrupeds of North America*. New York: Thomas Y. Crowell, 1951.
8. Ford, A., ed. *Audubon, by Himself: A Profile of John James Audubon, from Writings Selected, Arranged and Edited by Alice Ford*. Garden City, N. Y.: The Natural History Press, 1969.
9. Herrick, F. H. *Audubon the Naturalist: A History of His Life and Times*. 2 vols. New York: D. Appleton & Co., 1917.
10. McDermott, J. F., ed. *Up the Missouri with Audubon, by Edward Harris*. Norman: Univ. of Oklahoma Press, 1951.
11. McDermott, J. F., ed. *Audubon in the West*. Norman: Univ. of Oklahoma Press, 1965.
12. McKelvey, S. D. *Botanical Explorations of the Trans-Mississippi West, 1790-1850*. Jamaica Plains, Mass.: Arnold Arboretum of Harvard University, 1955.
13. Roosevelt, T., et al. *The Deer Family*. London: MacMillan & Co., 1902.
14. Sprague, I. Unpublished journal, entry for July 28, 1843. Library of the Boston Athenaeum.
15. Thwaites, R. G., ed. *Original Journals of the Lewis and Clark Expedition, 1804-06*. 8 vols. New York: Antiquarian Press, Ltd., 1959.
16. Walcheck, K. "Audubon Bighorn Sheep." *Montana Outdoors* 11(Jan.-Feb., 1980):17-21.

# CHAPTER 8

# John Palliser and Thomas Blakiston

*During his first visit to the northern Great Plains in 1847 and 1848, Irishman John Palliser learned the dangerous sport of high-speed bison hunting. A decade later he was to lead a serious scientific expedition across southern Canada and northwestern Montana.* (COURTESY, MONTANA HISTORICAL SOCIETY)

News of the upper Missouri River drainage and of the wonders of the vast wilderness interior of North America spread throughout Europe in the 1840s. Maximilian's lavish edition of his *Travels* illustrated with Bodmer's handcolored aquatint engravings was first published in 1839 and was read by European aristocrats. Audubon's account of the amazing abundance of game animals also reached England and must have presented an irresistible enticement to sportsmen, naturalists, adventurers, and the idle aristocracy.

Among the Europeans lured to Montana by these tales of untamed wilderness and herds of game rivaling those of Africa was an Irish country gentleman named John Palliser. Palliser, born in Dublin in 1817, was the oldest son of an eminent and respected family, and, as heir to a rather large estate, was independently wealthy. Palliser had received little formal scientific training, and had been less than a diligent student. Typical of the European aristocracy of his time, he preferred sport and travel to study, and on the slightest provocation would gladly leave his "dull books and duller tutors for a burst after the partridges, or for the more noble and exciting pursuit of the antlered lords of the forest and mountain." (5:1) Nevertheless, he had an inquisitive mind and his studies left him with a sincere although distant fascination with scientific pursuits. He eventually became one of the most famous explorers of the northern Great Plains.

The quest for adventure flowed in the blood of the Palliser family, and John's five brothers pursued their fair share. One brother died on an expedition to the North Pole; two others hunted big game in Ceylon; one sailed the China seas and rescued a damsel from pirates; and another roamed the wilderness of the Australian Outback. Perhaps it was inevitable that John, too, would be drawn into the pattern of exploring faraway and unknown lands. Palliser's future brother-in-law, William Fairholm, provided the impetus for a journey to the North American wilderness. Fairholm had hunted big game along the Missouri River in 1840, and his tales, together no doubt with those of Prince Maximilian, George Catlin, and John James Audubon, proved an irresistible allurement to the spirited Irishman. In 1847 Palliser set out from Liverpool for adventures in the wilds of the Upper Missouri.

Once on the North American continent, Palliser was anxious to head west. Travel in those days, however, was considerably more complicated than it is today. Palliser's trip westward followed a roundabout path from Boston to New York to Philadelphia to Baltimore to Wheeling to Louisville to Cairo and finally by Mississippi steamer to New Orleans. Part of this trip was made in the company of P. T. Barnum and the famous midget, Tom Thumb, whom Palliser got to know quite well.

From New Orleans, Palliser traveled back up the Mississippi and Arkansas Rivers to hunt the Arkansas country. There, he camped alone for the first time. He was yet a country gentleman, still somewhat soft, and a far cry from the lean wilderness wanderer he would be in the months and years to come. "It is only when left to our own resources," he wrote, "that we sportsmen of England feel how very little we are in the habit of doing for ourselves, and how helpless we are rendered by all our civilisation." (5:55)

Palliser's summer travels included the Mammoth Caves of Kentucky, where he claimed to have traveled 19 miles underground. He caught several of the strange blind cave fish there, which were, as he described them, "by a wonderful dispensation of nature, without eyes or any organ adapted to the reception of light." (5:68)

In the fall of 1847, Palliser joined the American Fur Company's annual fall expedition to the trading posts on the upper Missouri and Yellowstone Rivers. In those days, the 2,000-mile ascent of the Missouri by steamer from St. Louis to Ft. Union took seven or eight weeks, while the return could be accomplished in eight or nine days (depending on the season). This route took him through the region of the tall-grass prairie, and he was impressed by this "gigantic vegetation," as he called it. In these virgin prairies, the grass grew "over thousands of acres from five to eight feet high," and among the "huge coarse grass" were "weeds that I never saw before, rank and tangled in their unchecked growth." (5:87) Palliser was later to contrast this lush grassland with the arid, desolate, short-grass plains occurring just north of the Montana border, an area now known as "Palliser's Triangle."

Palliser's journey by steamer ended at Ft. Union, the busy trading post near the mouth of the Yellowstone River, which in the previous 15 years had been home to Prince Paul, Prince Maximilian, Father De Smet, and John James Audubon. Palliser rested from his travels only a couple of days before striking out on his first buffalo-hunting foray. To read Palliser's account of his stay at Fort Union, which is reminiscent of Audubon's narrative, leaves little doubt that bison-hunting was the goal he had dreamed about while in Ireland. It also leaves the impression that while in Montana Palliser did little else except hunt or think about hunting.

"Buffalo-hunting is a noble sport," he wrote. "The first object in approaching a herd of buffalo should be to get as close as possible before charging them; then, rush in with your horse at full speed, single out one animal, and detatch him from the herd, which you will soon do, and after a turn or two be able to get a broadside shot, when you should endeavour to strike him behind the fore-shoulder." (5:111)

*Blue grama, a dominant grass species of the short-grass plains of "Palliser's Triangle."* (KRISTI DuBOIS)

Palliser became an expert at high-speed buffalo-hunting. He would carry the bullets in his mouth and shoot while standing in the stirrups of his galloping horse. On one hunt he and his horse somersaulted over a bison that had fallen across their path. On another, he was charged and tossed by an angry bison bull. This was quite a different hunting experience than he was accustomed to in England. There, he wrote, "you rise in the morning, not too early, and shave with hot water; a substantial breakfast with a cup of delicious cream-softened tea awaits you in the breakfast-room; your guns are as clean as if they had not been used at all the day before; and you take them without the slightest compunction from the hands of that invaluable individual called the gamekeeper, who is to attend you throughout the day, and who tells you not to trouble yourself by carrying too great a weight of shot, as he has a supply with which to replenish your little two pound Sykes' ...." (5:56)

At Fort Union, Palliser learned to stalk bison in the snow by hiding under a white blanket. Describing one such hunt, he wrote: "I crept forward on my hands and knees covered by the blanket, which prevented them from distinguishing me amidst the surrounding snow, and enabled me to approach until I came within shot. I continued creeping about and around them, singling out the best and fattest of the cows for upwards of an hour, and it was not until I had laid five of their number low that they smelt a rat, and bolted off ...." (5:117-18)

Palliser was convinced that there were three species of wolf, "the large white wolf, or buffalo wolf, the grey wolf, and the kit wolf," (5:136) although he acknowledged that naturalists of the day recognized only one species that occurred in many color phases from white to almost black. He considered wolves, which were still quite common around Fort Union, to be excellent hunting, especially since the hides brought up to $2 apiece at the Fort. "Generally speaking," he observed, "the colder the climate the more valuable the fur. Even the same animal in the same region, will bear a far more valuable fur if the winter reaches a greater intensity of cold than what is ordinary in the districts; so much so that connoisseurs in furs will talk of the winters of '34 and '46, as connoisseurs in wine do of the great vintages of '36 and '42." (5:80)

By the time of Palliser's visit, the beaver trade had declined drastically, and Palliser noted that beaver trappers were "a race now rapidly becoming extinct, owing to the great fall in the price of beaver, from the recent introduction of silk into the manufacture of hats." (5:121) Palliser developed a fondness for the beaver during his wanderings in Montana. The little animal showed a skill and intelligence, he thought, "greater than that which instinct can dictate, not merely in choosing its timber, but also by cutting the tree down with its indefatigable little tusks, in such a way as to make it fall exactly in the direction it wishes, above the intended place of residence; so that, when it cuts it up into lengths, it can swim downstream, steering the logs to their destination." After watching "the helpless struggles of these poor intelligent little creatures" in traps, he was "seized with remorse, and determined forthwith that there should be no more beaver trapping." (5:225)

The Great Plains, which some people regarded with disdain, were a source of almost religious attraction for Palliser. "The eternal illimitable sweep of the undulating prairie," he wrote, "impressed on me a sense of vastness quite overwhelming. ... I know not when I have felt so forcibly conscious of my own insignificance, as when struggling through this immense waste, and feeling as though I were suddenly carried backward into some remote and long past age, and as though I were encroaching on the territories of the Mammoth and the Mastodon." (5:87-88) The air in these high plains, according to Palliser, "is extremely healthy, and its effect upon the constitution something wonderful; so much so, that persons never suffer from coughs or colds; the complaint is quite unknown." (5:105)

Palliser spent most of the winter (1847-1848) hunting the prairie around Fort Union, working the Lower Yellowstone River (where much to his delight he encountered his first elk, a herd of 100) and harvesting large mammals in impressive numbers. As winter progressed, however, the confinement of the Fort became too much for him. He began planning a solitary excursion along the Missouri River to Fort McKenzie (probably not the same fort at the mouth of the Marias River visited by Prince Maximilian 15 years before, but another in present-day North Dakota). (6) As a traveling companion, he selected a mongrel dog, half "buffalo wolf" and half Indian dog, which had been howling about Fort Union all winter and which had attracted his admiration. Ishmah, as he named the dog, was fitted with an Indian-style travois and carried all Palliser's effects.

Striking out in January, 1848, Palliser followed a party of voyageurs along the Missouri for a while, and then set out on his own, with only his dog for company. Palliser followed the ice at the river's edge, realizing that to be lost in a storm on the open prairie meant certain death. These weeks alone in a bitter wintertime wilderness developed the survival skills and determination that would be so critical during his years in the Canadian wilderness. The dangers he faced during this solitary adventure seemed to forge within his spirit a desire for even greater challenge.

On one occasion during this lonely march, Ishmah spotted a wolf across the ice and bolted after it, carrying with him all of Palliser's survival gear. As dog and wolf disappeared in the distance at a full run, Palliser immediately realized the seriousness of the situation. He was alone, a hundred miles from the nearest habitation, without food or blankets, and with only two bullets in his pouch. He followed the trail of the two animals until nightfall, then gave up and returned to the river's edge. There he sat and lamented his fate. Looking to the North Star, Palliser calculated that it must be about ten o'clock, "the time at which in England we have our knees under the mahogany, surrounded by friends, discussing a bottle of the best and awaiting a summons to tea in the drawing-room." (5:159) An arctic wind froze the perspiration on his face, forming icicles on his beard. Palliser's relief was immense when hours later his dog returned to camp, still carrying an intact travois. On another occasion, Palliser avoided hypothermia in a blizzard by holding

*Palliser's dog Ishmah once saved his master's life during a blizzard, earning a place of honor on the title page of Palliser's book,* Solitary Rambles and Adventures of the Hunter in the Prairies.

Ishmah close to his body, allowing "the caloric, as it issued from him, [to] preserve my body from turning into stone." (5:194)

Palliser finally made it to Fort McKenzie, and after a brief stay returned to Fort Union, arriving there April 1, 1848. From there, he traveled up the Yellowstone River with a small party as far as the mouth of the Bighorn River. The farther upstream he traveled, the more abundant the game animals became. In the *Mauvaises Terres* or badlands, probably near present-day Makoshika State Park, he bagged his first "grosse corne," Audubon's bighorn sheep. The ridiculously massive horns and heavy skull bones of the rams amused Palliser; he figured they were built so sturdily "as to enable the animal safely to fling himself on his head from very considerable heights." (5:219) Actually, this feature in the male mountain sheep is an adaptation to the spectacular headbutting ritual of the fall rut.

During this Yellowstone trip, Palliser wrote the following account of the group behavior of the pronghorn. "These march in line, sometimes for several miles together, and, by imitating the movements of their leader, exhibit the most striking effects, resembling military evolutions; they simultaneously whirl round their white breasts and red flanks, like the 'Right face! — Left face!' of a regiment on parade. Obedient to the motions of their leader; when he stops, all stop: he stamps and advances a step, the slight similar impulse waves all down along the line; he then gives a right wheel, and round go all their heads for one last look; finally, he gives the right face about, and away 'their ranks break up like clouds before a Biscay gale'." (5:217-18)

Palliser and his small party camped at the mouth of the Bighorn River, where they lived like kings in the wilderness. According to Palliser, a typical day's supper included "buffalo-beef, elk-meat, venison, antelope's-liver, and wild mutton, besides the luxuries of cat-fish and marrow-bones." (5:232) Palliser especially enjoyed the channel catfish which inhabit the Yellowstone, calling it "one of the finest flavored I ever ate." He described this fish, known to the men as a "barbue," as a "quaint little fish, like a miniature dolphin; has double fins, besides those on its back, and a preposterously long beard-like excrescence from each side of its mouth." (5:229) When the party finally returned down the river to Fort Union, the men had to construct two boats of willows and hides to transport their sizeable booty of skins and furs.

Palliser's botanical observations made along the Yellowstone reveal an awareness of the rich diversity of the floodplain community, although his lack of botanical training is painfully evident. Of the Yellowstone River Valley he wrote, "the trees were all different from our European ones, but bearing in their foliage the character of ash, oak, alder, and birch, besides those less known to us, as cocoa and rhododendrons, which were now beginning to blow, and presented a beautiful appearance .... Willows were, as usual, in abundance, pushing in advance of the timber like the tirailleurs and skirmishers thrown out in the van of an advancing army; at the end of the point they commenced like osiers thickly crowded, the switches increasing in size until they became timber, and sufficiently large to contend for air and light with the other forest trees." (5:239-40)

To his regret, Palliser still had not seen a real live grizzly bear by the time he left Fort Union on his return voyage down the Missouri River, although he had seen numerous tracks along the Yellowstone River. In North Dakota, however, he found more grizzly bears than he could handle. Between the Turtle Mountains and the mouth of the Little Missouri he bagged the trophy

*This map, published in 1846, shows what was known about the geography of the region that was to be Montana at about the time of Palliser's first journey to the West.*

*In 1848 Palliser believed the heads of bighorn rams were built so sturdily "as to enable the animal safely to fling himself on his head from very considerable heights."* (TOM ULRICH)

specimens that to him made the adventure a complete success. From the wilds of the Upper Missouri, Palliser sent to Ireland a live black bear, three bison, two white-tailed deer, a pronghorn, and his dog, Ishmah. While in transit aboard the ship, the bear, drenched by rain, broke its chain and climbed into the pilot's bed, where he "rolled himself comfortably up in the blankets." (5:305)

Palliser returned to his homeland in late 1848, after taking a side trip to Panama and crossing the Isthmus to the Pacific Ocean. His account of his adventures created a sensation among his family and friends, and at their urging he published in 1853 a narrative of his North American travels entitled *Solitary Rambles and Adventures of a Hunter in the Prairies.* (5) In the introduction to this account, Palliser provides abundant practical advice on wilderness outfitting to fellow adventurers, describing in detail the requirements for guns, horses, knives, clothing, powder, and provisions — advice he would himself find ample opportunity to follow again in a few years.

In Ireland, Palliser flourished amid the luxury and comfort of his secure position in the aristocracy. But he soon began to thirst for the adventure and danger of wilderness travel and the heady thrill of exploring unknown lands. As he had written in *Solitary Rambles,* he had "left the Indians and the Upper Missouri with great regret." (5:289) On his return journey from America, Palliser had learned of the exploring expeditions and railroad surveys that were being initiated in the western United States. He took this idea home with him, and eventually decided to approach the Exploration Committee of the Royal Geographical Society with a plan for similar exploration of the then-unknown wilds of western Canada. Palliser probably envisioned another solitary ramble, this time justified by some serious geographical observations interspersed among the stalking and hunting. The Society responded to his idea with enthusiasm, but had something a little more structured in mind. The Society finally approved an expenditure of 5,000 pounds sterling for what was to be dubbed the British North American Expedition, to be led by Palliser, and to include a botanist, a naturalist-geologist, a magnetic observer, and an astronomical observer. In 1857 the expedition began a three-year journey through the wilds of western Canada and parts of the adjacent United States (including northwestern Montana).

At the time of the British North American Expedition, the result of David Thompson's extensive explorations in the Canadian plains and Rockies some four decades earlier were almost totally unknown. Thompson's careful journals and maps had been kept secret by officials of the North West Company. Thompson, 86 years old, nearly blind, and quite unknown, was still living in the Montreal area at the time Palliser began his expedition. In fact, it was not until the late 1880s that Dr. Joseph Tyrell, a field assistant to Canadian geologist George Dawson, finally uncovered Thompson's hidden journals. By that time, of course, the region first explored by Thompson had been fairly well re-explored, first by Palliser and later by others. It is interesting to speculate how the history of the West might have changed had the two explorers conferred; Thompson believed that most of the Pacific Northwest south of the 49th Parallel rightfully belonged to the British Empire, and his explorations — if publicized — might have reinforced that claim.

Although the focus of the British North American Expedition was primarily geographical, much in the way of natural history exploration was accomplished. The British government was keenly interested in knowing what natural resources existed in this vast and unknown landscape, and in learning what potential the interior held for settlement and agriculture. Thus the Society insisted that trained scientists accompany the expedition. Actually, by the time the expedition was in full swing, everyone, including Palliser, was contributing to the study of plant and animal life. As one observer said about the party, "they did not let a flower or a fly or an insect escape their spectacles and nets .... The collection of bugs and plants that they made would have filled a museum." (8:ci)

Part of the success of the expedition in this regard was because of the humor and contagious enthusiasm of the botanist, Eugene Bourgeau. Bourgeau hailed from the high Alps and could not speak a word of English. He had collected extensively in France, the Canary Islands, Spain, and North Africa. Although he had not received formal academic training in botany, he was one of the most respected collectors in Europe and was famous for his meticulously prepared herbarium specimens. As one observer wrote of Bourgeau, "The Botanist's enthusiasm was almost as great as a gold miner in the discovery of a big nugget. It gave me a lot of amused satisfaction to watch his delight when he found a new species. I watched for new plants in my travels and when I was fortunate enough to bring an addition to his collection I was treated to a lesson of *interesting* information .... His excited observations opened a vast knowledge that catalogued each growing plant as a matter of supreme importance to the overall purpose of nature .... I could never again heedlessly trample plants, without reminding myself of this man's gentle and almost reverent handling of a rarity in plant life." (8:xxvii)

Unfortunately, Bourgeau left the expedition in the spring of 1859 to go collecting in the Caucasus Mountains and never made it as far as the borders of Montana. By the time he returned home, however, he had collected 10,000 dried plants representing 819 species for the Herbarium at Kew. He also had collected mammal skins and birds' eggs, and had even provided data on soil temperatures and the temperatures inside trees.

Scientists in England lamented that no ornithologist had been assigned to the expedition, but two of the party members did quite well in this field. James Hector, M.D., was the geologist-naturalist of the expedition and, by default, the official ornithologist. Hector, a Scotsman, recorded much information in his journal not only about birds but also about mammals, reptiles, and insects. He was a capable botanist, and continued botanizing after Bourgeau's departure. He gathered many alpine plants, estimating their altitude by measuring the temperature of boiling water.

The real ornithologist of the expedition, however, was not Hector but a stormy Englishman, Lieutenant Thomas Wright Blakiston. Blakiston was a well-trained military man, born in England in 1832, a grandson of a baronet. His official assignment on Palliser's British American Expedition was as "magnetic observer," which meant that his duty was to make hourly measurements of the earth's magnetic field, as was the scientific vogue at the time. Yet he was an ornithologist at heart, and had once contacted Charles Darwin for employment in the field. As a member of Palliser's expedition, his official duties, as he put it, "were widely different from those of a zoologist; in fact, I had properly nothing to do with natural history, my work being of a nature which required the use of the sextant more than the following-piece, the pen and pencil instead of the dissecting-knife, and observations of the movements of magnets rather than of birds. It was consequently only spare moments at uncertain times that I was able to devote to my favourite pursuit, ornithology." (1:V,155)

From the start Blakiston did not get along well with the other members of the exploring expedition. He may have been resentful that Hector had been named official naturalist rather than himself. When Palliser named Hector, a civilian, instead of Lieutenant Blakiston as second in command of the expedition things quickly grew intolerable. Thus, in August of 1858, Blakiston resigned from the expedition in a huff. He had previously promised Palliser, however, that he would explore the Kootenai River country, and being a true English gentleman, kept his word, although he did not send a map or any of his ornithological findings to Palliser afterwards.

In the fall of 1858, Blakiston — traveling with a trio of "Red River half-breed voyageurs," (8:557) a Thickwood Cree guide named James, and a dozen of Palliser's horses — set out for the Kootenai. He crossed the Continental Divide at North Kootenai Pass north of Glacier Park and dropped south of the international boundary into the valley of the North Fork of the Flathead River in present-day Montana.

Blakiston was euphoric at his accomplishment on being the first white man to cross what might someday become a historic pass. It was there that he encountered a strange variety of grouse while "following an Indian trail through the thick pine-woods .... I do not know what induced me to shoot the bird," he wrote, "for it was not my custom to waste ammunition; but it may have been that I was in better humour than usual for having just crossed the watershed of the Rocky Mountains, and that, too, by a pass hitherto untrodden by any white man." (1:V,122-23) Blakiston wrote a detailed description of this grouse, believing it to be a distinct species from the spruce grouse of the East; today it is considered merely a race of the same species. He also noted a hummingbird in the same area, although he was unable to identify it as to species, and a red-tailed hawk, which he dubbed "the squealing buzzard." (1:III,318)

Blakiston's party next ascended the North Fork of the Flathead to its head, dropped into the Kootenai River drainage, and "camped, for the first time, in a Columbian forest." (8:568) Blakiston was impressed by the change in vegetation on the west side of the divide, as other naturalists before and since have been. He described several new species of trees, including the western red cedar (which he called "the Columbian Cedar"), western larch, and subalpine fir. Blakiston spent a few days with the Indians at Tobacco Plains, the relatively dry, grassy area near present-day Eureka.

*The Palliser expedition approached Chief Mountain, in present-day Glacier National Park, from the north.* (LARRY THOMPSON)

There he found western meadowlarks, a turkey vulture feeding on a dead horse, and cedar waxwings whose "stomachs were filled with a delicious berry, called by the Cree Indians and half breeds the 'Sasketoon'." (1:V,65) The party then continued eastward up Grave Creek, a tributary of the Kootenai River, then descended Yakinikak (also known as Trail) Creek to the North Fork of the Flathead River. He then ascended Kishenehn Creek to a pass he called Boundary Pass, "so named by me on account of its western end being in United States territory, while the eastern is on the British side of the line." (1:V,73) Today it is known as South Kootenay Pass.

On September 6, near the summit of Boundary Pass, Blakiston made a remarkable discovery. It had been storming for days, and the party was plowing through two feet of fresh snow with drifts to four feet when Blakiston "espied a bird on some open ground where the snow had been nearly all drifted away by the wind. All I had to do was to pull my gun out of its cover, and discharge the barrel which contained shot, ... and I secured a specimen of this Bunting. Of course I did not know what species it was at the time, and, considering the situation and circumstances, did not stop to inquire, but tied the bird up as nicely as I could, and commenced the descent." (1:V,74) Months later, back in civilization, Blakiston examined the bird carefully and found it to be a Smith's longspur, a drab, nondescript little bird that breeds in the arctic and winters in Texas. This was the first record of this bird in Montana, and in fact this bird is so rare in the state — passing through only in migration, and then almost always in eastern Montana — that it has only been seen four times since.

Blakiston's small party continued down the east slope of Boundary Pass and followed eastward along the Montana border, re-crossing the Continental

*The blue grouse (left), Steller's jay (center) and yellow-headed blackbird were among the many Montana bird species carefully described by English ornithologist Thomas Blakiston.* (FROM LEFT: ED WOLFE, G.R. HIGBEE, TOM ULRICH)

Divide to Waterton Lake, which Blakiston discovered and named after the recently-deceased British naturalist, Charles Waterton. While in route, he collected many plants, especially ferns, which he eventually gave to Bourgeau. He also noted a new species of pine, whitebark pine, which Bourgeau, whose path had not crossed its range, had not yet encountered. Blakiston spent two days in the Waterton Lake area where, he noted, "game was abundant, including grisly bears." In this area, Blakiston was "much struck by the comparative greenness of the prairies on this side, after the burned up appearance of the Tobacco Plains, which we had left but a few days." (8:578)

Blakiston prepared a detailed map of his discoveries in the Kootenai country but never gave a copy of it or a report to Palliser. Upon his return to England, he wrote of his ornithological findings in the prestigious English journal *The Ibis*, attempting to make "as complete a list as possible of the birds inhabiting the interior portion of the vast tract stretching from ocean to ocean, known as British North America ... the wild uncultivated region ... tenanted by few besides the aboriginal Indian tribes." (1:V,39-40) His preparation of the report was interrupted by an expedition to China, during which he traveled nearly a thousand miles farther up the Yangtze River than had any other European. Upon his return to England, he seems to have taken his ornithological pursuits much more seriously. The continuation of his report of Canadian birds became more authoritative after his return, and he drew "from every reliable authority within my reach." (1:V,155) Blakiston tended to be a "splitter," preferring to recognize different races of subspecies of birds as distinct species. He justified this philosophy on the basis that "we shall not get men to sacrifice their comfort, and perhaps risk their lives, in collecting abroad, if, when they return home, their species are to be called mere varieties." (1:V,155) Blakiston became very defensive and apologetic about his report on birds, perhaps because he lacked formal training in ornithology, and wrote, "To say that I am aware of its defects would be to criminate myself, because it might be in justice remarked, why did not I rectify them?" He appeared overly sensitive to criticism, even in advance: "I will therefore conclude with the simple request that if any censoriously inclined naturalist meditate severe criticism, he will be guided by the memorable advice of 'Punch' — questionable perhaps in the case in which it was offered, but often so very appropriate — 'Don't!'" (1:V,155)

Blakiston eventually settled in Japan, where he spent 20 years as a merchant, and became a respected ornithologist of international renown. His book on the seabirds of Japan was considered definitive, and his work on biogeography led to defining what was to be known as "Blakiston's Line," separating the biological regions of Manchuria and Siberia. After a tour of Australia and New Zealand, Blakiston retired to the United States, where, at age 53, he married an Ohio girl and settled in New Mexico, and where his continued ornithological work brought him some renown. He died in 1891.

But to return to Palliser: In the fall of 1859, Hector and Palliser, traveling separately, also passed through northwestern Montana, following the Kootenai River downstream and making the famous portage around Kootenai Falls. Palliser, like Blakiston, was impressed by the vegetative differences between the east and west sides of the Divide, and noted near Kootenai Falls that the current year's growth of the elderberry bushes was nearly 12 feet.

Of all the observations made by the expedition, certainly the most famous is Palliser's description of the dry, treeless extension of the northern Great Plains into southern Canada, the area that came to be known as "Palliser's Triangle." This area was bounded to the west by the forests of the Rocky Mountains and the north and east by the boreal "park belt" of aspen, which Palliser correctly surmised was due to the success of prairie fires in holding back the invasion of conifers. This area is dry enough to support certain species that are typical of Great Basin deserts and that reach their northern limits here, including the scorpion, the eastern short-horned lizard, big sagebrush, and Nuttall's saltbush. For decades settlers shunned this "Great American Desert," which had received such bad press in Palliser's report.

Traveling through this region, the expedition had touched the Montana border near the Milk River north of the Sweetgrass Hills, those prominent landmarks just south of the international border.

Following the completion of the expedition and its return to England, Palliser spent a year back in America, this time helping the Confederates smuggle contraband through Yankee blockades in the Civil War. He never returned to his former wilderness haunts.

By the end of the Civil War, the Mullan Road had been completed from Fort Benton to Fort Walla Walla, the Federal Homestead Act had been passed by Congress, Montana was officially a territory, and the discovery of gold had drawn people by the thousands, first to Gold Creek (1862) and then to Grasshopper Creek (1862), Alder Gulch (1863), and Last Chance Gulch (1864). The great herds of bison and elk were thinning; the pristine wilderness had been violated by civilization. In short, the habitat in Montana was no longer suitable for this dying species, the great European explorer-naturalist of the mid-1800s.

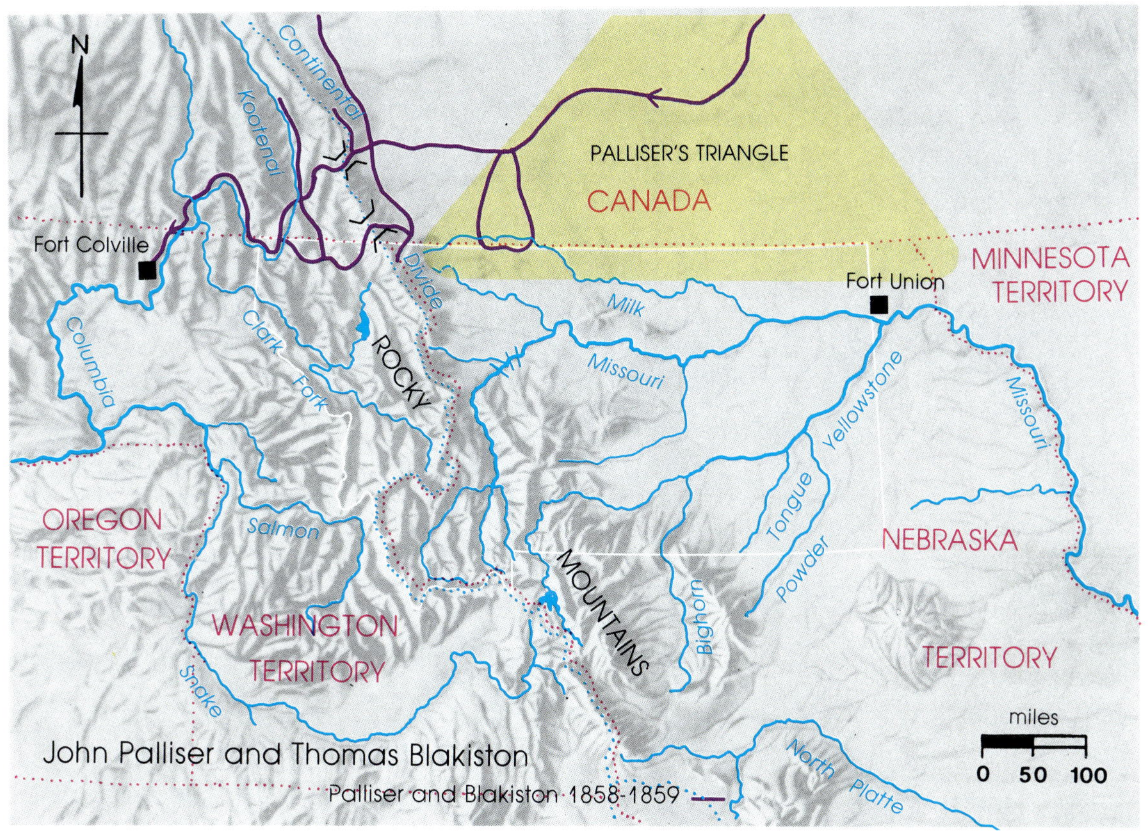


## Sources


1. Blakiston, T. W. "On Birds Collected and Observed in the Interior of British North America." *The Ibis* 3(1861):314-20, 4(1862):3-10, 5(1863):39-87. 121-55.
2. Blakiston, T. "Report of the Exploration of the Kootenie and Boundary Passes of the Rocky Mountains in 1858." *Occasional Papers of the Royal Artillery Institution* (London). I(1859):237-54.
3. Holmgren, E. J. "Thomas Blakiston, Explorer." *Alberta History* 24(1976):15-22.
4. Palliser, J. *Exploration — British North America.* London: Eyre and Spotteswoode, for H. M. Stationery Office, 1863.
5. Palliser, J. *Solitary Rambles and Adventures of a Hunter in the Prairies.* London: John Murray, 1853.
6. Spry, I. M. "Did Palliser Visit Saskatchewan in 1848?" *Saskatchewan History* 16(1963):22-6.
7. Spry, I. M. *The Palliser Expedition: An Account of John Palliser's British North American Expedition, 1857-1860.* Toronto: The MacMillan Co., 1963.
8. Spry, I. M., ed. *The Papers of the Palliser Expedition, 1857-1860.* Vol. XLIV. Toronto: The Champlain Society, 1968.

CHAPTER 9

# The Pacific Railroad Surveys

*In May of 1854, Lieutenant Mullan of the Stevens Railroad Survey lost nearly "his whole party and property ... in using a raft unmanageable in the swift current" of the Clark Fork River near present-day Missoula. This incident, typical of the hardships of wilderness travel at that time, was captured by German artist Gustavus Sohon.*

By the early 1850s, pressure was mounting for the U.S. government to lend its aid in the construction of a transcontinental railroad that would extend rails from their eastern terminus in the midwest to the Pacific Ocean and tie the country together from coast to coast. Such a railroad was needed to transport goods from Eastern trade centers to the Western gold fields, to move natural resources from west to east, to transport military equipment and personnel into the Indian lands, and to provide a safer and easier means of travel for settlers heading west. Furthermore a transcontinental railroad would help solidify the American claim to the still-disputed lands of the West by providing a strong American presence, and would provide a channel of communication between the eastern states and the isolated settlements along the Pacific Coast. Without such a railroad, there were three choices available to a person wishing to head west: join a dangerous and tedious seasonal wagon train, hack through the malaria-infested jungles of Panama, or travel 13,000 miles by sea around Cape Horn.

On March 2, 1853, Congress passed a bill ordering the Secretary of War, Jefferson Davis, to conduct field surveys and to prepare a full report of all practicable routes between the Canadian and Mexican borders for a transcontinental railroad. Davis had little time to think about his assignment, since Congress wanted the full report no later than the first Monday in January, 1854.

Davis wasted no time in organizing the surveys. He divided the entire West into four tiers, the exploration of each to be commanded by a different officer. The northern tier, extending from St. Paul, Minnesota, to the Pacific Ocean, encompassed a swath of land 150 miles wide between the 47th and 49th parallels, including all of northern Montana. (The region between the 45th and 47th parallels — an area including southern Montana — was not surveyed until 1856, although as it turned out the first railroad across Montana was to be built through this area.)

To head the survey of the northern tier, Davis appointed Isaac Stevens, governor of the newly-created Washington Territory, which at that time included what is now Montana west of the Continental Divide. Stevens was a brilliant young lieutenant in a division of the Corps of Engineers attached to the Pacific Coast Survey, and had resigned his commission to become governor. Stevens was described by George Suckley, who served as naturalist under his command, as "a smart, active, ubiquitous little man, very come-at-able, [who] wears a red shirt and helps pull on the rope when we get stuck in a mud hole." (10:278-79)

Governor Stevens received his assignment on April 8, 1853. His charge required him "to examine carefully the passes of the several mountain ranges, the geography and meteorology of the whole intermediate region, the character, as avenues of trade and transportation, of the Missouri and Columbia Rivers, the rains and snows of the route, especially in the mountain passes, and, in short, to collect every species of information bearing upon the question of railroad practicability." Stevens realized that his path would take him deep into the heart of hostile Indian territory, and he wrote that "it was necessary, moreover, to give great attention to the Indian tribes, as their friendship was important to be secured, and bore directly upon the question both of the Pacific Railroad and the safety of my party." (17:XII,31)

Stevens divided his immense territory into eastern and western divisions. To the western division, including parts of present-day Washington, Oregon, and Idaho, he assigned Captain G.B. McClellan. Stevens assumed control of the eastern division, which included Montana.

The "natural history apparatus" of the expedition had been wisely placed under the very capable directorship of Spencer Fullerton Baird of the Smithsonian Institution, and Baird not only provided field instructions for collecting plant and animal specimens, but also hand-picked many of the naturalists for the various survey parties. In his general instructions for the expedition, Stevens ordered that "Each officer and scientific man of the expedition will keep a daily journal, noting everything worthy of observation of a general character. These journals will be deemed a part of the results of the expedition, will be turned over as a part of its archives, and will be made use of in preparing the report ... The naturalists and collectors, for full information in reference to their duties, are referred to [Baird's] printed notes prepared for this expedition, and his printed directions prepared for the Smithsonian Institution. The collections will all be sent to him in Washington for the purpose of that portion of the report." Baird's field instructions contained directions such as the following: "As the expedition will pass through the breeding-ground of many species of birds whose nidification and eggs are not known, attention should be paid to securing abundant specimens of the nests and eggs. As far as possible the skin of the bird to which each set of eggs may belong should be secured, and have a mark attached common to it and the egg." (13:5)

To the western division of the Stevens Survey, under the command of Captain McClellan, was assigned Dr. James Graham Cooper as naturalist. Cooper was the son of a distinguished New York City naturalist named William Cooper, the man for whom the Cooper's hawk is named. James, born in 1830, could be expected to share an interest in natural history since his father's

*Artist John Mix Stanley created this magnificent lithograph depicting Governor Isaac Stevens, en route to Fort Benton, reading a dispatch on September 11, 1853 from Lieutenant Grover explaining that a proposed route over the Continental Divide could not be traversed by wagons.*

friends included John James Audubon, Thomas Nuttall, John Torrey and Spencer Fullerton Baird. As a boy he assembled a respectable collection of shells, nests, and snakes, and kept a menagerie of wild animals as pets. In 1851 Cooper graduated from the College of Physicians and Surgeons (now Columbia University) in New York. Two years later, with the help of his father's friend Baird, he was hired as a contractor to serve as surgeon-naturalist to the Stevens Survey under McClellan.

Assigned as naturalist to the eastern division under the direct supervision of Stevens himself was Dr. George Suckley. Suckley, also from New York City, was the same age as Cooper and also had graduated from the College of Physicians and Surgeons the same year as Cooper. He was serving as resident surgeon at the New York Hospital when he was tapped for the Stevens Survey.

In addition to the naturalists, two artists accompanied the expedition. One of these men, John Mix Stanley, was already a famous artist at the time he signed with the eastern divison under Stevens. The other, the German artist Gustavus Sohon, was assigned to Captain McClellan's western division. He was later to transfer to Stevens' command when Stanley headed east.

Stevens' main party left St. Paul, Minnesota, on June 8, 1853, and proceeded westward in the general direction of Fort Union. The Stevens Party was the first into the field. Lieutenants Andrew Jackson Donelson and John Mullan, separating from the main Stevens party, took a steamer to Fort Union, arriving there on July 3. Stevens and the main party, traveling overland much of the way, did not make it to Fort Union until August 1. The entire group was reassembled at Fort Union, which served as temporary headquarters while

*On September 6, 1853, A. W. Tinkham of the Stevens Survey ascended the summit of one of the Sweetgrass Hills and saw the distant Front Range of the Rockies, presenting a "seeming unbroken front" through which the expedition was to site a railroad route.* (KRISTI DuBOIS)

supplies were readied for the push westward. Suckley took a side trip from Fort Union that took him to the head of the Souris River in Canada.

On August 9, the group left for Fort Benton, traveling overland along the Missouri River to the mouth of the Milk River, then up the Milk River to the vicinity of present-day Havre and south through the old dry channel of the Missouri River to Fort Benton. Fort Benton was reached September 8, 1853.

Fort Benton served as the base camp from which several small groups sortied in different directions to explore mountain passes and valleys. Lieutenant Mullan headed south to explore the Musselshell River drainage, then continued west. Assistant Engineer A. W. Tinkham took a side trip to the Sweetgrass Hills and became the first white man to climb the two summits of East Butte. "Our ascent had been one of continued excitement and interest," he wrote in his report. "For months we had been confined to the monotony of the smooth bleak prairie, and had missed the rocks and trees, the hills, and brooks, to which we were accustomed, and as we again were suddenly thrown among them with all their novelty and pleasant associations, our spirits were strangely exhilarated, and every familiar stone and shrub possessed a rare charm." (17:I,226)

Game was abundant in the Sweetgrass Hills; a large elk was shot, mule deer and bighorn sheep were seen, and pronghorn were abundant. From the summit Tinkham could see for a hundred miles or more in all directions — the Cypress Hills of Canada were visible, as were the Bear Paw Mountains, the Highwoods, and the Little Belts. To the west, the Rocky Mountain Front was visible, an "imposing mass abruptly opposing itself like a forbidding wall, ... gorgeous with its glittering peaks and flashing snow-fields, lit up with unusual brilliancy by the evening sun." It was through this "seeming unbroken front" that the expedition was supposed to find a route for a railroad. (17:I,228)

Suckley, meanwhile, was busy collecting plant and animal specimens of all sorts. To search the prairies for frogs he hired a professional who had previously made his living catching bullfrogs for restaurants. To capture specimens of birds, Suckley employed a bullwhip in the style of Indiana Jones. In the Milk River Suckley collected a variety of sucker that was believed to be a new species. It was named *Catostomus sucklii* in honor of its collector, but today it is considered to be merely a variety of the white sucker. He also collected a new plant, now known as *Suckleya suckleyana*, along the Milk River.

On September 22, 1853, Stevens and his party left Fort Benton and traveled by way of Cadotte Pass (a few miles north of Rogers Pass) to the site of De Smet's St. Mary's Mission in the Bitterroot Valley. There, near the site of present-day Stevensville, a temporary camp called "Cantonment Stevens" was established as winter headquarters for the party. Mullan, having traversed a winding path taking him from the Musselshell River to the Deer Lodge Valley to Horse Prairie Creek near present-day Dillon and over the Divide into the Bitterroot Valley, met the Stevens party there. Stevens continued westward toward the Pacific Ocean.

On October 2, 1853, Suckley received a letter from Governor Stevens: "You will proceed in a canoe," Stevens ordered, "down the Bitter Root and St. Mary's rivers ... and down Clark's fork of the Columbia river to the main river ... and from that point make your way by the most practicable route to Olympia. During your stay at this place you will employ your time to the best advantage, collecting such specimens in zoology, botany, ichthyology, &c., as may be rare and interesting.... My object in this is to inform you, so far as I learn of the dangers ahead, that you may not be exposed to unnecessary risk." (13:422-4)

On October 15, Suckley pushed off down the Bitterroot River in a makeshift boat made of three bullocks' hides. Two white soldiers and an Indian guide were his companions. A somewhat battered Suckley finally arrived at Fort Vancouver on December 6, having endured, during his 1,049-mile marathon, rapids, the wreckage of the boat, near-starvation, and various Indian skirmishes. There he met his friend Cooper. Mullan, who wintered at Cantonment Stevens, made extensive natural history collections the following year and shipped them to Suckley.

The Stevens Survey was officially disbanded on April 1, 1854. After the disbandment, Cooper and Suckley spent some time collecting plants together in what is now western Washington State, then met in Panama to do some more exploring together. The extensive collections made by Cooper and Suckley in Panama were sent to Baird at the Smithsonian but lost in shipment.

Meanwhile, explorations for the railroad route in Montana continued. Tinkham, in October of 1853,

ably, Hayden severed his connections with Hall, cutting his only source of scientific funding.

The lack of money did not dampen Hayden's determination. In early 1854, Hayden hitched a ride on an American Fur Company steamer and ascended the Missouri River as far upstream as Fort Benton. During the next two years he collected extensively in Montana and the Dakotas, concentrating on fossils but carefully observing and collecting plants and animals as well. He subsisted on whatever meager earnings he could procure by doing odd jobs for the Company or for the unruly fur traders who were scattered through the Montana wilds. He also ascended the Yellowstone River to the mouth of the Big Horn River near present-day Hysham, furiously collecting specimens on shore while the slow Fur Company boats labored upstream. The Indians gave Hayden wide berth. They called him "the man who picks up stones while running," (9:35) and thought he was insane, and, therefore, a holy man, not to be harmed.

While descending the Yellowstone in the summer of 1854, a distance of more than 400 miles, Hayden and his party were never out of sight of large bands of bison. On one occasion, the party came across an old bison bull lying on the river bank, "surrounded with wolves, who had already deprived him of his nose and tail. He had evidently yielded to his fate, but pitying the poor animal, we hallooed and fired a charge of shot among the wolves, which dispersed them. The old bull revived, started down the bank, and swam across the river to a sandbar, where he fell exhausted. Before we were out of sight, the wolves had surrounded him again, and undoubtedly nothing was left of him in a few hours but a parcel of bones distributed over the prairie." (5:141) Hayden estimated that about 250,000 bison were being destroyed in the northern Great Plains each year, about 100,000 for robes alone. Among the survivors, males outnumbered the females ten to one, since only cow skins were used for robes and cow meat was preferred for food. This impact on the bison population structure no doubt accelerated the speedy demise of these noble prairie monarchs.

By far the greatest findings of Hayden's first Montana surveys (1854-5) were the fossils, which he transported back to St. Louis in huge quantities. Dr. Joseph Leidy and Hayden's old collecting companion Meek jointly published the descriptions of the bizarre creatures discovered. Among the fossil discoveries made by Hayden in Montana during this low-budget labor of love were the remains of fantastic creatures the likes of which the world had never imagined. Among the fossil bones that Hayden brought back from his 1855 Montana explorations were some strange, saw-edged teeth. Joseph Leidy, the Philadelphia anatomist who examined these teeth, named the animals that grew them *Troodon* and *Palaeoscinus*. These were the first American dinosaurs to be described and named.

*Hayden searched the badlands and breaks along the Missouri and Yellowstone rivers for fossils, which he used to correlate ages of geological strata. Shown are the badlands along the Yellowstone River near Fallon.* (ROBERT SCHERTING)

Hayden's reputation as a scientist was immediately and firmly established, and his fame spread among the scientific community. Shortly after he arrived in St. Louis in early 1856, Hayden was contacted by a young lieutenant of the small but elite group known as the U.S. Topographical Engineers. Lieutenant Gouverneur Kemble Warren was a dashing, eloquent, and brilliant man, wearing a black moustache and long, flowing Custer-style locks. Trained as a civil engineer, Warren had graduated second in his class at West Point in 1850 and had an amateur's love of natural history. He was described by Missouri River steamboat captain Joseph La Barge as "a handsome man, with a fine head and clear eye, at that time rather slender, but well built and erect. He was always pleasant, and was liked by his men, but was nevertheless a strict disciplinarian." (2:208-09) Warren asked Hayden to prepare a report on the geology and topography of the unknown regions that Hayden had so thoroughly studied during the

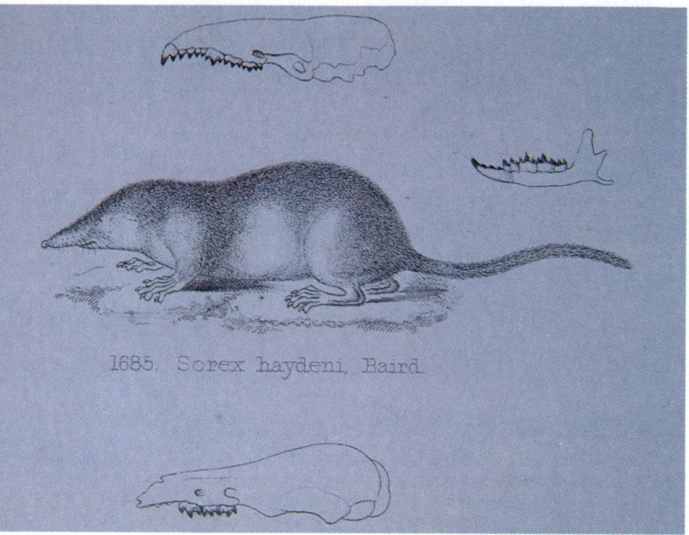


*Hayden collected everything in his path in his early days — fossils, plants, birds, mammals, fish. Although he came to specialize in marine invertebrate fossils (shown here is a brachiopod, an extinct mollusc-like organism), a mammal, the Hayden shrew, now bears his name.* (KRISTI DuBOIS PHOTO; PACIFIC RAILROAD SURVEY DRAWING)

previous three years. Hayden obliged, and his report was incorporated into Warren's report of an 1855 expedition into the Dakota country.

Warren was duly impressed by the young Hayden and his work, and when Warren received his orders in 1856 to travel to the wilds of the Yellowstone River Valley, he asked Hayden to accompany him as an assistant. Hayden accepted without hesitation. Warren's assignment was to explore the upper Missouri and Yellowstone country, to examine potential sites for military posts, to chart possible routes for military roads, and to gather other pertinent scientific information that may have been of use to the government. Warren's party ascended the Missouri in a steamboat and arrived at Fort Union on July 10, 1856.

After a brief sojourn at Fort Union, the Warren Expedition continued some 60 miles up the Missouri, about as far as present-day Wolf Point, on Captain Joseph La Barge's steamer, the *St. Mary*. This was by now familiar territory to Hayden, and he no doubt scraped away at some of his favorite fossil-collecting sites from the previous years. Returning to Fort Union, Warren crossed paths with the notorious St. George Gore, who was wrapping up his extravagant hunting trip. The encounter proved beneficial for Warren: He picked up some mules and used wagons from Gore, and employed one of Gore's most valuable assets, Jim Bridger, the famous mountain man.

On July 25, Warren and his crew began the arduous overland ascent of the Yellowstone Valley using Gore's wagons and pack animals. Hayden collected plants, fossils, snakes, birds, mice, snails, whatever conceivably could be grabbed, trapped, pressed or pickled, identified, and carried back to the scientific museums in the East. Warren himself helped collect and preserve many of the animal specimens, and kept an eye out for unusual species that may have been of interest to Hayden. The expedition proceeded only as far as the mouth of the Powder River near Terry, about 100 miles short of Hayden's ascent of 1854, then turned back, part of the party floating on the river in bullboats, the rest returning overland with the wagons and mules. On September 1, the party left Fort Union with crates of specimens, bound for civilization.

The Warren Survey of 1856 did not accomplish much in the way of meeting its intended military objectives, but as a scientific expedition, it was a success. Among Hayden's collections — the most extensive made in Montana to this time — were specimens of nearly 600 plant species, 47 mammals, 186 birds, 24 fish, and 28 reptiles and amphibians, not to mention quantities of unidentified bugs, and mosses and lichens. Among the mammal specimens were four complete elk skeletons, two deer skeletons, and dozens of hides, skulls and antlers. The greatest contribution to science, however, were Hayden's fossil specimens. Of the 77 species of fossil vertebrates he collected, more than 50 were new to science; of the 251 fossil molluscs, 186 were new; and *every one* of the 70 fossil plants he brought back from the Yellowstone was new to science.

Upon his return to Washington, D.C., Hayden quickly set about the task of engaging specialists for identification of his extensive specimen collection and of preparing an official report. In sorting out and identifying these extensive collections, Hayden enlisted and received the help of some of the most eminent specialists of the day: Spencer Fullerton Baird of the Smithsonian helped out with the mammals; John Torrey, John S. Newberry, George Engelmann, and Hayden's old field partner Fielding B. Meek, looked over the plants and fossils. Captain A. A. Humphreys, Warren's boss, paid Hayden a high compliment for making scientific collections that "are esteemed to be of high scientific value ... without interfering with the immediate practical objects of the explorations, and reflect credit on the labors of Lieutenant Warren and his assistants." (15:7)

Hayden accompanied Warren on another expedition to the Black Hills region in the summer of 1857. That same year, a detailed and accurate map of the western United States was published in the Pacific Railroad Survey. This map, the most sophisticated map of the West up to that date, was prepared by Warren. Drawing on all available sources, including Hayden's explorations of 1853 and 1854, Warren prepared this cartographic masterwork when only 26 years of age. It was to become the roadmap for the flurry of military and scientific expeditions which poured into the region after the Civil War.

One notable feature of Warren's famous map was a nagging blank spot in the area near the headwaters of the Yellowstone River, the source of many legends and the focus of explorers' dreams. When the preliminary report of his explorations of 1855-1857 was finally published in 1858, as an appendix to the Secretary of War's annual report, Warren laid out a blueprint for an expedition to penetrate this maddening holdout of legend and myth. "The expedition should be completely organized and equipped for the field by the 1st of May, 1859, and remain in the field until the 1st of December, 1860," wrote Warren. His expedition should proceed overland from Fort Pierre to the Powder River and up the Yellowstone to the mouth of the Big Horn River, he suggested. A party then should be sent to examine "the mountain region about the sources of the Yellowstone and Missouri" (15:10-11) — namely, the vicinity of present-day Yellowstone Park. On the return, one party should descend the Missouri and another the Yellowstone, the two meeting at Fort Union and proceeding from there back to civilization.

In May of 1859 an expedition was ready to proceed, exactly as specified by Warren. However, Warren was not in charge. He had been replaced by one William F. Raynolds, a West Point graduate and now the captain of the elite Corps of Topographical Engineers. Warren was assigned to the Military Academy at West Point, where he became assistant professor of mathematics — to an Army explorer, the equivalent of an assignment to Siberia. Warren served as a major general in the Civil War and became a hero at Gettysburg, but his western explorations were through.

Captain Raynolds, showing decidedly good judgment, appointed Hayden as surgeon-naturalist to the expedition and Jim Bridger as official guide. Also accompanying the expedition were Lieutenant H. E. Maynadier of the Topographical Engineers, and Dr. M. C. Hines, surgeon and assistant naturalist. Leaving St. Louis in the spring of 1859, Raynolds followed almost to the letter the blueprint laid out in Warren's 1858 report. Upon arriving at Fort Pierre, the expedition struck out overland and proceeded westward toward the Yellowstone River by way of the Powder River. Raynolds' mission was twofold. First, he was to assess the Indian situation, the climate, and the natural resources of the area. His second mission was to investigate four possible wagon routes: Fort Laramie to Fort Union, from the Yellowstone River to South Pass in Wyoming, from the sources of the Wind River in Wyoming to the sources of the Missouri, and from Fort Laramie to Fort Benton. This latter route was to connect with the Mullan Road, which was under construction during that very season.

On July 21, 1859, the expedition entered Montana, crossing the divide between the Little Missouri and Powder Rivers near present-day Alzada. The party then continued overland to Fort Sarpy on the Yellowstone River near present-day Forsyth. On the way, Hayden and some of the men took an unauthorized leave from the main group to explore the intriguing range of hills known as the Wolf Mountains near Rosebud Creek. Raynolds was quite upset, and upon their return, issued an order forbidding anyone to leave the party overnight without express permission.

Crossing the Powder and Tongue River drainages, the party found the grassland so severely overgrazed by bison that no grass was left for the mules. The men had to cut cottonwoods to feed bark and twigs to the starving animals. As they descended Armell's Creek toward the Yellowstone, the men witnessed an amazing sight. "From the summit of the hill," wrote Raynolds, "we obtained our first view of the Yellowstone Valley itself, of which over 50 square miles

*Hayden scoured the badlands of Eastern Montana in search of fossils. Top: Prairie country southwest of Baker.* (KRISTI DuBOIS) *Bottom: Winter in Makoshika State Park near Glendive.* (ROBERT SCHERTING)

was visible, literally black with buffalo, grazing in an enormous herd whose numbers defy computation, but must be estimated by hundreds of thousands." (11:45) On one occasion, three large bison bulls charged the party, "to the great alarm of one of the escorts, who dropped his gun, and, raising his hands, exclaimed, in all the accents of mortal terror, 'Elephants! elephants! my God! I did not know there were elephants in this country!' On another occasion as a band of bison was passing close by the train, one of the teams started in full pursuit, and was with great difficulty checked. It was probably the first buffalo chase on record with a six-mule team." (11:34)

The party camped for 12 days at Fort Sarpy, then split on August 31 as it headed south into what is now Wyoming. Raynolds headed up the Bighorn River to explore its sources, and Maynadier proceeded toward the headwaters of Rosebud Creek. While the party was plodding along, a sow grizzly with three cubs charged out of a plum thicket and knocked one of the men to the ground; fortunately, he was not injured. Both parties continued to a rendezvous at a dismal winter camp on the North Platte River in Wyoming, where a bleak and boring winter was passed.

Raynolds was somewhat of a religious zealot, and always observed the Sabbath, delivering his own wilderness sermons. The men appreciated this respite from the march, but Raynolds' sermons were sparsely attended. Raynolds seemed to pick on Hayden as a prime subject, and the patient geologist was treated to daily sermons from his captain.

When the spring of 1860 finally arrived, the party was once again divided. Maynadier was to proceed northwestward along the eastern edge of the Yellowstone Plateau and back into the Yellowstone River Valley. Raynolds, meanwhile, was to proceed west toward Jackson Hole and explore the legendary wonders around the sources of the Yellowstone River. Hayden traveled with the Raynolds party. They were to rendezvous at the Three Forks on June 30.

Maynadier encountered many difficulties. In attempting to cross the raging Shoshone River in Wyoming, the mules were swept downstream and drowned, and much of the gear including the precious surveying instruments was lost. Raynolds' progress did not go exactly as planned either. Bridger had told him repeatedly that it would be impossible to explore the headwaters of the Yellowstone from the south, and that to reach this land of wonders it would be necessary to cross into the upper Madison River drainage and double back into the present-day Park area.

On May 30, 1860 Raynolds acknowledged gracefully but with much regret that he had been defeated in his plans to be the first man to lead a scientific expedition into the Yellowstone headwaters. "Directly across our route," he wrote, "lies a basaltic ridge, rising not less than 5,000 feet above us, its walls apparently vertical with no visible pass nor even canon. On the opposite side of this are the headwaters of the Yellowstone. Bridger remarked triumphantly and forcibly to me upon reaching this spot, 'I told you you could not go through. A bird can't fly over that without taking a supply of grub along.' I had no reply to offer, and mentally conceded the accuracy of the information of 'the old man of the mountains'." (11:86)

*Plains pricklypear dominated much of the eastern Montana landscape crossed by Hayden, particularly areas that had been heavily trampled or overgrazed by bison.* (BRUCE SELYEM)

Floundering slowly through deep snow around the south side of Yellowstone, Raynolds and Hayden "were compelled to content [themselves] with listening to marvellous tales of burning plains, immense lakes, and boiling springs, without being able to verify these words." (11:10) It would be more than a decade before Hayden himself was to lead the first fully-staffed scientific expedition into this legendary region.

Crossing into Montana over the pass that now bears Raynolds' name, Raynolds and his party proceeded down the Madison River to the Three Forks, arriving at the rendezvous on June 29, 1860. There they impatiently waited until Maynadier finally appeared four days later. Splitting the party for a third time, Raynolds transferred Lieutenant Mullins [not to be confused with Lieut. Mullan] to his party and sent Maynadier down the Yellowstone River to Fort Union in a half-putrefied bison-skin boat, which had been cached a few days earlier. It was affectionately nicknamed "the Rose of Cashmere." Raynolds and crew proceeded to Fort Benton.

Near Fort Benton, the party crossed paths with some of the advance scouts of Lt. Mullan's road-building expedition, which was nearing the end of two years of grueling work on the wagon road from the Bitterroot Valley to Fort Benton. For the fourth time, the Raynolds party split, with Raynolds following the Missouri River downstream, and Hayden and Bridger accompanying an overland detachment under Lt. Mullins to explore the divide between the Yellowstone and Missouri Rivers. Hayden thus had the opportunity to traverse some of the most interesting fossil-producing country in the West. Drinking water was scarce; Hayden estimated that "one-third of the fluid that we dignified by the name of water was buffalo urine." (11:166) On August 3, the camp was charged by 250 Crow Indians who announced "our hearts being black, we have come to fight *you*." (11:167) Mullins' party consisted of 14 men, and could easily have been overrun by the Indians. But the attackers fired only 30 shots, then left. The three parties — Raynolds, Maynadier, and Mullins — met at Fort Union August 11, and from there steamed down the Missouri and back to civilization.

Raynolds began work upon his report shortly after his return, but the Civil War broke out, delaying such less-urgent projects. Hayden, likewise, was forced to set aside his cases of specimens and head to war. Hayden served as a surgeon in the Union army, while Raynolds became a brevet brigadier general. Because of the war, Raynolds' report was not published until 1868, (11) and Hayden's report on the geology of the region did not appear until a year later. (6)

Although Hayden was the official naturalist of the Raynolds' expedition, and although he continued to collect zoological and botanical specimens, his interest increasingly was on geology. Upon his return in 1860, Hayden had sent the extensive biological collections made by himself and by Dr. Hines to another impressive array of experts, including Elliott Coues for birds, J. S. Newberry for fossil plants, and George Engelmann for living plants. As with the collections of the Warren Survey, nothing was ignored — sedges, mosses and liverworts were painstakingly described, as were insects and molluscs. Unfortunately, the reports on natural history, other than the observations included in Raynolds' and Hayden's narratives, were never published (with the exception of the bird collections).

Hayden's geologic report, (6) one of the landmarks of western geology, synthesizes the results of his 15 years of work on the rocks of the West. Hayden's report contained the first full-color geologic map of the West, and was destined to become a scientific classic. Raynolds' report, while interesting in its accurate description of the regions traversed, failed to describe an easy route for a wagon road to connect with the Mullan Road, as had the Warren Survey before. However, Raynolds' recommendation for a railroad route up the Yellowstone River and into the Three Forks area was to become a reality in the early 1880s.

While his primary interest was in geology and fossils, Hayden made many observations and collections of wildlife and plants during his travels with Warren and Raynolds. He found that "formidable animal," (4:92) the grizzly bear, to be still quite abundant around the sources of the Missouri. At Fort Union, he captured the first specimen of Hayden's shrew known to science. He noted that house mice, introduced to the North American continent from Europe, were already common at all the fur-trading posts on the Missouri. The coyote, Hayden wrote, "is much more abundant on the Upper Missouri than the large wolf, and collects in larger bands, which seem to act in concert in taking their prey. They are said to station themselves, when in pursuit of antelope, in such a manner, that when one becomes wearied, a fresh one appears and takes up the chase, until the antelope is captured. They are also said to be very expert in cutting the hamstrings of buffalo, deer, and not unfrequently of horses. They are great enemies of the prairie dog. Multitudes may be seen at all times in their villages, waiting patiently for the dogs to make their appearance. At night, they fill the air with their terrible music. With the Indians, their barking at night always forebodes evil of some kind, and the voyager is reminded of a lurking enemy." (5:141)

Beaver populations were recovering well from fur-era overtrapping, reported Hayden, and the "Yellowstone River, from mouth to source, as well as its tributaries, contained myriads, so that they consume literally acres of the small cottonwood trees which skirt the streams." (5:146) One beaver dam Hayden encountered produced a waterfall of four feet in height. An albino beaver with bright red eyes and a cream-colored pelt was found in the Musselshell River. Beaver meat "is eaten to some extent by the Indians and traders," wrote Hayden, "and in the absence of other meat is considered quite a delicacy." (4:91)

The bird life of the lower Yellowstone Valley was somewhat different during Hayden's time than it is today. Trumpeter swans, now confined mainly to the Red Rocks Lakes and Yellowstone Park regions, were seen nesting in the lower Yellowstone Valley in 1856. Flocks of now-extinct passenger pigeons could still be seen feeding on wild berries. Ravens, today rare on the eastern Montana plains, were commonly seen by Hayden following the large herds of bison, waiting to share a kill with a wolf or grizzly. Hooded mergansers, rarely seen on the Yellowstone today, were reported by Hayden, as were least terns, which have been seen in Montana only twice since.

Hayden was a crack shot and collected birds in numbers Audubon would have been proud of. He collected 21 specimens of the hybrid flicker alone and seemed to enjoy shooting birds of prey, a sport that no respectable conservationist would pursue today. The sparrow hawk, he wrote, is such an "exceedingly noisy and saucy bird" that it seems to demand being shot at, "when silence would have enabled it to have escaped unnoticed." Likewise, Hayden found that the red-tailed hawk also "presents itself a fine mark for the gun." (5:152-3)

Hayden observed the pure-white figures of snowy owls, standing out like bleached bison skulls against the prairies which had been blackened by autumn fires, and mistakenly assumed that these were great horned owls that had turned white for the winter. Snowy owls are found in Montana only in winter, and great horned owls do not molt into white winter plumage. Nevertheless, this common misconception persists to this day, and Hayden is perhaps to be excused for an honest mistake. He also observed the much smaller and diurnal burrowing owl, and correctly inferred that "it probably consumes no nobler prey than insects or small mice." (5:154)

While big game was still abundant in the Yellowstone River Valley in 1856, Hayden noted a definite decline in overall numbers of some species since his explorations of 1853 and 1854. "Some of the larger animals on the Upper Missouri ... are fast passing away, and in a few years must become extinct," he wrote. "The buffalo, which has been so important an agent in the preservation of the Indians, is now gradually gathering into a smaller area; and although in the valley of the Yellowstone and along the Upper Missouri thousands may yet be seen, they are annually decreasing at a rapid rate ... probably at this time all the larger animals, as buffalo, elk, deer, antelope, bighorn, and beaver, are more abundant in the valley of the Yellowstone than in any other portion of the Upper Missouri." (4:90) Elk and deer were apparently still as abundant as they had been during Captain Clark's 1806 descent of the Yellowstone.

Hayden's plant collections were impressive. Professor Chester Dewey, of the University of Rochester, New York, — at age 74, the grand old man of sedges — wrote Hayden with admiration: "I only wonder that, with your other objects of special attention, you were able to seize upon so many of these ... and yet I know they are only a small portion of the plants you have thus preserved ...." (4:122-3) Sedges are well known to beginning botanists as one of the most difficult of all plant groups to identify; yet Hayden succeeded in procuring specimens of 53 different species, including four that Dewey believed were new to science. One of these was named *Carex haydeni* after its discoverer and another *Carex meekii* after his cohort, although these names are no longer used. Another plant, persistentsepal yellowcress *(Rorippa calycina)*, discovered by Hayden on the Yellowstone and described by George Engelmann from Hayden's specimen, remains today one of the rarest of Montana plants.

*In 1860 Hayden traveled cross-country from Fort Benton to Fort Union, exploring the divide between the Yellowstone and Missouri rivers, country dominated by featureless plains and rough coulees like this one near present-day Circle.* (MARK THOMPSON)

Hayden noted that prairie-dog towns support a distinct flora in contrast to the grasslands of the surrounding country; this is explained by the simple observation that the plants that prairie dogs do not like to eat thrive while the rest are chewed to oblivion. Some of the plants Hayden found abundant in prairie-dog towns are cut-leaved nightshade, bracted verbena, pennyroyal, ellisea, and dyssoidea. These same plants are common in large prairie-dog towns today.

"One of the most interesting portions of the country," wrote Hayden, "is in the region surrounding Fort Union, not only on account of its geological peculiarities, but also from the number and variety of its fossils," including "shells of mollusca in a fine state of preservation," and "silicified wood ... in the same perfect state of preservation. Throughout the region of

*Hayden was the first to describe the "island" mountain ranges of eastern Montana, such as the Moccasin (left) and the Highwood (right) mountains as volcanic in origin. Geologic features known as dikes provided the evidence.* (LEFT, RIGHT, MARK THOMPSON; CENTER, ROBERT GILDART)

the Yellowstone," he continued, "silicified wood is found in the greatest abundance, so that many portions have been called by the trappers 'petrified forests.' There is everywhere evidence of an exceedingly luxuriant growth of timber during the tertiary period." (5:95-8)

Hayden was also fascinated by the beds of lignite coal he found in the Yellowstone region, especially beds that were burning from natural causes. "The spontaneous ignition of the lignite beds, and its influence on the contiguous strata, is nowhere better exhibited that in the country bordering upon the Yellowstone. Often ranges of hills extending back from the river into the interior for several miles, form a series of high bluff ledges of the fused or semifused rocks, somewhat variegated, but mostly of a lively red color, giving the country the appearance of the ruins of a large city. The light vesicular pumice-like masses have been scattered by the wind over the plateaus surrounding these hills, and are sometimes carried a mile or more from the original position. Even at the present time, I observed several places where the lignite beds were in a state of combustion, both on the Missouri and on the Yellowstone, and the atmosphere is filled with smoke and the sulphurous smell which issues from these fires is exceedingly offensive to the traveller." (5:98-9)

Hayden also noticed "myriads of spherical concretions ... from half an inch to several feet in diameter ... formed of thin layers of sandstone, concentrically arranged about a nucleus. They contain much ferruginous matter, of a grayish color internally, but becoming of a reddish iron-rust color on exposure." (5:97) These strange formations comprise the "buckshot soil" found in many of the sandstone areas of eastern Montana.

But the natural objects of greatest fascination to Hayden were the fossil molluscs. Although these lack the glamour of dinosaurs and huge sea serpents, they provide the paleontologist with a valuable tool with which to determine the relative age of sedimentary rock formations. Hayden found that particular beds of rock supported species of fossil molluscs that were entirely different from those in other beds. More important, he found that the different layers, each with their different mollusc faunas, formed a chronological sequence, and that the sequences could be correlated from one area to the next. This allowed Hayden to correlate the different strata he encountered throughout the West. The result was the determination of a standard stratigraphic column with which geologists working in other areas could make comparisons. There were nine layers in Hayden's stratigraphic column, each layer named for the prominent locale where it could be seen, and each layer corresponding to an epoch of geologic time.

"It will be seen, therefore," boasted Hayden in his report on the Warren Survey, "that no department of the geology and natural history of the Upper Missouri has been neglected in our explorations." (4:109) Hayden's study of the natural history of Montana was meticulous, and his eclectic and all-embracing enthusiasm was to characterize his later reports when he was leader of the "Hayden Surveys" conducted by the U. S. Geological and Geographical Survey of the Territories.

Although Warren and Hayden fell in love with the landscapes of the Missouri and Yellowstone regions, they did not hold great hopes for their future. "There is no disguising the fact," wrote Warren, "that a great portion of it is irreclaimable desert, with only a little wood and cultivable land along the streams." (15:28) So severe is the climate, he continued, that "we find the cedar unable to support itself above the ground, and, spreading itself over the surface, presents the appearance on the hill-sides of grass or moss."* (15:34)

The reasons for this barrenness of the Great Plains landscape, according to Warren, were "1st, an insufficiency of timely rains; 2nd, over large areas the soil does not possess the proper constituents; 3rd, the

*Warren was referring to horizontal juniper, a creeping species that is quite distinct from the tree-like Rocky Mountain juniper.

severity of the long cold winters and short summers; and a 4th might be included in the clouds of grasshoppers that ... are nearly the same as the locusts of Egypt." (15:28) Much of the drought of this region, Hayden surmised, is because the Rocky Mountains wring out most of the moisture from air masses blown eastward from the Pacific Ocean.

In all, Hayden's early work in Montana provided the foundation for all of the geological exploration that was to follow. Hayden was the first to describe the isolated mountain ranges of eastern Montana — the Belts, Highwoods, Judith, Bear Paw, and Little Rockies — as igneous intrusions ... congealed "blisters" of magma, which were thrust by volcanic forces through the sedimentary strata of the Great Plains. Hayden also inferred that, since tropical plants are found in Montana fossils from the Tertiary Age, a tropical climate must have existed at that time, and that when these tertiary deposits were laid down "the lofty barrier of the Rocky Mountains did not exist." This was quite a bold assertion in a time when many scientific minds of the world were attacking Darwin's newly-published theory of evolution with fervor. Hayden deduced on the basis of the fossils species of mollusc he discovered that much of eastern Montana must have once been a huge inland sea, and that vast estuaries existed along its shore just east of the current Rocky Mountain Front.

He was the first to show that much of the sediment on the Great Plains contains volcanic ash. Hayden also described in detail the river terraces and glacial drift, which are evidence of the recent ice ages, and glaciers are mentioned in his 1869 report. Before Hayden who would ever have believed that just a few thousand years ago much of Montana was covered with huge sheets of ice thousands of feet thick? Also, by showing that species once existed that are now extinct, Hayden's findings provided evidence for the brand new and highly controversial theory of evolution, published by Charles Darwin in 1858, the same year as Hayden's report on the Warren Surveys. If mountain ranges could be shown to have formed and to have disappeared over the ages as Hayden surmised, perhaps it was not inconceivable that living species too had evolved and been extingushed as Darwin postulated.

In his final report on the expedition of 1859-1860, Raynolds wrote that "I regard the valley of the upper Yellowstone as the most interesting unexplored district in our widely expanded country." This land of "burning plains, immense lakes, and boiling springs," (11:10-11) so sought after by decades of explorers, and so nearly penetrated by Raynolds and Hayden in 1860, was finally to be opened to scientific exploration in 1871, and Hayden was to lead the assault.

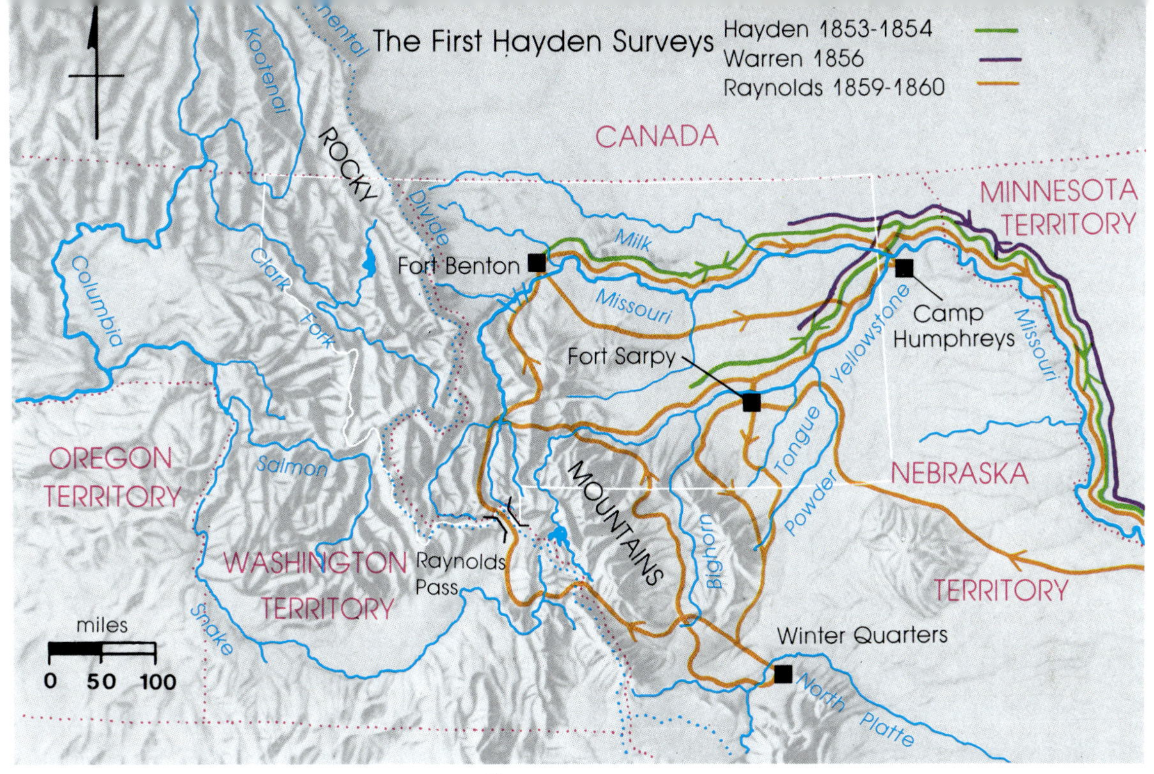


## Sources


1. Brown, M. H. *The Plainsmen of the Yellowstone*. New York: G. P. Putnam's Sons, 1961.
2. Chittenden, H. M. *History of Early Steamboat Navigation of the Missouri River*. New York: Francis P. Harper, 1903.
3. Dunraven, W. *The Great Divide*. London: Chatto and Winders, 1876.
4. Hayden, F. V. "Catalogue of the Collections in Geology and Natural History, Obtained by the Expedition Under Command of Lieut. G. K. Warren, Topographical Engineers, by F. V. Hayden, M. D." Included in Warren, *Preliminary Report* ... [see below].
5. Hayden, F. V. "On the Geology and Natural History of the Upper Missouri." *Transactions of the American Philosophical Society* new series 12 (1862):1-183.
6. Hayden, F. V. *Geological Report of the Exploration of the Yellowstone and Missouri Rivers Under the Direction of Captain W. F. Raynolds, Corps of Engineers, 1859-'60*. Washington: U. S. Government Printing Office, 1869.
7. Heldt, F. G. "Sir St. George Gore's Expedition." *Montana Historical Society Contributions*. Vol. I. Helena: State Publishing Co., 1876:144-8.
8. Koch, E. "Big Game in Montana from Early Historical Records." *Journal of Wildlife Management* 5(1941):357-70.
9. Lanham, U. N. *The Bone Hunters*. New York: Columbia Univ. Press, 1973.
10. Powell, J. W. "Ferdinand Vandiveer Hayden." *Ninth Annual Report of the U. S. Geological Survey to the Secretary of the Interior, 1887-1888*. Washington: U. S. Government Printing Office, 1889.
11. Raynolds, W. F. *Report on the Exploration of the Yellowstone and Missouri Rivers in 1859-1860*. Senate Executive Document 77, 40th Congress, 2nd Sess., Series 1317. Washington: U. S. Government Printing Office, 1868.
12. Roberts, J. *The Amazing Adventures of Lord Gore*. Silverton, Colo: Sundance Publishing Co., 1977.
13. Sanders, H. F. *A History of Montana*. Chicago: Lewis Pub. Co., 1913.
14. Schubert, F. N., ed. *Explorer on the Northern Plains: Lieutenant Gouverneur K. Warren's Preliminary Report of Explorations in Nebraska and Dakota in the Years 1855-'56-'57*. Engineer Historical Studies, No. 2. Washington, D.C.: Office of the Chief of Engineers, 1981.
15. Warren, G. K. *Preliminary Report of Explorations in Nebraska and Dakota, in the Years 1855-'56-'57*. Washington: U.S. Government Printing Office, 1858.
16. White, C. A. "Memoir of Ferdinand Vandiveer Hayden, 1839-1887." *National Academy of Science Biographical Memoirs*. 3(1895):395-413.

CHAPTER 11

# The Northwest Boundary Survey

*The watercolors of artist James Madison Alden provide us with some of the very few surviving records of the Northwest Boundary Survey of 1857-1861. This view of Waterton Lake, looking south into what is now Glacier National Park, was painted in 1860.* (NATIONAL ARCHIVES)

In 1846 the United States and Great Britain settled a long-standing dispute over the ownership of the Pacific Northwest by signing the Oregon Treaty. Before this time, Great Britain had laid claim to lands west of the Continental Divide as far south as the 42nd parallel (the current northern boundary of California), while the United States had claimed land as far north as 54 degrees 40 minutes (the present southern boundary of Alaska). The Oregon Treaty solved this dispute by extending the 49th parallel westward from the Rocky Mountains as the boundary between Oregon Territory on the south and British Columbia on the north. The northern boundary of the United States was thus a straight line of latitude all the way from the Lake of the Woods in present-day northern Minnesota to the Pacific Ocean. What could be simpler?

The clean, straight line on the map, it turned out, was somewhat more difficult to locate on the ground.

Toward the closing years of the 19th century, as settlers were moving into northern Washington, Idaho, and Montana, the need for clearly-surveyed and marked boundary lines became apparent to Congress, and the government directed the United States Geological Survey (U.S.G.S.) in 1897 to survey the Montana-Idaho boundary from the 49th parallel south to a point near the Clark's Fork River. This would require a determination of the location of the 49th parallel.

As the U.S.G.S. prepared for its survey, officials dimly remembered that the 49th parallel from the Pacific Ocean to the crest of the Rockies (in what is now Glacier National Park) had already been surveyed nearly 40 years earlier. A complete and detailed survey had been made during the period 1857-1861, not only by an American party, but by a British party working right behind the Americans. However, nothing but a few scattered notes could be found of the results of that survey.

The plot soon began to thicken. The survey's few records suggested the unbelievable: it appeared that more than a million dollars had been spent by the two governments in the survey; separate lengthy reports had been prepared by the respective commissioners and jointly signed by the Americans and the British. The reports had been submitted to high government officials, then lost. No trace of either report was to be found.

Both governments began a search to find the lost documents, and began considering the unthinkable, an ultimate resurvey of the boundary line. The United States government assigned Marcus Baker of the U.S.G.S. the impossible job of tracking down the long-lost reports, and Otto Klotz was given a similar assignment by the Canadian government.

Both men conducted a feverish search of all possible government archives and document repositories in an attempt to find the missing reports. Klotz combed government offices in Ottawa, Ontario and London, England, but to no avail. Then, one day, while Klotz was visiting the Royal Observatory at Greenwich, England, on other business, he happened to glance at some old boxes that were stacked high on top of the library shelves. The boxes bore the initials "B.N.A.," which he interpreted as "British North American." He asked the librarian what the boxes contained. "He did not know," wrote Klotz, "they had been there a long time. By request the janitor was called with step ladder; the boxes were brought down, the dust removed as well as the lid, and there lay before my bulging eyes the records of the 49° parallel west of the Rockie Mountains — the records that had been looked for the past 30 years! A happy man was I." (8:17)

Baker was not so lucky. He succeeded in gathering various memoranda, plus the maps and a large number of watercolor landscape paintings of the country crossed by the surveys. But the final report was never found, and its whereabouts remains unknown. The magnitude of this loss to the scientific community was great, because the reports contained extensive natural history findings — reports on birds, botany, insects, molluscs — apparently illustrated after the fashion of the great Pacific Railroad Survey reports. Among the lost documents was a "copious synopsis of the species of American salmon and trout," (1:62) prepared by George Suckley, and catalogues of fossils discovered during the survey. Not since the loss of the papers of Prince Paul's second journey had such a loss befallen the study of the natural history of Montana.

From the rescued British report and the journals and publications of the various members of the two expeditions, it is possible to reconstruct a fairly complete picture of Northwest Boundary Survey of 1857-1861.

In early 1857 Archibald Campbell was appointed U.S. Commissioner of the Northwest Boundary Commission, and Colonel J. S. Hawkins of the Royal Engineers was appointed by Queen Victoria as Campbell's British counterpart. Campbell's party arrived at Victoria, on the Canadian territories' west coast, via Panama in the summer of 1857, and immediately began pushing eastward toward the Continental Divide. The British party assigned to establish the boundary in the Puget Sound area was already there when the Americans arrived, but the British land crew was not to appear until the following year. The British and American land surveys thus proceeded independently from the Ocean to the Rockies.

*Alden painted this waterfall near Starvation Peak a few miles north of Kintla Lakes.* (NATIONAL ARCHIVES)

## THE AMERICAN SURVEY

In mid-1857 the American survey party under Campbell began its four-year journey to the Rockies, cutting a 40-foot swath through the dense timber as it progressed eastward. Lieutenant John G. Parke was Campbell's chief astronomer and surveyor and became his right-hand man during the survey. Also along on the American survey were Joseph S. Harris, assistant astronomer and naturalist; George Gibbs, geologist and interpreter of Indian languages; Dr. C. B. R. Kennerly, surgeon and naturalist; and James Madison Alden, artist to the survey. The party was eventually to clear about one-half of the 400-mile length of the boundary.

Little is known about the progress of the American expedition as it hacked its way eastward through the coniferous jungles of Washington and Idaho. Yet by October of 1859 it had progressed as far as the Colville River, near present-day Midway, Washington, for in that month Captain John Palliser, who was heading west from the Rockies, encountered a soldier in an American uniform chasing some wild ducks on the river, and soon met the main survey party. After a brief visit, Palliser turned back, because the Commission had been so thorough in working the boundary line west of that point that there was no use in his continuing.

A year later, in the fall of 1860, the American Commission finally scaled the summit of the Rockies in present-day Glacier Park. Fortunately James Alden's magnificent watercolors of the Kootenai River, Kootenai Falls, the Tobacco Plains, and the high mountains survive among the few remaining records of the American survey. Arriving at the summit in October of 1860, Alden first painted a view looking westward along the path over which they had labored so many years. He then turned around, and painted a view looking east across Waterton Lake. He finished just in time, for snow began falling just after he completed his last sketch of the Montana Rockies.

Having completed most of its task, the Commission turned back and began the long, slow return down the Kootenai River to civilization. In 1861 the Commission finally returned to Washington D.C. via Panama, laden with 24 large crates of natural-history specimens. Some laborers remained behind until late in 1861.

Bad luck befell the Commission almost immediately. Dr. Kennerly, the expedition's naturalist, died on the return trip, without having had a chance to prepare his findings for publication. The remainder of the commission members started preparation of the scientific reports as best they could, but by the time the reports were completed, the Civil War had broken out, and all work stopped on the project. After the war, some sporadic work on the reports continued, and by 1869 a splendid final U.S. report was ready for submission to the Secretary of State. But as a result of the Civil War, which had drained the country of much of its energy and financial strength, the government could no longer afford the luxury of colorful and expensive reports. According to Marcus Baker, "The reason [the report] was not published, I am informed, is that Mr. Fish, Secretary of State at that time, deemed its publication too expensive. The war had brought a mountain of debt, and under these conditions he refused to sanction so costly a publication." (1:18)

So the unpublished manuscript of the report was shuffled from office to office in Washington. In 1872 Archibald Campbell himself was appointed Commissioner of a new boundary commission, this time called the *Northern* Boundary Commission.*

This commission was responsible for surveying the United States-Canada boundary from the Lake of the

*Campbell had served on the *Northwest* Boundary Commission previous to that time.

*Photographs on this and opposite page were taken by Jerry DeSanto from nearly the same location as Alden's watercolors and show that, although Alden used a bit of artistic license, his landscapes were generally very accurate.* (WATERCOLORS COURTESY OF NATIONAL ARCHIVES) ***Above:*** *View looking southwest along Kishenehna Valley from Kishenehna Pass, British Columbia, a few miles north of Kintla Lakes.* ***Below:*** *View from the monument atop the Continental Divide looking west along the international boundary.*

Woods to the Continental Divide. The papers of the preceding Northwest Boundary Commission were sent to Campbell's new office with the Northern Boundary Commission and have not been seen since. Alden's magnificent paintings of the glorious Glacier region did not reach the public for more than a decade after the end of the survey.

## THE BRITISH SURVEY

The records of the British Commission's work on the Northwest Boundary Survey, so miraculously rescued from oblivion by Klotz, leave a much more detailed record of activities in Montana. Although the British Commission supposedly was working out of Canada, a great deal of its time was spent south of the international boundary, especially in Montana, where the Kootenai River was used as the primary route for supplies and travel. Also, a number of personal journals and books from the British expedition survive, and, together with Alden's watercolors, give us a vivid picture of this howling wilderness in the early 1860s.

*South Kootenai Trail, Waterton Lakes National Park, Alberta.*

In 1858, after the American crew was already a year ahead of the British, Colonel John Summerfield Hawkins and his crew arrived in Victoria. Captain Robert Walsely Haig was the senior astronomer and surveyor under Hawkins. Fortunately for science, three very capable naturalists and observers were assigned to Hawkins' command. First, the official surgeon and naturalist of the expedition was David Lyall, M. D., a botanist. Lyall had accompanied an expedition to the Arctic in 1852-1854 and had been appointed at the suggestion of Sir William Hooker of the Royal Botanical Gardens at Kew, England. Second, the Commission's assistant naturalist and veterinary surgeon was a formidable-looking Englishman named John Keast Lord, M.R.C.V.S. A very capable observer and collector, Lord had been educated at the Royal Veterinary College in London and had conducted archaeological and scientific research for the Viceroy of Egypt. Finally, Lieutenant Charles W. Wilson, Secretary to the Commission, kept a detailed journal and made a number of competent watercolor illustrations, which give a clear record of the day-to-day activities of the Commission.

The fact that the Americans had already covered the terrain ahead of them was of little help to the members of the British Commission. In many places, astronomical observations did not match those of the Americans, and a separate swath had to be cut through the timber, parallel to the American line. In some places, a third swath had to be cut. There was little contact between the two commissioners; they met officially at Fort Colville in November of 1859, and unofficially in the field, but both surveys proceeded independently. During the winter of 1860-1861, after the American survey was almost completed, the British Commission wintered at Fort Colville, and there invited the Americans to a grand ball hosted by the Hudson's Bay Company. Of the 28 astronomically determined stations installed along the parallel, 14 were set by the Americans, 11 by the British, and 3 jointly.

In the spring of 1861 Colonel Hawkins again set his crews in motion. The Americans had been finished for almost a year, and Hawkins wanted to finish his job by the first snowfall. Hawkins broke the crews into three sections: west of the Tobacco Plains; from the Tobacco Plains over the "Galton Mountains" (Whitefish Range) to the Flathead Drainage; and from the Flathead to the Continental Divide. Lt. Charles Wilson was assigned the job of getting supplies to all three working parties, and Lord and Lyall, the naturalists, moved about freely among all three sections. Hawkins worked his crews hard to finish during the 1861 season.

Wilson used the Kootenai River as a supply line for the two eastern contingents and had to traverse the arduous Kootenai Falls portage so vividly described by Thompson and DeSmet. After fording the Yaak River, Wilson stopped to take a bath and to catch some trout. Wilson found abundant serviceberries in the area. They were an important source of vitamin C to the men, and no doubt prevented many a case of scurvy.

In the Tobacco Plains, Lord and Lyall were surprised to find plant and animal species characteristic of the dry palouse prairies of eastern Washington, including sharp-tailed grouse, long-billed curlews, and sagebrush. Again in the Flathead Valley, small patches of arid sagebrush-grassland, so different from the verdant forests that surround them, are found. These can still be seen in the Big Prairie region near Polebridge.

In the densely forested mountains, the naturalists found that the trunks of most of the young lodgepole pines had been stripped of their bark to a height of seven feet. As Lyall reported, "This is done by the Indians, during their annual hunting-excursions from the Kootenay and Kalispelm country to the Buffalo Plains on the east side of the Rocky Mountains, for the sake of the inner bark, which they use as food, as well in its fresh state as when compressed into thick cakes so as to render it portable." (7:141) Lord noted that woodland caribou were found in the Galton Mountains, and he found several pair of shed moose antlers on the Flathead side of the range.

The high point of the expedition was the ascent of the Lewis Range to the Continental Divide. The trail led up Kishenehn Creek, a drainage to the north of Kintla Lake in present-day Glacier National Park, and took the party to an elevation of 7,000 feet. "Wild and beautiful is the scenery on every side," wrote Lord. "Right and left stupendous pinnacle-like hills, white with snow, seem to reach to the clouds; ridge follows ridge, each seeming to be more craggy and massive than its fellow, as far as the eye can scan this wondrous landscape ... One is puzzled to imagine how such masses of rock could have been up-heaved to so great an altitude." (5:II,185-6)

Wilson climbed one of the peaks to a height of about 8,200 feet and was equally enthusiastic in his description of the scene: "...a glorious view, a perfect sea of peaks all around us and running off to the north and south, whilst on the west we looked into the valley of the Flathead, small lakes of the most brilliant blue, with their borders of bright green herbage lay

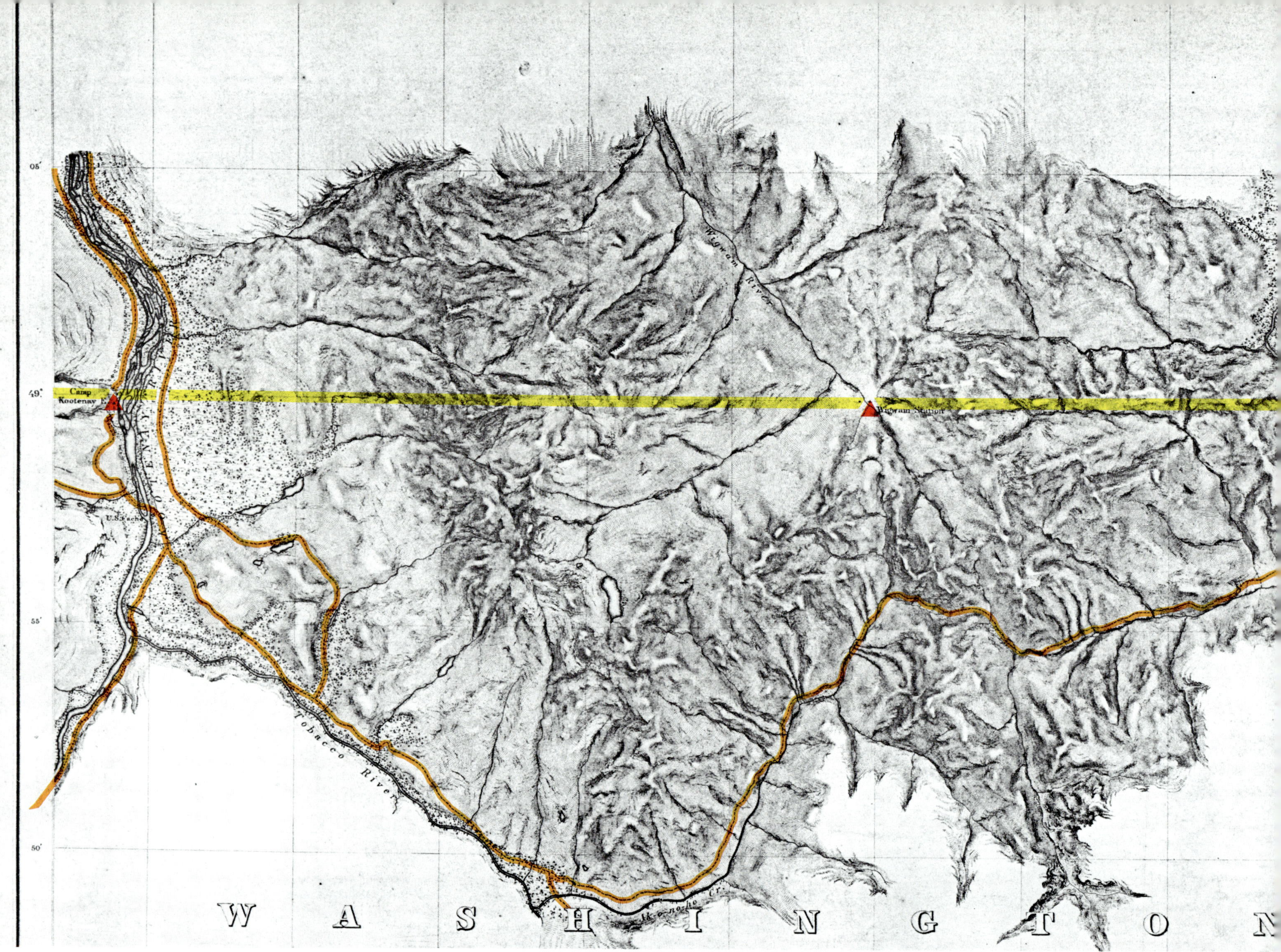


*This previously unpublished map shows the main supply routes traveled by the American survey party in 1859 and 1860 while surveying the international boundary*

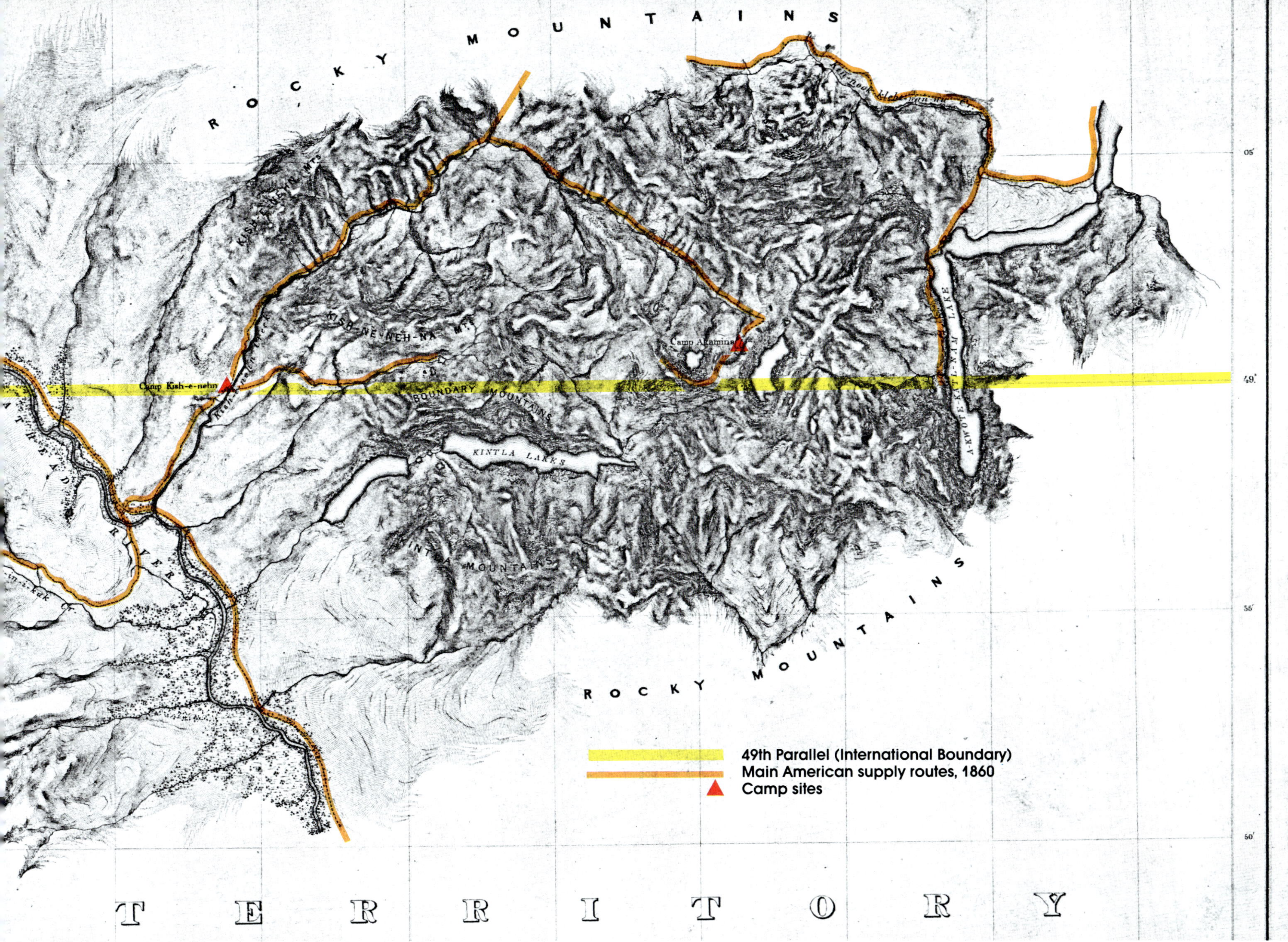


*between Montana and British Columbia.* (NATIONAL ARCHIVES)

scattered in all directions in the hollows, hundreds of feet beneath us and (where it could still cling) some patches of snow and small glaciers heightened the beauty of the scene; so rugged and precipitous are the mountains that at this great altitude no snow remains except in hollows and on some benches, which have a tolerably level surface. In the spring the snow must all come off at once or nearly so; the effects of the avalanches appear to be tremendous and the rocky glens are in some places piled high with the debris of tree and rock." (8:156-7)

Many strange new plants and animals greeted the explorers on these alpine ridges. Here were pikas, hoary marmots, rosy finches, and mountain goats. Lord busily collected and described these little-known species. After one of the party killed a mother white-tailed ptarmigan, Wilson felt obligated to adopt her orphaned chicks. "Poor things," wrote Wilson, "their end soon followed their mother's! For after carrying them about the whole day and bringing them safely into camp (with the intention of rearing them) while my back was turned, their box was broken into by some lean hungry hound who made very short work of my pets." (8:159) Lord collected and mounted specimens of adult ptarmigan as well as chicks; these eventually were sent to the Royal Museum at Kensington.

High on the mountainside, Wilson and Lyall found alpine wildflowers that reminded them of familiar favorites from England. "Fancy our delight," wrote Wilson, "at finding on a grassy spot, close to a huge bank of the dear old 'Forget-me-not' which carried our thoughts far away from the wild mountains to many a pleasant spring day of 'Auld lang syne' in 'merrie England'; I send you some which I gathered right on the summit." (8:160) The "London Pride" in fact was a new species of saxifrage, which Sir Hooker later named *Saxifraga lyallii* in honor of its discoverer. Lyall collected no fewer than 6,700 plant specimens, representing some 1,375 species, during his tour with the Commission. Many of these were new to science and today bear his name; among these are subalpine larch *(Larix lyallii)*, common at high elevations in northwestern Montana along the border, Lyall's phacelia *(Phacelia lyallii)* and Lyall's penstemon *(Penstemon lyallii)*. In addition to the new species, many of the alpines were familiar and well-known from arctic and alpine regions around the world, such as mountain-avens.

On July 26 Lyall and Wilson, with Bauerman the geologist, undertook a hurried side trip to the Great Plains, which were visible in the distance from the summit viewpoint. On the east side, they noticed, the trees were sparse and stunted, so different from the magnificent forest monarchs found just a few miles to the west. Finally they encountered the first bison skulls and bones bleaching in the sun. Lyall collected some prairie plants, but all but one, showy crazyweed, had been collected earlier on the expedition to the west of the Rockies. Unfortunately, the explorers had to return to camp and never did get a glimpse of the prairie bison they so longed to see.

*Subalpine larch* (Larix lyallii) *is one of several plant species named after David Lyall of the British Survey Party.* (CHARLES KAY)

Wilson reported that the fishing in the tributaries along the eastern slope of the Continental Divide "has quite beaten anything we have seen before; the streams are literally alive with the most delicious trout of all weights, from about 4 oz. to 2½ lbs and they are the most ravenous fish I ever met with ... Of course our fishing is done in a very rough way as we cannot carry about rods, reels and all the etceteras of a fisherman; a young larch tree or a piece of willow for a rod, some 15 or 20 feet of line and a roughly tied fly of grouse feathers are our weapons and though rough are very effectual." (8:157) Lyall was the best of the fishermen; he landed nine dozen trout in about four hours.

The British Commission finished its job on schedule, by the fall of 1861, and returned to Fort Colville to spend another miserable winter. All the ink froze, making writing impossible, and worse, the wine and treacle supply froze solid. By the next April, the trip to Fort Vancouver was under way, and by July, 1862, the party was back in England.

Prominent among the scientific accomplishments of the British expedition were Lord's collections and detailed descriptions of the wildlife of the regions traversed. He wrote detailed and accurate — if bombastic — descriptions of the habitat characteristics and behavior of the common bird and mammal species of the Northwest. These were published in a magnificent, two-volume book entitled *The Naturalist in Vancouver Island and British Columbia,* (5) published in London in 1866. Lord intended this book *not* "to be a book on Natural History merely; neither does the Author desire to weary his readers with tedious descriptions of genera and species. Comparative anatomy ... can be acquired at home, but *habits* are only discoverable by those who devote themselves to the rough though pleasant life of a wanderer ... the Author has purposely avoided any definite system of arrangement, preferring a pleasant gossip, chatting, as it were, by the fireside about North-Western Wilds." (5:I,v-vi)

Ten years later, Lord expanded a chapter in his earlier book and wrote a guidebook for wilderness outfitters and travelers, entitled *At Home In The Wilderness: What To Do There and How To Do It.* (6) In this book, he purports to offer "a few practical hints on the general details of travelling, trusting the rough suggestions I shall offer may prove of use to those who are disposed to venture into a distant country wherein wheels, steam, iron and macadamised roads, are unknown luxuries ...." (6:viii)

Lord was an eager, enthusiastic, and capable naturalist, although sometimes overzealous in his popularized descriptions, and he deserves more recognition than he has been given. His Montana explorations are not described in Montana history books, and his work in Glacier Park seems to have been similarly ignored.

In all, the Northwest Boundary Surveys could easily have rivalled the Pacific Railroad Surveys in historical and scientific importance. Certainly the landscapes of Alden might have had a great impact on the public's perception of the remote mountainous area that is now Glacier Park — had they been published in the manner of the Railroad Survey lithographs. It is one of the ironies of history that these pioneering expeditions through some of the West's most fascinating country have been all but forgotten.

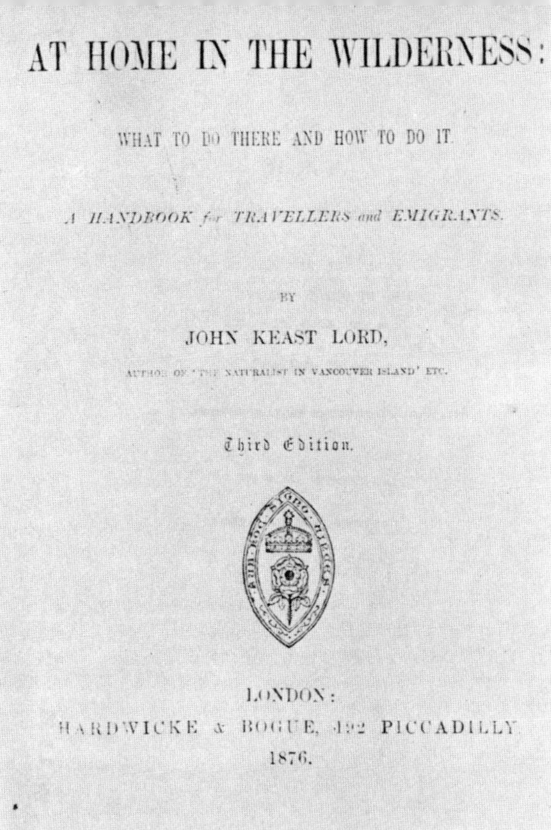

AT HOME IN THE WILDERNESS:

WHAT TO DO THERE AND HOW TO DO IT.

*A HANDBOOK for TRAVELLERS and EMIGRANTS.*

BY

JOHN KEAST LORD,

AUTHOR OF 'THE NATURALIST IN VANCOUVER ISLAND' ETC.

Third Edition.

LONDON:
HARDWICKE & BOGUE, 192 PICCADILLY.
1876.

*Naturalist John Keast Lord of the British survey party wrote two books based on his explorations in Canada and Montana. The illustration of sharp-tailed grouse at right is from his little-known work,* The Naturalist in Vancouver Island and British Columbia, *which contains many descriptions of wildlife species seen in Montana.* (LEFT, COURTESY, WHITMAN COLLEGE LIBRARY; RIGHT, UNIVERSITY OF IDAHO LIBRARY)

"There is a strange indescribable delight in discovery," wrote Lord, "and in finding animals for the first time in their native haunts, animals that before one had vaguely heard or only read of; thus digging, as it were, from Nature's exhaustless mine, fresh wonders of Divine handiwork on which eye had not before gazed ... if we ask ourselves, Why was this or that made? how seldom can we answer the question! Why did He, who made the world, the sun, and the stars, deck the butterfly's wing with tiny scales, that by a simple change in arrangement produce patterns beside which the most finished painting is a bungling daub? Why exist those microscopic wonders, (diatoms and infusoria,) formed with shells of purest flint, and of the quaintest devices? Why were these atomies, that tenant every roadside pool, which dance in the sunbeam, and float on the wings of the breeze? Why all the prodigal variety of strange forms crowding the sea, forms more wonderful than the poet's wildest dreams ever pictured? Who can tell?" (5:I,358)

Who, indeed?

## SHARP-TAILED GROUSE

In 1861 John Keast Lord found the Sharp-tailed Grouse, that characteristic bird of the eastern Montana plains, to be "particularly abundant on the tobacco plains near the Kootanie River" near present-day Eureka, west of the Continental Divide. Lord found these birds to offer sport-shooting as fine as any English birds, and wrote that "for delicacy of flavour ... I'll back [it] against any other bird of the Western wilds." Lord's description of the bird was characteristically flamboyant: "The singular mixture of colours (white, black, and brownish-yellow), the dark blotches, transverse bars, and V-shaped marks of dark-brown, exactly resemble the ground on which the bird is destined to pass its life. The ochreish-yellow angular twigs and dead leaves of the Artemisia, or wild-sage; the sandy soil, dried and bleached to a dingy-white; the brown of the withered bunch-grass; the weather-beaten fragments of rock, clad in liveries of sombre-coloured lichens, admirably harmonise with the colours in which Nature has wisely robed this feathered tenant of the wilderness." But Lord was most enthusiastic in his description of the grouse's spring mating-dance, and his description stands today as one of the most colorful of the many passages that have been written about this strange spring ritual: "... their love-meetings are celebrated in a somewhat curious fashion ... Their usual time of assembling is about sunrise, and late in the afternoon; they select a high round-topped mound; and often, ere the fair are wooed and won, and the happy couple start on their domestic cares, the mound is trampled and beaten bare as a road.

"I had often longed to be present at one of these chicken-dances; and it so happened that, riding up into the hills early one spring morning, my most ardent wishes were fully realised. The peculiar 'chuck-chuck' came clear and shrill upon the crisp frosty air, and told me a dance was afoot. I tied up my horse and my dog, and crept quietly along towards the knoll from whence the sound appeared to come. Taking advantage of some rocks, I weasled myself along, and, without exciting observation, gained the shelter of an old pine-stump close to the summit of a hillock; and there, sure enough, the ball was at its height.

"Reader, can you go back to the days of your first pantomime, your first Punch-and-Judy, or bring to your remembrance the fresh, bounding, joyous delight that you felt in the days of your youth, when you had before your eyes some long and deeply-wished-for novelty? If you can, you will be able to imagine my childish pleasure when looking for the first time on a chicken-dance. There were about eighteen or twenty birds present on this occasion, and it was almost impossible to distinguish the males from the females, the plumage being so nearly alike; but I imagined the females were the passive ones. The four birds nearest to me were head to head, like gamecocks in fighting attitude — the neck-feathers ruffed up, the little sharp tail elevated straight on end, the wings dropped close to the ground, but keeping up by a rapid vibration a continued throbbing or drumming sound. They circled round and round each other in slow waltzing-time, always maintaining the same attitude, but never striking at or grappling with each other; then the pace increased, and one hotly pursued the other until he faced about, and tete-a-tete went waltzing round again; then they did a sort of 'Cure' performance, jumping about two feet into the air until they were winded; and then they strutted about and 'struck an attitude,' like an acrobat after a successful tumble. There were others marching about, with their tails and heads as high as they could stick them up, evidently doing the 'heavy swell;' others, again, did not appear to have any well-defined ideas what they ought to do, and kept flying up and pitching down again, and were manifestly restless and excited — perhaps rejected suitors contemplating something desperate. The music to this eccentric dance was the loud 'chuck-chuck' continuously repeated, and the strange throbbing sound produced by the vibrating wings. I saw several balls after this, but in every one the same series of strange evolutions were carried out." (5:I,301-10)

These dancing grounds are called "leks" by biologists. Leks are arenas where male animals congregate and display to attract females, and are among the most highly-organized of the social functions of birds.

***Left:*** *Lord described the "series of strange evolutions" carried out by sharp-tailed grouse on their leks or breeding grounds.* (TOM ULRICH) ***Right:*** *He saw in the protective coloration of the pika, a close relative of rabbits, evidence for divine intervention.* (LARRY THOMPSON)

## PIKA

High on the talus fields of the Rocky Mountains, Lord came across a species of animal that was unfamiliar to him: "As I contemplated this heap of rocks, a cry like a plaintive whistle suddenly attracted my attention; it evidently came from amongst the stones. I listened and kept quiet. Again and again came the whistle, but nowhere could I see the whistler. A slight movement at length betrayed him, and I could clearly make out a little animal sitting bolt upright, like a begging dog, his seat a flat stone in the middle of the heap.

"I had a load of small-shot in one barrel, intended for ptarmigan; raising my gun slowly and cautiously to my shoulder, I fired as I lay on the ground. The sharp ringing crack as I touched the trigger — the first, perhaps, that had ever awoke the echoes of the mountain — was the death-knell of the poor little musician.

"I picked him up, and imagine my delight when for the first time I held a new Lagomys in my hand."

Lord believed that he had discovered a new, smaller species of pika, which he named *Lagomys minimus*. Actually, it was the common North American pika, *Ochotona princeps*. Having identified the mountain whistler, Lord set out to "find what they did, and how they passed their time in their stony citadel." His behavioral observations were very astute and generally accurate, although he incorrectly surmised that pikas hibernate over the winter. Actually the pika (a close relative of rabbits and hares) stays active all winter, and subsists on the "haystacks" of sun-dried vegetation, which it busily gathers during the brief alpine summer. "I had not long to wait," wrote Lord, "they soon came peeping slily out of their hiding-places, and, inferring safety from silence, sat upon the stones and cheerily chorused to each other. The least noise, and the whistle was sounded sharper and more shrill — the danger signal, when one and all took headers among the stones.

"I soon observed they were busy at work, carrying in dry grass, fir-fronds, roots, and moss, and constructing a nest in the clefts between the stones, clearly for winter-quarters. The nests were of large size, some of them consisting of as much material as would fill a good-sized basket. One nest was evidently the combined work of several little labourers, and destined for their joint habitation.

"There were no provisions stored away, neither do I think they garner any for winter use, but simply hybernate in the warm nest; which, of course, is thickly covered with snow during the intense cold of these northern latitudes, thus more effectually preventing radiation and waste of animal heat. Their food consists entirely of grass, which they nibble much after the fashion of our common rabbit. They never burrow or dig holes in the ground, but pass their lives among the loose stones."

The "nests" described by Lord were actually the pika's winter food supply. Lord also commented on the effectiveness of the pika's drab, protective coloration: "Who can fail to trace the evidence of Divine care in colouring the fur of this defenceless creature in a garb exactly resembling the grey lichen-covered fragments amongst which he is destined to pass his life? So closely does the animal approximate in appearance to an angular piece of rock when sitting up, that unless he moves it takes sharp eyes to see him; and the cry or whistle is so deceptive that I imagined it far distant, when the animal was close to me." (5:I,323-8)

## HUMMINGBIRDS

John Keast Lord had spent considerable time in the tropics, and there came to associate the hummingbirds with the bananas, palms, and grotesque orchids of the tropics. Imagine his surprise when he discovered *three* species of these "gems of the air" along the western slopes of the Rockies.

"Away from the tropics and its feathered wonders, to the wild solitudes of the Rocky Mountains, — it is there I want you in imagination to wander with me, and to picture to yourself, which you can easily do if you possess a naturalist's love of discovery, the delight I experienced when, for the first time, I saw hummingbirds up in the very regions of the 'Ice King'." Chasing each other in sheer sport, with a rapidity of flight and intricacy of evolution impossible for the eye to follow — through the bushes, and over the water, everywhere — they darted about like meteors. Often meeting in mid-air, a furious battle would ensue; their tiny crests and throat-plumes erect and blazing, they were altogether pictures of the most violent passions. Then one would perch himself on a dead spray, and leisurely smooth his ruffled feathers, to be suddenly rushed at and assaulted by some quarrel-some comrade. Feeding, fighting, and frolicking seemed to occupy their entire time."

Devoted naturalist that he was, Lord spent two long days shooting specimens and skinning them for the Royal Museum. His guilt was evidently great, and he wondered if it was worth it to dispatch such creatures of beauty even for the sake of science. "I daresay hard epithets will be heaped upon me, — cruel man, hard-hearted savage, miserable destroyer, and similar epithets, — when I confess to shooting numbers of these burnished beauties. Some of them are before me at this moment as I write; but what miserable things are these stuffed remains, as compared to the living bird! The brilliant crests are rigid and immoveable; the throat-feathers, that open and shut with a flash like coloured light, lose in the stillness of death all those charms so beautiful in life; the tail, clumsily spread, or bent similar to the abdomen of a wasp about to sting, no more resembles the same organ in the live bird, than a fan of peacock's feathers is like to the expanded tail of that bird when strutting proudly in the sun."

*Lord accurately described the habitat preferences of three northwestern Montana hummingbird species. Although he thought himself a "miserable destroyer," he felt compelled to take specimens of these "gems of the air."* (UNIVERSITY OF IDAHO LIBRARY)

Lord noted that hummingbirds do not feed exclusively on nectar; he watched several feeding on insects that were trapped in birch and alder sap. "Busily occupied in picking off these captives were several very sombre-looking hummingbirds. They poised themselves just as the others did over the flowers, and deftly nipped, as with delicate forceps, the helpless insects ... Were any proof needed to establish the fact of hummingbirds being insect-feeders, this should be sufficient. I saw the bird, not only on this occasion but dozens of times afterwards, pick the insect from off the tree, often killing it in the act; and found the stomach, on being opened, filled with various species of winged insects."

The three species of hummingbirds encountered by Lord in the primeval forests of northwestern Montana can still be found there in abundance: the Rufous, Calliope, and Black-chinned Hummingbirds. Lord carefully noted the differences in the habitat preferences of the three: "The habits of the three species differ widely. The [Rufous] Hummingbird loves to flit over the open prairies, stopping at every tempting flower, to catch some idler lurking in its nectar-cells. Building its nest generally in a low shrub, and close to the rippling stream, it finds pleasant music in its ceaseless splash. Minute Calliope, on the other hand, prefers rocky hillsides at great altitudes, where only pine-trees, rock-plants, and an alpine flora 'struggle for existence.' I have frequently killed this bird above the line of perpetual snow. Its favourite resting-place is on the extreme point of a dead pine-tree, where, if undisturbed, it will sit for hours. The site chosen for the nest is usually the branch of a young pine; artfully concealed amidst the fronds at the very end, it is rocked like a cradle by every passing breeze.

"The [Black-chinned] Hummingbird lingers around lakes, pools, and swamps where its favourite trapping-tree grows. I have occasionally, though very rarely, seen it hovering over flowers; this, I apprehend, is only when the storehouse is empty, and the sap too dry to capture the insects. They generally build in the birch or alder, selecting the fork of a branch high up ... The [Black-chinned] Hummingbird arrives about a week or ten days after the other two."

Lord was duly impressed by the prospect of these tiny creatures migrating hundreds or thousands of miles, and arriving on the breeding grounds at precisely the time when their preferred food plants, the currants, were in bloom. "Marvellous is the instinct that guides and the power that sustains these birds (not larger than a good sized bumblebee) over such an immense tract of country; and even more wonderful still is their arrival, timed so accurately, that the only flower adapted to its wants thus early in the year opens its hoards, ready to supply the wanderer's necessities after so tedious a migration!

"It seems to me vastly like design, and Foreseeing Wisdom, that a shrub indigenous and widely distributed should be so fashioned as to produce its blossoms long before its leaves; and that this very plant alone blooms ere the snow has melted off the land, and that too at the exact period when hummingbirds arrive. It cannot be chance, but the work of the Almighty Architect —who shaped them both, whose handiwork we discover at every step, and of whose sublime conceptions we everywhere observe the manifestations in the admirably-balanced systems of creation!" (5:I,328-36)

*John Keast Lord wrote of the butterfly's "wonderful displays of brillant colouring," but he thought of the equally beautiful black-billed magpies as murderers after watching the birds kill mules and horses.* (ABOVE, WILL KERLING; RIGHT, TIM CHRISTIE)

## BUTTERFLIES

John Keast Lord wrote extensively not only of birds and mammals but also of insects. He was puzzled by the tendency of butterflies to congregate, as they do, on mud-puddles or animal droppings. "Few more wonderful displays of brilliant colouring can be imagined than an assemblage of butterflies. 'Knights' and 'chevaliers' have a habit, in North and North-western America, of pitching together on the ground, choosing damp bare places for their gatherings; many hundreds of these brilliantly-coloured insects might be seen every day on these meadow-like river-banks, out-vying in variety of tints any grouping of flowers the most skilful gardener could produce. For what purpose they thus congregate I am at a loss to imagine." (5:II,158)

## BLACK-BILLED MAGPIE

The black-billed magpie, a beautiful and common bird throughout Montana, is not often thought of as a predator on big-game animals. Nevertheless, magpies are cunning and ruthless predators, especially in winter, when deer and elk are in poor condition and mired in deep snow. Lord witnessed the magpie's grisly behavior while on the Boundary Survey. "I call them murderers," he wrote, "because I have seen them kill mules, and worse than that, pick the eyes out of a living animal when, wounded and helpless, it lay down to die; and pounce on maimed birds, break in their skulls, and deliberately devour their brains whilst the muscles still quivered with life.

"To the packer the magpies are dire enemies. If a pack-mule or horse has a gall, and happens to be turned out to graze with the wound uncovered, down come the magpies on its back; clinging with their sharp claws, reckless of every effort to displace them, they peck away at the wound; the tortured beast rolls madly, and for a short time the scoundrels are obliged to let go, but only to swoop down again the instant a chance offers. This repeated agony soon kills an animal, unless the packers rescue it."

Magpies became an unbearable pest at the expedition's mule-camp, and Lord performed the following experiment with a quantity of strychnine. The magpies had accumulated "until they were in hundreds. Shooting at them was only wasting valuable ammunition. The packers were driven almost into a state of revolt. We had an old maimed suffering mule which was to be killed, so the packers gave it a ball containing a large dose of strychnine; death was immediate, and the carcase, ere ten minutes had elapsed, was covered with magpies working at the eyes, lips, sores, and soft skin inside the thighs. It was the most singular spectacle I ever witnessed. One after the other the birds rolled from off the dead mule, and as they fell and died, others greedily took their vacant places; and so this terrible slaughter went on, until the heaps of dead magpies nearly buried the body of the mule. Two foxes, one coyote, several Indian dogs, and a large wolf, on the day following the mule's demise, lay dead by the side of the poisoned birds. It was a terrible revenge — how far justifiable is a matter of opinion. The packers, of course, were in wild glee at the entire success of the scheme." (5:II,71-3)

## STRIPED SKUNK

The striped skunk, one of the constant companions of the Northwest Boundary Commission from the Pacific Ocean to the crest of the Rockies, was not Lord's favorite animal. Lord's Russian setter had a propensity for killing skunks, and, according to Lord, "For days, nay weeks, after one of these encounters, I could hardly bear him near me; the sickening foetor seemed to gain in strength as it exhaled from the dog, volatilised by the heat of his body ... Mix the very worst mud from the Thames on a summer-day, at low-water, with Rimmel's shop, a gasworks, fellmonger's yard, and knacker's boiling-furnace; and I will venture to assert that the odour produced, even if concentrated by the subtle power of chemistry, would be a mild and pleasant perfume, when matched against that of the skunk."

Lord wrote the following description of a skunk preying on ducks, which may or may not have been based on actual observation: "Ducks are his favourite birds; but, you ask, how can he possibly catch them? In this way. His instinct guides him to reside near the pools on which water-birds come to sleep and pass the night. When everything is still and hushed, and the unsuspecting birds are floating in fancied security, with their heads tucked under their wings, then out steals the crafty skunk, and creeping noiselessly down his roadways, swims, without the slightest splash, towards the drowsy birds, dives under the one that suits his taste, seizes it by the breast, and, spite of all its flapping, quacking, and struggling, drags the victim ashore, kills, and eats it. He seldom gets more than one in the night; for the other birds take timely warning, and leave for some safer retreat." (5:II,4-8)

*Golden-mantled ground squirrel.* (LARRY THOMPSON)

## GOLDEN-MANTLED GROUND SQUIRREL

Sharing the chipmunk's rocky habitats in northwestern Montana is a beautifully colored, striped ground squirrel, which many people today mistake for a chipmunk. John Keast Lord did not make this mistake, and wrote the following accurate description of the golden-mantled ground squirrel: "Two broad stripes of jet-black mark each side of the animal, and extend from the shoulders to the thighs; between each pair of stripes is a line of equal width, of a yellowish-white. The medium region of the back is a rich grey; chestnut-brown, mottled with yellow and black, colours half the thighs, and extends over the hips, shading away into the grey on the back. The tail is rather short, but very brushy; the under-surface, coloured a bright yellow-brown, is margined with a much lighter tint of the same colour. Above the tail is grey, like the back. Length about seven inches; tail four inches without the terminating hairs."

Lord described in detail the food habits, habitat, and behavior of this little mountain animal. "It feeds principally on young grass and the juicy stalks of succulent plants; extending from the holes or clefts where they reside, trails beaten like footpaths lead in the direction of the favourite herbage. It is a most active and watchful squirrel: at the slightest noise it bounds with astonishing speed, and takes leaps almost equal to those of the flying-squirrel to reach its hole, uttering as it runs a low plaintive whistle. Conspicuous as this squirrel's coloration appears when viewed apart from its habitat, nevertheless, it admirably accords with the light and dark markings peculiar to the slaty rocks amidst which I saw it; when the animal is perfectly still, it is quite impossible to make it out to be other than a portion of the rock, until by moving it betrays itself." (5:II,187-8)

## CHIPMUNK

The chipmunk was another constant companion of the Northwest Boundary Commission from the ocean to the Rockies. Lord called it "the Store-keeper, ... One of the liveliest, prettiest, merriest, and, to judge from appearances, the happiest little animal one meets with in the North-western wilds ...." Lord was amazed at the ability with which the little animal was able to adapt to every kind of habitat imaginable. "This squirrel seems to live everywhere," he wrote. "Dive into the dark shadow of the pine-forest, where mouldy life holds high festival — where huge fungoid growths and giant agarics spring in flabby clusters from the oozy logs — where the pools, thick and slimy, are covered with the green fleshy leaves of the 'skunk cabbage,' and each branch and spray, draped with the black lichen (*Lichen jubatus*), seem mourning over death and decay on every side — in these damp solitudes lives the 'Store-keeper,' merry and quarrelsome, as in brighter scenes. Climb the mountain-side, and scramble through the rock-walled ravine, where the pine clings to the stones rather than grows from their clefts; where no murmuring streamlet cools and refreshes thirsty Nature, or breaks the solemn silence with its rippling music; and not even the footfall of the savage disturb its echoes; and naught living, save the denizens of the air, that peep into its weird depths from the tree-tops, ever visits it: yet in the very loneliest of these glens the 'Store-keeper' is sure to be met with. Climb on — higher, higher — to the perpetual snow-line, marking the boundary betwixt life and icy desolation; and there too, on the very frontier, he bounds, and jumps from rock to rock, ever scolding, laughing, whistling, and toiling, to garner in his harvest." (5:II,48-50)

Adaptable as the chipmunk may be, Lord actually saw three different species in Montana. These species are known to invade different vegetation zones on a mountainside, so that only one species is generally found in a given patch of habitat. In the lower grasslands and open ponderosa pine forests of the Tobacco Plains, for example, one finds the yellow-pine chipmunk. Higher up the mountainsides, in denser forests of spruce and fir, the red-tailed chipmunk holds reign. Finally, high on the alpine tundra of Glacier Park, where the boundary-line crossed the Continental Divide, is found the least chipmunk. Scientists have found that these little animals actually defend the boundaries of their species' range, fighting off any intruders of another species.

## MOSQUITOES

The literature of western exploration is full of references to that tyrant of the bottomlands, the mosquito. Nearly every explorer, from Lewis and Clark on, has commented on the tortures that these creatures inflict on the already miserable wilderness traveler. But few writers have so vividly captured the agony of a mid-summer mosquito infestation as John Keast Lord. Their numbers along the route of the Boundary Survey, he wrote, were "something beyond all belief, and really terrible. I can convey no idea of the numbers, except by saying they were in dense clouds truly, and not figuratively, a thick fog of mosquitos. Night or day it was just the same; the hum of these bloodthirsty tyrants was incessant. We ate them, drank them, breathed them; nothing but the very thickest leathern clothing was of the slightest use as a protection against their lancets. The trousers had to be tied tightly round the ankle, and the coat-sleeve round the wrist, to prevent their getting in; but if one more crafty than the others found out a needle-hole, or a thin spot, it would have your blood in a second. We lighted huge fires, fumigated the tents, tried every expedient we could think of, but all in vain. They seemed to be quite happy in a smoke that would stifle anything mortal, and, what was worse, they grew thicker every day.

"Human endurance has its limits. A man cannot stand being eaten alive. It was utterly impossible to work; one's whole time was occupied in slapping viciously at face, head, and body, stamping, grumbling, and savagely slaughtering hecatombs of mosquitos. Faces rapidly assumed an irregularity of outline anything but consonant with the strict lines of beauty; each one looked as if he had gone in for a heavy fight, and lost. Hands increased in size with *painful* rapidity, and ... one was in a *knobby* state from head to heel."

The outcome was that the camp had to be abandoned: "we were completely vanquished and driven away — the work of about a hundred men stopped by tiny flies." Nevertheless, Lord collected specimens of his foe, and on his return to England found one of them to be a species new to science, which he named *Culex pinguis*, "because it was fatter and rounder than any of its known brethren." Lord's field notebook was "a mausoleum of scores of my enemies; there they lay, dry and flat; round some of them a stain of blood tells how richly they merited their untimely end." (5:I,316-18)

*John Keast Lord wrote the first detailed accounts of the habits of the hoary marmot, a seldom seen alpine mammal of northwest Montana.* (TOM ULRICH PHOTOS)

## HOARY MARMOT

High on the wind-swept summit of the Rocky Mountains, in the tundra zone of what is now Glacier National Park, John Keast Lord encountered an exciting and seldom-seen animal, the Hoary Marmot. Unlike its low-elevation relative the yellow-bellied marmot, which was common in the rocky outcrops along the Tobacco Plains, the Hoary Marmot is restricted to the highest peaks. Describing its habitat, Lord wrote, "If there is a spot on the face of the globe more dismal, solitary, inhospitable, and uninviting than another, that spot is where this most accomplished siffleur resides; and it is not by any means a matter to be wondered at, that so very little is to be found, in works on Natural History, relating to this little anchorite's habits."

Lord gives us a vivid description of the thrill of his first discovery of the Hoary Marmot in the high mountains of Glacier: "My purpose being to climb the craggy ascent that led up to the watershed — not by any means a dangerous thing to do; it was simply leg-aching, tiresome, scrambling work. The grass

being dry, it polished the soles of my mocassins, until they became like burnished metal; so that progression, up the long green slopes, was much the same as it would have been up an ice-slant, with skates on. I got up at last, and, feeling somewhat fagged, seated myself on a flat rock, unslung my gun, lighted my pipe, and had a good look at everything round about me.

"The sun had crept steadily up unto the clear sky, unflecked by a single cloud; the mists, that in the early morning hung about the ravines, and partially veiled the peaks and angles of the vast piles of rocks, had vanished, revealing them in all their immensity. Below me was a lake, smooth as a mirror, but the dark-green cold look of the water hinted at unfathomable depth. Tiny rivulets, fed by the snow, wound their way, like threads of silver, between the rocks and through the grass, to reach the lake.

"I was not so much impressed with the beauty of the landscape, as awed by its substantial magnificence. Few living things were to be seen save a group of ptarmigan, sunning themselves on a ledge of rocks, a couple of mountain-goats browsing by the lake, and a few grey-crowned linnets, — birds seldom seen but at great altitudes. There were also the recent traces of a grizzly, or black bear, that had been munching down the wild angelica. A solemn stillness intensified the slightest sound to a supernatural loudness — even a loosened stone rattling down the hillside made me start; there was no buzz and hum of busy insects, or chirp of birds, or splash of torrents, to break the silence; the very wind seemed afraid to moan: it was deathlike silence to the very letter.

"As I smoked away, silent as all about me, suddenly a sharp clear whistle, that awoke the echoes far and near, thoroughly roused me, and sent all other thoughts to the rout. As I could see nothing, I deemed it expedient to remain quiet. Cocking my rifle, I lay on the grass, and waited patiently for a repetition of the performance. I had not long to tax my patience: again came the same sound, then others joined in the refrain, until the place, instead of being steeped in silence, resembled the gallery of a theatre on boxing-night.

"I very soon spied one of the performers, seated on the top of a large rock; its position was that of a dog when begging. With his forefeet he was busy cleaning his whiskers, smoothing his fur, and clearly going in for a somewhat elaborate toilet: perhaps he was going a wooing, or to a morning concert, or for a constitutional, or a lounge on the 'Marmot's mile;' but whatever his intentions were, I regret to say they were frustrated. Solely in the cause of science I had to stop him; resting my rifle on a flat rock, as I lay on the ground, I fired, and the sharp crack, as it rang amid the rocks, was the whistler's death-knell.

"Rapidly reloading, I scampered off to secure my prize. I am afraid there was not much pity felt — delight at getting a new animal was uppermost. Smoothing his fur, I plugged the shot-holes, examined him closely, measured him; admired his handsome shape, bright-grey coat, and brushy tail; investigated his teeth and claws, walked back, and had a look at him from a distance; then set to work, and skinned him. You can see him also, if you like to visit the British Museum, where this very victim is 'set up,' and placed amidst the Marmots; his name, together with that of his destroyer, black-lettered on the board to which he is affixed. At the sound of the rifle, every one of his companions took sensation-headers into their holes, and did not come out again during my stay on this occasion.

"In habits marmots are essentially sociable animals, inasmuch as they live in little colonies; but, unlike some of the prairie marmots, these rock-whistlers, when married, have a house of their own; and if blessed with a family — a blessing seldom denied them — they kick out the youthful pledges of affection as soon as they can nibble up a living for themselves. The burrow, which is quite two feet in diameter, is dug invariably in a slanting direction, generally at the base of a rock, standing up like a pedestal, on which they love to sit and whistle. Wide trails, bare-like roads, lead in all directions from their holes to the feeding and drinking-places; their hours of repast, sensibly chosen, are early in the morning, when the grass and herbage is wet with dew.

"For only a few months, during summer, is this quaint little miner permitted to revel in the luxury of light; for seven dreary months out of the twelve does he sleep out his drowsy existence. What a wise and wonderful provision, to secure from utter extinction animals compelled to live in these icy regions, is hybernation! Growing wondrously fat during the summer, they retire, when the nipping cold and deep snow comes, into burrows lined with soft warm bedding; there become semi-torpid, and literally a living stove; for the fuel, stored as fat, is slowly burned up in the lungs, giving out heat just as coal would in a fire-grate. Thus the rock-whistler heeds not the chilly blasts that sweep through gorge and glen, and so sleeps on safe from harm, until Sol comes to set him free."

Lord's careful description of the Hoary Marmot is surprisingly accurate and was the first published ecological study of this remarkable animal. Lord goes on to describe how the marmot may be cooked, and he considered it something of a delicacy: "When skinned a long peeled stick is thrust through the body, from tail to head; then placed slantwise, one end being fast in the ground, the treasured morsel is slowly roasted over a gentle fire.

"I can bear testimony to the delicacy of roasted marmot; it beats Ostend rabbit hollow; all honour to the redskin's taste! A dinner off a roasted rock-whistler, washed down with a pull at the crystal stream, is a repast not to be despised." (5:II,190-95)

*Waterton Lake in the country traversed by the Northwest Boundary Survey.* (CHARLES KAY)

## Sources


1. Baker, M. *Survey of the Northwestern Boundary of the United States, 1857-1861.* Geological Survey Bulletin No. 174. Washington: U. S. Dept. of the Interior, 1900.
2. Deutsch, H. J. "A Contemporary Report on the 49° Boundary Survey." *Pacific Northwest Quarterly* 53(1962):17-33.
3. Klotz, O. *Certain Correspondence of the Foreign Office and of the Hudson's Bay Company.* Ottawa: Government Printing Bureau for the Canadian Department of the Interior, Office of the Chief Astronomer, 1899.
4. Klotz, O. "The History of the Forty-Ninth Parallel Survey West of the Rocky Mountains." Geographical Review 3(1917):382-7.
5. Lord, J. K. *The Naturalist in Vancouver Island and British Columbia.* 2 vols. London: Richard Bentley, 1866.
6. Lord, J. K. *At Home in the Wilderness: What To Do There and How To Do It: A Handbook for Travellers and Emigrants.* London: Hardwicke and Rogue, 1876.
7. Lyall, D. "Account of the Botanical Collections Made by David Lyall, M.D., R.N., F.L.S., Surgeon and Naturalist to the North American Boundary Commission." *Journal of the Linnaean Society of London* 7(1863):124-144.
8. Stanley, G. F., ed. *Mapping the Frontier: Charles Wilson's Diary of the Survey of the 49th Parallel, 1858-1862, While Secretary of the British Boundary Commission.* Seattle: Univ. of Washington Press, 1970.
9. Stenzel, F. *James M. Alden: Yankee Artist of the Pacific Coast, 1854-60.* Fort Worth: Amon Carter Museum, 1975.
10. Watson, C. M. *The Life of Major-General Sir Charles William Wilson.* London: publisher unidentified, 1909.

## Next in the Montana Geographic Series

**Montana's Indians Yesterday and Today**

Books abound on Montana's Indians in the past, but this is the first book to combine a colorful, accurate, concise history of the Indians that occupied what is now Montana and also to review the lifestyle, resource base, leadership and aspirations of Montana's Indians today. By William Bryan with photography by Michael Crummett.

**The Yellowstone River**

High in Yellowstone Park near Younts Peak is born the last major free-flowing river in the contiguous United States. Undammed but not uncontroversial, the Yellowstone is the backbone of tens of thousands of square miles of southern Montana. It races through some of Montana's most rugged high country, creating a cold water fishery of international acclaim, yet as it flows from Montana the Yellowstone plods along laden with silt. It is no less important to the economy of southeastern Montana and no less cherished for its unusual warm-water fishery and diverse riparian wildlife. From west to east are communities as disparate as Red Lodge, Billings and Miles City, wild back country, irrigated bottom land, and miles of dry cattle country — all influenced by the wild Yellowstone.

**Other Titles in Planning and Production**
**The Continental Divide——by Bill Cunningham**
**Eastern Montana's Mountain Ranges——Mark Meloy**
**The Rocky Mountain Front——by Rick Graetz and Gus Wolfe**

The Montana Geographic Series

| | |
|---|---|
| Volume 1 | Montana's Mountain Ranges |
| Volume 2 | Eastern Montana: A Portrait of the Land and the People |
| Volume 3 | Montana Wildlife |
| Volume 4 | Glacier Country: Montana's Glacier National Park |
| Volume 5 | Western Montana: A Portrait of the Land and the People |
| Volume 6 | Greater Yellowstone: the National Park and Adjacent Wild Lands |
| Volume 7 | Beartooth Country: Montana's Absaroka-Beartooth Mountains |
| Volume 8 | The Missouri River |

# MONTANA MAGAZINE

## Tells The Whole Montana Story

The history, the wild back country, the people, the wildlife, the towns, the lifestyles, the travel — these things are Montana — unique among the states. Montana Magazine brings you the Montana story six times a year in a beautiful, long-lasting magazine.

Its hallmark is full-page color photography of Montana from the peaks to the prairies.

### REGULARLY FEATURED DEPARTMENTS:

WEATHER
GEOLOGY
HUNTING AND FISHING
OUTDOOR RECREATION
HUMOR
PERSONALITY
GARDENING
DINING OUT

Montana Magazine
Because You Are
A Montanan

For subscription information write:
**MONTANA MAGAZINE**
Box 5630
Helena, MT 59604

**Volume II of Montana explorers will contain a complete index and a list of the scientific and common names mentioned in both volumes.**

**CONTENTS OF VOLUME II**



**Front Cover Photos:**

Along the Missouri River near Loess Ferry. (TIM CHURCH)
Mountain Lions. (JOHN JAMES AUDUBON)
View of Highwood Mountains from Fort McKenzie (KARL BODMER, INTERNORTH FOUNDATION, JOSLYN ART MUSEUM, OMAHA, NEBRASKA)
Bitterroot. (LARRY THOMPSON)
Flathead River. (GEORGE WUERTHNER)